The Regulation of Animal Health and Welfare

The Regulation of Animal Health and Welfare draws on the research of scientists, lawyers, economists and political scientists to address the current and future regulatory problems posed by the issues of animal health and disease. Recent events, such as the outbreak of BSE, epidemics of foot and mouth disease, concerns about bluetongue in sheep and the entry into the food chain of the offspring of cloned cattle, have heightened awareness of the issues of regulation in animal disease and welfare. This book critically appraises the existing regulatory institutions and guiding principles of how best to maintain animal health in the context of social change and a developing global economy. Addressing considerations of sound science, the role of risk management and the allocation of responsibilities, it also takes up the theoretical and practical challenges which here – and elsewhere – attend the co-operation of scientists, social scientists, lawyers and policy makers. Indeed, the collaboration of scientists and social scientists in determined and regulatory contexts, such as that of animal disease, is an issue of ever-increasing importance. This book will be of considerable value to those with interests in this issue, as well as those concerned with the law and policy relating to animal health and welfare.

John McEldowney is professor of law at the School of Law at the University of Warwick. His research interests in the field of public law include regulation and accountability. He has written extensively in the field of public law and was one of the investigators on the Governance of Livestock Disease (GOLD) project.

Wyn Grant is part-time professor of politics at the University of Warwick. He has written extensively on comparative public policy in advanced industrial countries with special reference to agricultural policy and environmental policy. He has over 40 years' experience of university teaching and research.

Graham Medley is professor of infectious disease epidemiology at the University of Warwick, and was the principal investigator of the Governance of Livestock Disease (GOLD) project that led to this book. He has published extensively on a diverse range of infectious diseases of humans and livestock.

Law, science and society

General editors

John Paterson
University of Aberdeen, UK

Julian Webb
University of Warwick, UK

Law's role has often been understood as one of implementing political decisions concerning the relationship between science and society. Increasingly, however, as our understanding of the complex dynamic between law, science and society deepens, this instrumental characterisation is seen to be inadequate, but as yet we have only a limited conception of what might take its place. If progress is to be made in our legal and scientific understanding of the problems society faces, then there needs to be space for innovative and radical thinking about law and science. *Law, Science and Society* is intended to provide that space.

The overarching aim of the series is to support the publication of new and groundbreaking empirical or theoretical contributions that will advance understanding between the disciplines of law, and the social, pure and applied sciences. General topics relevant to the series include studies of:

- law and the international trade in science and technology;
- risk and the regulation of science and technology;
- law, science and the environment;
- the reception of scientific discourses by law and the legal process;
- law, chaos and complexity;
- law and the brain.

Titles in the series:

Absent Environments
Theorising environmental law and the city
Andreas Philippopoulos-Mihalopoulos

Uncertain Risks Regulated
Edited by Ellen Vos and Michelle Everson

Knowledge, Technology and Law
At the intersection of socio-legal and science & technology studies
Edited by Emilie Cloatre and Martyn Pickersgill (forthcoming, January 2014)

The Regulation of Animal Health and Welfare

Science, law and policy

By John McEldowney, Wyn Grant and Graham Medley

With

David Carslake, Jonathan Cave, Justin Greaves, Laura Green, Matthew Keeling, Amy KilBride and Habtu Weldegebriel

Routledge
Taylor & Francis Group
a GlassHouse Book

First published 2013
by Routledge
2 Park Square, Milton Park, Abingdon, Oxon OX14 4RN
A GlassHouse Book

Simultaneously published in the USA and Canada
by Routledge
711 Third Avenue, New York, NY 10017

Routledge is an imprint of the Taylor & Francis Group, an informa business

British Library Cataloguing in Publication Data
A catalogue record for this book is available from the British Library

Library of Congress Cataloging in Publication Data
The regulation of animal health and welfare : science, law and policy /
Edited by John McEldowney, Wyn Grant and Graham Medley.
   pages cm
Includes bibliographical references.
ISBN 978-0-415-50474-4 (hbk) – ISBN 978-0-203-52260-8 (ebk)
1. Veterinary hygiene–Law and legislation–Great Britain. 2. Animal
welfare–Law and legislation–Great Britain. 3. Domestic animals–Law and
legislation–Great Britain. I. McEldowney, John F., editor. II. Grant, Wyn,
editor. III. Medley, Graham, editor.
KD3420.R44 2013
344.4104'9–dc23   2013005750

ISBN: 978-0-415-50474-4 (hbk)
ISBN: 978-0-203-52260-8 (ebk)

Typeset in Times New Roman
by Cenveo Publisher Services

Printed and bound in Great Britain by
TJ International Ltd, Padstow, Cornwall

Contents

Contributors

David Carslake is an ecologist by background, and currently a research associate at the School of Social and Community Medicine at the University of Bristol.

Dr Jonathan Cave is a senior tutor and senior lecturer in the Department of Economics at the University of Warwick, and Research Leader at the Rand Corporation, UK. His research interests include multidisciplinary research, telecommunication regulation and regulatory theory.

Dr Justin Greaves is the director of student experience and progression in the Department of Politics and International Studies at the University of Warwick. His research interests include interdisciplinary research and theories of welfare and justice.

Professor Laura Green is a professor at the School of Life Sciences at Warwick and a visiting professor at the University of Nottingham. Her research aims are to improve the health and welfare of farmed livestock using epidemiological approaches in multidisciplinary settings.

Professor Matt Keeling holds a joint appointment with Mathematics and Life Sciences at the University of Warwick. His interests span epidemiology, ecology and evolution. He focuses on the roles of spatial interactions and stochasticity (randomness), and how these can affect the dynamics, control and persistence of biological organisms.

Amy KilBride is a post-doctoral researcher at Warwick University using multidisciplinary approaches to address questions of how to improve the welfare of farmed animals.

Habtu Weldegebriel is an agricultural economist and currently working at the EPIC Centre of Expertise on Animal Disease Outbreaks in Scotland.

Preface

The governance of disease in farmed livestock is the subject of this book, drawing on the results of a multi-disciplinary research project funded by the Rural Economy and Land Use Programme (RELU).[1] RELU support for the project enabled consideration of the impact of biological, economic and political processes and legal arrangements on the efforts of producers and government to control animal disease or mitigate its consequences. Persistent or 'endemic' diseases of livestock are numerous and common, and set many challenges for policy makers and regulators. Various aspects of the regulation of animal health and welfare that address animal diseases are relevant to the study. Often, disease is exacerbated by livestock movement and limited control measures taken by the individual farmer. There are a wide range of shared responsibilities in the control of animal diseases that fall on the private and public sectors.

The research findings of the study indicate that there is a need for a radical rethink of basic principles and that risk analysis must be more reliably based on and inclusive of socio-economic evidence. The legal framework is an essential consideration in applying the appropriate economic analysis to the regulation of animal diseases, and legal rules are ultimately a critical factor in ensuring the effectiveness of prevention and cure. Legal rules are also influential in the implementation of policy making and in the formulation of policy. Policy makers must also factor in different public perceptions about animal diseases. The political profile of a disease is largely related to the question of whether or not it can cause disease in humans, and bovine spongiform encephalopathy (BSE) and brucellosis are two examples where this is possible. Foot and mouth disease (FMD) does not generally cause disease in humans but has a very high public profile. Public awareness of some diseases that affect only animals but have economic consequences for farmers is sometimes more limited, as with diseases

---

1 RELU was a UK-wide research programme supporting interdisciplinary research on the multiple challenges facing rural areas. The RELU research programme received over £26.5 million between 2004 and 2013 aimed at encouraging an understanding of the social, economic, environmental and technological challenges faced by rural areas. It is also intended to enhance the capabilities for integrative, interdisciplinary research in rural issues.

such as mastitis or bovine rhinotracheitis. These attract little government funding and media attention, and many view such diseases as 'production diseases' and to be treated as problems for the farming industry.

There are many biological factors at work for a pathogen or infection to survive in a herd. These include carrier animals, environmental contamination or through wild animals, such as the bacteria that cause Johne's disease. There are many economic factors that should be considered by farmers in their commercial undertakings – disease may impact on production levels and farmers must conform to legal and regulatory obligations. The availability of subsidies and compensation for disease may influence the choices made by farmers. Such choices are reflected in different responses to disease and its control; for example consumer choices may determine market decisions and influence political and stakeholder choices. Interwoven into this complex system of decision-making are global influences.

Account must also be taken of a decline in UK public finances and vulnerability in the agricultural sector attributable to climate change. The latter is unpredictable, but relatively small changes in global mean temperature may have profound significance. More extreme weather events are predicted, such as frequent droughts and changes in rainfall. Changes in temperature patterns are likely to result in an increased risk of pests and disease in animals. The agricultural sector in general must be proactive in adapting to change. Specific sectors are particularly vulnerable. Heat stress on animals may lead to lost milk production, poultry may suffer higher mortality rates and produce fewer eggs, and transportation of animals at times of heat waves may pose major risks to their health and welfare.

The control of endemic diseases is often undermined by the disconnects between the biological and economic domains. There are differences in aims and objectives, methodology and the pre-eminence of market forces. Endemic diseases are controlled at the herd level by the individual farmer. Information networks including veterinary advice, government policy and the role of stakeholders, such as supermarkets, influence behaviour, but are all underlined by market forces. There are many variables at work including the technical ability to diagnose and treat diseases. Vaccination and other approaches to disease are also influenced by economic choices and policy implications. Underpinning such considerations are the complications of the available preferences and the difficulties of making appropriate choices. Farmers without disease in their herd have a competitive advantage. Removal of disease from their herd or farm can result in an economic benefit, while other farmers may experience a benefit from a reduction in disease risk or infection. The elimination of the disease from a herd may not always be effective due to the risk of reintroduction of the disease. Uncertainties arising from the lack of a coherent policy can result in an increase in risk and ineffective use of resources.

Economic uncertainty, climate change, new disease threats and global pressures on food resources are all considered in the book. Regulating animal health and welfare is undergoing considerable change as a consequence of the setting up in November 2011 of the Animal Health and Welfare Board (AHWB) within the Department for Environment, Food and Rural Affairs (Defra). The AHWB has the policy role within Defra of reducing the risk and cost of animal disease and improving animal welfare. The creation of the new regulatory body coincides with considerable uncertainty over the complex chain of responsibility for animal health and welfare. Risk assessment and its appropriate regulation is also much in doubt and is influenced by the outcome of the financial crisis of 2008.

Understanding animal diseases in the context of interdisciplinarity highlights many of the benefits of knowledge exchange, supporting evidence-based policy and practice across a range of activities, both public and private. It helps to inform policy makers, engages with different stakeholders and aids collaboration and understanding. The advantages of an interdisciplinary approach include better risk appraisal and a more appropriate understanding of significant factors in animal health and welfare drawn from different disciplines, together with better organisational learning. Conclusions reached from the research are intended to support integrated policy making. It is hoped that this will favour continued support for policy makers drawn from a wide range of disciplines. The reaction of government and policy making to animal diseases is often influenced by factors such as the political profile of a disease centred around its prevalence. Elimination or control of an endemic pathogen requires a change in its environment and the political will to intervene; if an intervention programme is successful, the political profile of a disease is likely to fall. Animal health and welfare must promote governance that is appropriate to each pathogen, within an integrated approach to endemic disease.

Acknowledgements

We wish to thank the Rural Economy and Land Use Programme (RELU) RES-229-25-0016 for funding. We also wish to thank Professor Philip Lowe and David Salter (Warwick) for their contributions.

1 Introduction

Introduction

The subject of this book is the governance of disease in farmed livestock, which can be considered as anything that affects an animal's well being and welfare.[1] Generally, there are considerable differences between the management of infectious and non-infectious diseases. Infectious diseases are caused by pathogens (prions, viruses, bacteria, prions, parasites) that change their behaviour over time, in terms of patterns of transmission, and can alter genetically (e.g. the emergence of resistance to drugs). The recent outbreak of the Schmallenberg virus[2] previously unseen in the UK, which causes disease in sheep, cattle and goats, is a good example of the changing nature of the disease threat. Pathogens may be specific to one livestock species or may affect many species. Non-infectious diseases are caused by the management of the animal, for example poor physical resources, such as lying on hard concrete surfaces, which causes foot and limb injuries in all livestock species kept in such conditions, or poor diet, leading to deficiencies that cause metabolic disease. In this book, we concentrate on infectious endemic disease, although we believe that many of the insights are also relevant to non-infectious disease. Infectious epidemic (or exotic) diseases, such as foot and mouth disease (FMD), or emerging zoonotic diseases are used principally as comparisons, and we do not consider those directly. There is a considerable literature (both scientific and government reports) already

1 The research undertaken for this book was funded by a large RELU award and the study is cross-disciplinary, drawing on the research of scientists, lawyers, economists and political scientists.
2 The diseases are widespread throughout Germany, the Netherlands, northern and central Europe. It is an orthobunyavirus spread through midges and mosquitoes.

relating to the FMD epidemics of 2001[3] and 2007,[4] the bovine spongiform encephalopathy (BSE) epidemic[5] and bluetongue.[6]

As we shall see, the importance placed on a particular disease largely depends on who is setting the agenda. Considerations include the need to protect public health, to promote the welfare of animals and to address wider issues, such as international trade matters and the impact on the wider economy, environment and society. Setting priorities is made more complicated by the need to balance the interests of different stakeholders as well as the protection of the public interest.

The governance of animal diseases covers different regulatory approaches, and prevention and control measures, including cost sharing and responsibility. Governance arrangements must engage with various stakeholders – animal keepers, government, citizens and supermarkets. The financial crisis and public spending cuts raise difficult questions about the best way to allocate scarce resources to achieve satisfactory standards of animal health and welfare. Currently, the government bears the main cost of compensating farmers for animals compulsorily destroyed as a result of a notifiable disease outbreak. The 2001 FMD outbreak cost £6 billion to £9 billion and expenditure on bovine tuberculosis (bTB) in 2010/11 was £91 million. Public expenditure aside, animal disease may have a wider impact on public confidence. The BSE crisis in 1996 caused considerable public alarm and challenged the trust between government, the public and industry. Today, there is heightened concern of an increased threat of diseases amongst farmed animals in the UK. Climate change, the globalisation of trade and increased animal movements all have the potential to reduce the UK's capacity to control and prevent animal diseases.

One of the most significant developments in this area has been the setting up of the Animal Health and Welfare Board for England (AHWB)[7] within Defra in November 2011. The AHWB has the policy role within Defra of reducing the risk and cost of animal disease and improving animal welfare. The setting up of the AHWB makes it an opportune moment to consider the health and welfare of farmed animals. It raises questions about how law and legal regulation can ultimately help to achieve changes in public attitudes and popular culture. Sound science, the role of risk management and the allocation of responsibilities amongst those best able to undertake them are also important. How farmers and industry engage in the policy-making process and how regulatory burdens are discharged

3 Anderson, I., *Foot and Mouth Disease 2001: Lessons to be Learned Inquiry Report*, London: The Stationery Office, July 2002.
4 Anderson, I. *Foot and Mouth Disease 2007: A Review and Lessons Learned*, London: The Stationery Office, March 2008.
5 Phillips, L., Bridgeman, J. and Ferguson-Smith, M., *The BSE Inquiry: The Report*, London: The Stationery Office, 2000.
6 Defra, *UK Bluetongue Control Strategy*, PB13752, London: Defra, 1 December 2008.
7 See: www.defra.gov.uk/ahwbe.

are undergoing change. This is particularly important in the context of efficient and effective market solutions for developing a new partnership approach to animal health and welfare. Lastly, it is important to consider how the AHWB is accountable and responsible for its decisions.

The main geographical focus of the book is on England, although account is taken of Wales. Defra is the central government department, but responsibility in Wales, Scotland and Northern Ireland lies with the devolved administrations within a general the framework set by Defra. The book takes into account influences from the EU, such as the current *Animal Health Strategy 2007–2013*.[8] This provides a broad approach to future policy making, including additional prioritisation of EU intervention, a modern and appropriate animal health framework, better prevention, surveillance and crisis preparedness; and reliance on science, innovation and research. Recently, an EU policy document on the protection and welfare of animals[9] takes further steps in improving animal health and welfare throughout the Member States. Article 13 of the Treaty on the Functioning of the EU and affirmed by the Treaty of Lisbon has recognised the importance of animal welfare. Animals are regarded as 'sentient beings', a legal term that is associated with acknowledging that full regard must be given to the welfare requirements of animals while formulating EU policies. The application of the ordinary legislative procedure known as co-decision to agriculture and fisheries has resulted in greater transparency to decision making than in the past. There is likely to be a focus on food safety policy and consumers, which will need to be addressed by the farming community. There may also be a heated contest over scarce public finances with priorities being given to considerations such as food pricing rather than animal health and welfare considerations.

The book also addresses the general context in which animal health and welfare and the governance of endemic animal diseases is best considered. Almost €70 million annually is provided by the EU to support animal welfare, of which over 70 per cent goes to farmers in the form of welfare payments available from the EU Agricultural Fund for Rural Development.[10] Matters to be addressed in the strategy are enforcement, the dissemination of information amongst stakeholders and simplification of principles applicable to animal welfare.

---

8 See EU Commission, *A New Animal Health Strategy for the European Union (2007–2013) where 'Prevention is better than cure'* (COM 539 (2007) final).

9 See EU Commission, Communication on the European Union Strategy for the Protection and Welfare of Animals 2012–2015 (COM (2012) 6 final).

10 Houses of Parliament, POSTNOTE Number 392 October 2011, *Livestock Disease*, London: Parliamentary Office of Science and Technology. See Brownlie, J., Clarke, M.C., Howard, C.J. and Pocock, D.H., 'Pathogenesis and epidemiology of bovine virus infection of cattle' (1987) 18 *Annales de recherches vétérinaires* 157–166. Bennett, R., 'The "direct costs" of livestock disease: the development of a system of models for the analysis of 30 endemic livestock diseases in Great Britain' (2003) 54(1) *Journal of Agricultural Economics* 55–71.

Examining how to achieve appropriate standards of animal health and welfare is well suited to the interdisciplinary study on the governance of diseases in farmed livestock undertaken for this book. Disease threats to UK livestock drive up costs, severely impact on farming communities and undermine confidence in agriculture, as well as having an impact on the general economy. The book adopts a methodological approach that attempts to bring together the findings through an interdisciplinary perspective. The aim is to bring a fresh perspective to the way science is examined by social scientists, including lawyers, and to the way scientists think of the context of their work. This is consistent with the increasing expectation upon scientists to make their findings known in public forums outside their own disciplines.[11] It is also in line with the 1999 *Modernising Government* White Paper that 'policy decisions should be based on sound evidence'.[12] The common methodology is to examine the problems posed by animal health and disease using materials drawn from science, social science and relevant disciplines, in order to assess the operation of the regulations and control of diseases in the context of how issues of responsibility and cost sharing should be addressed. This orientation is pluralistic in style and content – it presents an applied view of science drawing on different disciplinary approaches that critically examine how science, law and policy address issues associated with animal health and welfare. It provides a useful case study of how different disciplines can be explained and developed, as well as how regulatory and policy issues can be managed in a sustainable way,[13] and this is explained further in Chapter 3.

It is also noteworthy how, during the period of research for the book, there has been an increasing awareness amongst policy makers of the impact of climate change on animal diseases.[14] Haskell and others[15] have shown the link between climate change and animal disease. Climate change, as a result of global warming and increasingly competitive markets, significantly affects UK agriculture. The effects of climate change have been linked to the spread of various viruses, for example bluetongue which, since 1998, has spread across Europe killing up to 1 million sheep. Bluetongue has also been found in the UK but has, to date, been successfully rebuffed. Tracking climate changes and mitigating their effects will be an important part of risk assessment and the adoption of the precautionary principle. Climate change will also affect the availability of water and may change agricultural practices. Increased storm events will also have a

---

11   Academy of Medical Sciences, www.acmedsci.ac.uk.
12   *Modernising Government*, Cm 4310, White Paper, London: The Stationery Office, 1999.
13   See Haack, S., *Defending Science within Reason: Between Scientism and Cynicism*, Amherst, NY: Prometheus Books, 2008, and *Evidence and Inquiry: Towards Reconstruction of Epistemology*, Oxford: Blackwell, 1993. Beecher-Monas, E., *Evaluating Scientific Evidence*, New York, NY: Cambridge University Press, 2007.
14   House of Commons Library, *Standard Note: Agriculture and Climate Change*, SN/SC/3763, 17 July 2012.
15   Haskell *et al.*, *Research Project: Animal Welfare and Climate Change: Impacts, Adaptations and Risks* (AW0513), Scottish Agricultural College, 2011.

potential impact. Animal health and welfare will be affected by the social, economic and environmental changes likely to be caused by climate change. In the UK it has proved particularly difficult to predict the effect of climate change, but extremes of weather – drought to flooding – are likely to create serious problems. However, the Meteorological Office struggles to predict short-term and longer-term change in the climate.

Making this study particularly relevant is the integration of different disciplines. This is the most effective way to provide analysis across distinct areas of expertise, ultimately encouraging the dissemination of information and more effective policy making. Relying on a small subset of specialists and a limited role for stakeholders' interests is unlikely to be effective in disease management. Decision making must be transparent and consider the range of interests if it is to be acceptable.

The role of science and scientists in collaboration with lawyers, economists and political scientists in reaching agreement on the criteria that should be considered by policy makers[16] is a recurrent theme throughout the book. The conclusions draw together the strands of analysis across the various disciplines and are intended to set the agenda for future research in this area. For example, this study may inform the approach adopted by the government and the AHWB in England. As an influential regulatory body, the AHWB should address how different disciplines[17] can best combine to promote effective control of animal diseases, protect animal health and improve regulation, as independent scientific information and its evaluation is crucial to its success. This sets a more general challenge[18] to facilitate the collaboration necessary for an understanding of the evidence-led policy making based around sound science. Interdisciplinary work fostering collaboration provides mutual understanding of complex multifaceted problems that policy makers and decision makers need to examine to ensure effective management of animal health and welfare.

First, we define what we mean by disease and discuss some biological and epidemiological characteristics that determine control. We go on to outline the management and regulation of animal diseases and what characterises appropriate regulation.[19]

16 Lowe, P. and Phillipson, J., 'Reflexive interdisciplinary research: the making of a research programme on the rural economy and land use' (2006) 57(2) *Journal of Agricultural Economics* 165–184.
17 Scott, C., 'Accountability in the regulatory state' (2000) 27(1) *Journal of Law and Society* 38–60.
18 See Greaves J. and Grant, W., 'Crossing the interdisciplinary divide: political science and biological science' (2010) 58(2) *Political Studies* 320–339.
19 The framework strategy is set out by Defra in 2004 in *Animal Health and Welfare Strategy for Great Britain*, London: Defra, 2004. The strategy addresses animal health and welfare by hoping to make 'joint working between industry and government a reality'. This involves making joint decisions about the prevention, control and elimination of animal diseases under the vision of a clear understanding of the roles and responsibilities that define the relationship between industry and government. In 2007, Defra published its influential *Responsibility and cost sharing for animal health and welfare: next steps Consultation Paper*, London: Defra, December 2007.

Defining animal health and welfare in a multidisciplinary study: a biological and epidemiological approach to animal diseases

In a multidisciplinary study of this kind, the management and regulation of animal health and welfare must take account of the biological and epidemiological characteristics that determine disease control. How science informs the analysis that contributes to the management and governance of animal diseases is considered.

As already outlined, disease in farmed livestock can be thought of as anything that affects an animal's well being and welfare. Considerable differences exist between the management of different infectious agents, therefore a short explanation of the terms and concepts is required for an understanding of the book.

Infectious and non-infectious diseases

A fundamental difference between infectious and non-infectious diseases is that infectious diseases are transmitted between hosts and spread through populations via direct and indirect contact.[20] In contrast, non-infectious diseases occur when there is an adverse factor affecting the host species. Consequently, the risk of an individual animal acquiring an infectious disease is dependent on the infection status of others in the population, whereas an individual's risk of aquiring a non-infectious disease is independent of other animals.[21] Generally, both infectious and non-infectious diseases cluster within farms (i.e. the on-farm incidence is higher or lower than chance when compared with the population of interest) because both the management and physical conditions and the presence of an infectious animal vary between farms. However, the presence of a non-infectious disease on one farm does not influence its presence on a neighbouring farm, whereas it might for an infectious disease.[22] The independence and non-independence of farm risks influence the regulation of diseases, which is discussed further below.

Biology of infectious diseases: introduction of a novel pathogen

No infectious disease exists everywhere all the time, so that there are farms, regions or nations that are free from some pathogens, either by deliberate action or natural circumstances. Such infection-free populations are at a particular risk

20 Barrett, S., 'Global disease eradication' (2003) 1(2–3) *Journal of the European Economic Association* 591–600.

21 One possible exception are the injurious behaviours inflicted by conspecifics, for example tail biting in pigs or feather pecking in hens, which might spread in a manner more similar to an infectious rather than a non-infectious disease within a herd/flock.

22 Hindmoor, A., 'Explaining networks through mechanisms: vaccination, priming and the 2001 Foot and Mouth Crisis' (2009) 57 *Political Studies* 75–94.

of an epidemic since all the constituent individuals, unless vaccinated, are susceptible to infection. A pathogen initially invades a naïve population of susceptible
individuals (in this case, farmed animals or livestock) by one or more of several
likely routes and infects susceptible individuals causing an epidemic, defined
as an increase in disease above the expected level (note that for a novel pathogen
the expected level of disease is zero). These individuals might or might not
show clinical signs of disease which, in turn, might range from a few days of ill
health to death. For those individuals that do not die, the next stage of the process
might be recovery and life-long immunity to that particular (strain of) pathogen,
recovery and partial immunity (i.e. they can be infected again) or a carrier status
where the individual remains infected for life and is permanently or occasionally
infectious to other hosts.[23]

Persistence of a pathogen

A pathogen persists in a population by infecting a continuing supply of susceptible hosts. Pathogens have many characteristics, including manipulating their host
or environment, to facilitate persistence. Once the initial susceptible population
has been exposed to a novel pathogen, the proportion of the population that is
susceptible declines and so constrains the disease to a lower prevalence. An
endemic disease is one in which each infected individual infects, on average, one
other susceptible individual. Typically, when a new pathogen enters a naïve
population, disease is more severe – or at least perceived to be more severe – than
after it has been in a population for many cycles of infection. Thus a pathogen
present in a population as an endemic disease often appears to be a mild disease
or is present at a relatively low prevalence or both. Such a disease does not
always cause an obvious financial cost to the farmer, but we argue that this is
principally due to accommodation and mitigation of endemic disease by farmers,
the agricultural industry and regulatory systems.

Spread of infectious diseases

Pathogens are an extremely varied group of organisms, relying on their hosts
to provide energy, shelter, etc. and potentially causing injury to their hosts in
the process. Pathogens vary in the number of host species they are able to infect
and the number of routes through which they are able to be passed to other
susceptible hosts. They also vary in their clinical presentation and severity of
disease caused, the duration of infectiousness of a host, their survival outside a
host, whether the host mounts a full immunity to the infection and whether this
immunity is life-long. Pathogens vary and mutate and use this as an evolutionary

---

23 Turvey, C.G., 'Conceptual issues in livestock insurance', Working Paper No. WP-0503-005,
    Food Policy Research Institute, Rutgers University, 2003.

mechanism for survival.[24] All these biological facets of a given pathogen influence how each disease is controlled or might be controlled.

Whilst the transmission of infection between individuals within a population is critical for invasion and persistence, for livestock disease there is an additional level of spread. Farmed livestock are typically kept in relatively small populations (herds or flocks), although the distribution of herd sizes is skewed. These populations have some contact with each other forming a meta-population, i.e. population of populations. Contact arises through movement of animals, personnel and equipment. In Chapter 4, we introduce the idea of the 'meta-herd': the herd of herds which is the national population of livestock. Consequently, how a pathogen invades and persists in the meta-population or meta-herd, not just the individual herd, is of great importance for regulation and management.

Developing strategies for the control of infectious diseases

The first infectious diseases to be eliminated[25] from the UK, namely contagious bovine pleuropneumonia (CBPP) and rinderpest, were recognised during the eighteenth century by the distinct clinical signs that were observed in diseased animals. Elimination was possible because these diseases (later known to be infectious diseases) only occurred in cattle, so they were host specific, did not survive outside the host in the environment and cattle were not infectious for a prolonged period before disease occurred. So, by killing animals diseased with CBPP and rinderpest, these pathogens were eliminated. To keep the diseases out of the UK, legislation was introduced to prevent the movement of livestock or their products (milk, cheese, meat or hides) into the UK.

Such elimination strategies were initiated in the mid-1700s when there were no vaccines or successful treatments, and elimination was the optimal way to maintain healthy livestock. These strategies continued for over a century, eliminating and keeping out of the UK sheep pox, rabies and FMD. Elimination was successful biologically because of the nature of the pathogens targeted, but the distribution of the hosts – relatively small isolated herds/flocks and the amount of contact between them – probably also aided both elimination and stamping out of re-introduced disease. As well as having no alternatives with which to control these diseases, there must also have been a societal and political willingness to achieve this control.

Disease labels: endemic and exotic and their consequences

An infectious disease that is not present in a country is described as exotic, i.e. exotic to that country, whilst a disease that is present in a country is described

---

24 There are a very small number of pathogens, including the human diseases measles, mumps and rubella, that appear to have much more limited diversity, but these are exceptional.

25 'Elimination' is the epidemiological term for regional removal of a pathogen, but still requiring control to prevent re-invasion. 'Eradication' describes the global removal of a pathogen – smallpox and rinderpest are the only pathogens to have been eradicated.

as endemic. As we argue in Chapter 4, these are political definitions or labels for a disease and are constructed. Diseases (pathogens) are not per se exotic or endemic; for example FMD is exotic in the UK but endemic in many parts of the world. Once this labelling has occurred, the political debate is framed around it, particularly in terms of how involved government should be in tackling the disease. Typically, exotic diseases have more political debate, more legislation and more estimates of economic impacts of introduction or control than endemic diseases. Endemic diseases are regarded more as part of the livestock landscape, to be accommodated and mitigated against rather than controlled through concerted effort. This situation is self-reinforcing, so that relatively little research is conducted on endemic disease, and its economic and welfare burden is relatively undefined so that the impetus for control is not as great as for exotic disease.

The label a disease carries determines the control that the disease receives and so its biological and economic behaviour in a population changes. One disease for which the political history has been described is FMD.[26] After initial introduction, FMD was eliminated (removed) from the UK in the late 1800s. From that time the pathogen has repeatedly entered the UK through introduction of infected animals, animal products and accidental release from UK laboratories. All political effort was towards keeping FMD as an exotic (i.e. non-endemic) disease. This drove the biological research agenda which targeted characterising the FMD virus, so that we are now able to identify where a particular incursion of virus came from. It also drove the biological agenda away from developing good vaccines that might have resulted in control of FMD through mass vaccination. As Woods points out in relation to FMD,[27] '[It] is simplistic to assume that the present-day image of FMD as a terrible plague emerged because it was obviously correct'. That is, we could have control by means other than exclusion.

The diseases that are not present in the UK now have been excluded for historic and practical reasons and we can consider them in distinct categories that are not necessarily biological. They include zoonoses (affecting man), for example *Brucella abortus*, rabies; economically important diseases, for example rinderpest, FMD and warble fly; and, additionally, diseases that are clinically indistinguishable from more important diseases, for example swine vesicular disease (which has clinical signs that are not distinguishable from FMD). It is quite possible that if some of these diseases were present in the UK now, they would be managed differently, possibly by vaccination.

Multidisciplinary study

Scientific understanding and technical knowledge are needed to control a disease, and economics can give us an estimate of the costs and benefits of control.

26 Woods, A., *A Manufactured Plague: The History of Foot and Mouth Disease in Britain*, London: Earthscan, 2004, p. 101.
27 Ibid., pps. 101–2.

However, these factors may be overruled by a political decision that is oppor-
tunistic rather than being evidence-based. The point Woods[28] makes about
FMD control could also be applied to other diseases: 'it was ... an ideological
affair that was closely bound up with the role and status of science in society,
the accountability of government bodies and Britain's international standing'.

Endemic diseases are themselves categorised by further political labels. These
include zoonotic diseases, economically important diseases, welfare-related
diseases and production diseases. These labels sometimes have some biological
meaning, but the category in which a disease is placed is not without contention.
In particular, diseases perceived to be a public health risk (to humans) attain
high political importance, especially those that can lead to an illness requiring
hospital treatment or that is potentially fatal. For example, BSE resulted in
governmental reorganisation (the formation of the Food Standards Agency and
Defra out of the former Ministry of Agriculture, Fisheries and Food (MAFF)[29]
was largely precipitated by the perceived failure to manage the epidemic), and
high expenditure. Currently, there is debate regarding the relationship between
Johne's disease (paratuberculosis) in cattle and Crohn's disease in humans, and
whether they have the same infectious cause: *Mycobacterium avium* subspp.
paratuberculosis[30] (MAP). Johne's disease is regarded as a typical endemic
infection, i.e. a production problem for the diary industry. However, MAP is
found in milk and if the public perception that MAP is a cause of Crohn's disease
strengthens, then the status of Johne's disease will change. Note that it is only the
perception that need change, not the scientific evidence to strengthen, although
there is probably some correlation between the two.

Endemic diseases that are not a risk to public health are left to the control of
the individual farmer with varying degrees of industry involvement and support.
This is an area where there is a clear regulatory gap. There is no clear legislation,
little political interest and few estimates of economic impact. Such categorisations
of diseases are not immutable and may change over time. An example of this is
bovine viral diarrhoea (BVD). Initially, this virus was named after it was associated with an episode of diarrhoea in cattle of three–four days' duration. Cattle
were infectious for a few days, made a full recovery and had life-long immunity.
The virus spread was uncontrolled and many herds became infected. Many years
later it was realised that the same BVD virus was responsible for spontaneous
abortions in cattle and death in a small proportion of young cattle. These young
cattle are immunotolerant to the virus and shed it onto the environment for many
months/years before ultimately dying from immune failure. This is the route for
persistence of the BVD virus. Infection with BVD can be diagnosed with a relatively simple blood test and disease can be controlled with a vaccine.

28 Ibid., p. 101.
29 Marsden, T., Lee, R., Flynn, A. and Thankappan, S., *The New Regulation and Governance of
    Food*, Abingdon: Routledge, 2010, pp. 79–80.
30 Greenstein, R.J., 'Is Crohn's disease caused by mycobacterium? Comparisons with leprosy,
    tuberculosis and Johne's disease' (2003) 3 *The Lancet Infectious Diseases* 507–514.

In the mid-1980s, the Scandinavian countries moved towards elimination of BVD. It was argued that the economic impact of BVD was far greater than was apparent on any one farm and that the behaviour of the virus and availability of diagnostic tests lent it to elimination. These countries approached control through segregation of herds free from BVD and gradual elimination of BVD from infected herds through vaccination and culling. By 2005, BVD was notifiable in seven[31] EU countries, and BVD was added to the World Organisation for Animal Health (OIE) list of diseases.[32] Thus interventions by international entities, including the EU but also international organisations – especially the sanitary and phytosaniatry rules of the World Trade Organization (WTO)[33] – may become more significant over time, influencing domestic decisions. These developments alter the pressure for control and may result in important changes relating to BVD control in the UK.

Non-infectious disease

Additionally to these categorisations, the management, regulation and policy related to non-infectious and infectious diseases differs, and the responsibility for a non-infectious disease is with the immediate carer who can influence its occurrence by changing the herd/flock environment. The limitation for reduction of non-infectious disease has been entirely economic, with the cost of improving a herd's environment having to be less than the financial benefit gained either through increased productivity or increased market value of the final product. Farmers, however, have different approaches to the amount of extra income that they use to improve the living conditions of their livestock. More recently in the UK, laws and codes[34] have been introduced to guide farmers on minimum standards for the environment of farmed livestock that are aimed at reducing non-infectious diseases and ensuring that livestock have some or all of the five freedoms used to define good animal welfare. Some of the legislation[35] in the UK is more prohibitive than in any other country in the world, for example it is illegal to house pregnant sows in individual stalls (crates): they must be kept in groups. The pig industry generally considers that this legal requirement makes it less able to compete on the international market.

---

31 Gunn, G.J., Saatkamp, H.W., Humphry, R.W. and Scott, A., 'Assessing economic and social pressure for the control of bovine viral diarrhoea virus' (2005) 72 *Preventive Veterinary Medicine* 149–162.

32 Ibid., p. 151.

33 Josling, T., Roberts, D. and Orden, D., *Food Regulation and Trade*, Washington, DC: Institute for International Economics, 2004, pp. 40–51.

34 See Defra for a list of relevant legislation, www.defra.gov.uk (accessed 27 March 2013), and also www.gov.uk (accessed 27 March 2013).

35 www.parliament.uk (accessed 27 March 2013).

Animal health and welfare board for England

As mentioned above, the Coalition Government has embarked on a programme of major changes in the way animal health policy and its funding are considered and this is also addressed in the book. Defra, the main government department responsible for animal health and welfare, has undertaken a major consultation process on strengthening governance and examining the financial aspects of animal health and welfare in the UK. This coincides with a cost sharing proposal that seeks to change the way animal health is funded. The Anderson Inquiry after the FMD outbreak in 2001 considered why costs should be paid by the general public. The cost to the taxpayer of the 2001 outbreak was around £6 billion to £9 billion. The aim of current policy making is to share costs between the main beneficiaries and risk managers. As part of the responsibility and cost sharing agenda, the aim is to develop partnerships to deal with a range of animal diseases.

As outlined above, the AHWB was set up in November 2011 and has a number of key objectives and roles. Its primary function is to advise ministers and ensure adequate communication with animal keepers. The advice covers strategic budget and policy priorities, as well as the implementation of effective disease risk assessment. There are also a number of important evaluations to be carried out, including assessment of operational plans and contingency arrangements. The government's budget and spending reductions are also within the terms of the AHWB. Defra has allocated £243,800,000 to the AHWB, with a planned reduction to £199,413,000 in 2012/15. The composition of the AHWB draws together external members who have long-standing connections and knowledge of the agricultural sector, and includes the Chief Veterinary Officer and his deputy as well as Defra-appointed directors. There are also plans to engage with stakeholders and develop links with industry and animal keepers.

The AHWB meets regularly and publishes its minutes online. It has agreed an allocation of responsibilities between Board members and intends to set up working groups amongst Board members. In developing its key strategies, the AHWB has set some priorities, including building trust and a working partnership between government and animal keepers. This will be based on best practice and value for money considerations, with the intention of developing self-reliance amongst the various stakeholders. In a time of public funding cuts, one of the greatest challenges is to achieve various aims and objectives, perhaps prioritising the main issues.

The effectiveness of the AHWB is largely dependent on its ability to earn trust and establish effective engagement with stakeholders.[36] It will be essential to work well with different agricultural sectors in order to provide both good policy making and effective strategic thinking. The AHWB must also consider how the public interest is best defined. In addition, the public need to be kept

---

36 Seals, M., *Animal Health and Welfare Board for England Presentation*, January 2012, www. defra.gov.uk/ahwbe (accessed 27 March 2013).

well informed. There are likely to be considerable tensions in reconciling different objectives, and there are many challenges to be met. For example, in certain areas, such as disease prevention, it may not be in the public interest to cut costs; careful consideration needs to be given to the EU policy making; economic considerations on each sector of agriculture may not be easy to reconcile; and controversial subjects need to be addressed, such as culling badgers or adopting a vaccination policy for certain diseases.

There are also methodological problems that arise from engaging with different specialisms. Gaining collaboration between science and social sciences is important, as is achieving public trust. There are certain sensitivities that arise such as the mix of government policy making and the use of sound science.[37] Scientific collaboration involving different disciplines highlights the need for independence and autonomy. The value of the collaboration is intended to foster shared values as well as a more nuanced understanding of policy and regulation in the ever changing political climate with rewarding outcomes, not least in defining a shared methodology as well as common values. Measuring the success or failure of science in collaboration with the social sciences may become one of the most important intellectual questions of the twenty-first century. It is strongly argued in this book that the broader analytically and more policy focused approach favoured by social scientists helps scientists recognise how science must engage with the policy implications of their findings. This has the potential to strengthen policy making. Social scientists may find that engaging with expert scientific evidence through cross-disciplinary collaboration is the most appropriate way to understand complex data and evaluations made from scientific judgements. This may help set priorities and lead to a better understanding of the underpinnings of social science research and the philosophical understanding of knowledge. Looking towards the future, there are many governance issues raised about the AHWB in its policy-making role, including how priorities need to be set and how the AHWB itself is open and accountable – it must gain public confidence and support before its legitimacy is accepted. This raises questions about effective parliamentary oversight of Defra, including an in-depth understanding of the AHWB and its role.

Organisation and approach of the book

Main themes and objectives

Many aspects of the governance of animal health are explored in this book. This is a challenging time, not least because of economic and social pressures on the

---

37 House of Commons, Science and Technology Committee, *The Government's review of the principles applying to the treatment of independent scientific advice provided to government*, Third Report of Session 2009–10, HC 158-I, London: The Stationery Office. The Government's review followed the sacking of Professor David Nutt as Chairman of the Advisory Council on the Misuse of Drugs (ACMD) on 30 October 2009.

agricultural sector – progress towards a sustainable future for livestock faces many challenges; climate change and disease risk is part of an overall consideration of threats to animal welfare; costs associated with animal welfare and disease need to be considered within changing circumstances; and the economics of the agricultural sector, particularly volatile prices such as low milk prices, need to be considered.

In Chapter 2, there is an historical explanation of how animal health and welfare has developed from the early era of the nineteenth century to the current approach to regulating animal health and welfare issue.

In Chapter 3, the main disciplinary issues and perspectives are discussed that make the case of greater communication at policy and implementation levels. The differing models for interdisciplinary research are studied and the challenges that meet researchers when addressing different methodologies considered. This chapter lays the foundations for the book that address how different disciplinary perspectives can be accommodated, and interact effectively, in consideration of a complex issue. It is relatively brief, and discusses the different models for interdisciplinary research, and the changes that face the researchers. Does the methodological approach adopted alter the outcomes? We believe that the interdisciplinary interaction's greatest strength is the framing of questions that should be addressed, rather than the selection of issues addressed. A recurring theme throughout the book is how governance including different ways to undertake risk assessment are critical to addressing animal health and welfare issues.

Chapter 4 addresses the interactions between the biological, social, economic, legal and political processes that determine the epidemiology of endemic disease. The chapter sets the scene for developing ideas that inform the current debate amongst agricultural stakeholders and engaging with future strategy for animal health and welfare in terms of risk management. This includes cost sharing and economic analysis of how best to assign responsibility for animal health and welfare.

Chapter 5 provides case studies of BVD, Johne's Disease and bTB, and deals with examples of endemic diseases. BVD is an endemic disease that is not a risk to public health. The control of BVD is left to the private farmer and for many years the virus spread and was uncontrolled. BVD is tackled in many countries through active controls and management strategies, and the UK has had to adopt different strategies than in the past including potential use of vaccination. The value of the chapter is that it shows how farmers follow each other in deciding what action to take, and analysis is provided of how a voluntary form of self-regulation may prove more cost-effective than individual responses that are largely *laissez faire*. What are the lessons to be learned? What might motivate self-regulation and how might the future be shaped by government regulation or oversight?

Chapter 6 concerns the law and economics of regulating animal health and welfare. The chapter examines legal regulation based on considerations of science and economics is discussed in the context of Europe and the political sensitivities of policy making. Conflicts between stakeholders are considered.

The debate between public and private sector solutions, and the different styles of regulation are considered in the context of the regulation of animal health and welfare based on sound science. The regulatory evaluation of animal health and welfare addresses risks and associated policy making in terms of costs and benefits. Disputes over the appropriate kind of risk assessment and management are one of the most controversial areas of law that interacts with animal health and welfare issues. The chapter also takes account of the precautionary principle and the principles of cost sharing and responsibility. The role of the precautionary principle is assessed, as well as the impact of policy making in this field especially in the light of the cost sharing and responsibility initiatives that are actively being pursued by the government. The chapter assesses how public opinion, stakeholders and costs are to be taken into consideration in the policy-making process. The analysis offered in the book is that the future regulatory framework for animal health and welfare goes beyond the combination of science, law, risk and safety, but espouses evaluation by the main stakeholders in the resolution of costs and efficiency gains. Reducing public spending on animal health and welfare is being undertaken. This marks a shift in ownership and responsibility related to a new framework for decision making that must take account of various stakeholders and the sensitivities of public opinion. Assessing risk and the precautionary principle is likely to be accommodated under different perspectives determined by who is paying. Inevitably, this is more likely to be conflict-driven because of competing interests and perspectives. The question of how to protect and define the public interest will be paramount. There is also an increasing politicisation of how to approach expert systems of analysis and this must be factored into the final policy-making agenda.

Chapter 7 addresses the policy-making process itself and what might inform the future strategy. The themes of risk management based on sound science, cost sharing drawing on economics and market solutions, and the political priorities embracing the various stakeholders are examined. Why are some diseases given higher priority by government than others? What are the values of various case studies, for example on bTB policy: the case of the 'rogue badger'. How do farmers view policy? What are the public perceptions of animal welfare and the relationship between animal health and welfare policy? How are the various interests of taxpayers, consumers, farmers and supermarkets considered in government policy making and approaches to animal diseases? The roles of EU and international organisations are considered. Proposals are put forward for the future of regulating animal health and welfare. These include better joined-up thinking to ensure that sound science is integral in the policy-making process; growth of confidence in the relationship between stakeholders and active consideration of different cost-sharing initiatives including the insurance principle; a wider public debate outside the stakeholders and better engagement with regulatory principles.

Lastly, Chapter 8 sets out the conclusions that bring the main analysis of the book together. The main thesis is that sound science is intrinsic to a better understanding of risk management and, consequently, it provides a better approach to law and regulation for animal health and welfare. To give the public a voice is only one part of the analysis; to ensure that well-informed debate is able to engage with regulation is another. As revealed in the book, the synergy between distinct disciplines is not easy to find in terms of a common methodology; sharing common values or ensuring that agreed procedures might be suitable for good decision making. The book advances the steps needed to ensure collaboration by first recognising that a commonly agreed and robust line of thinking when tackling animal health and welfare is not always possible. What is confirmed, however, is that critically appraising existing rules and principles, and investigating how institutions and concepts work, provide a means to secure dialogue, if not always agreement. Working within disputed areas of science and economics makes law making hazardous and outcomes unpredictable. In developing future policy, government must address contested values and opinions and, even if consensus is not agreed, sound science should inform the outcome. The question of how to 'advance' the regulation of animal health and welfare will be considered in light of an analysis that draws on all the disciplines involved in the study.

2 Historical and contemporary aspects of animal health and welfare

Introduction

In this chapter we begin by tracing the historical roots of contemporary approaches to animal health and welfare, primarily from the end of the nineteenth century until the present time. The main focus is on legislative developments. It was not until the development of high standards in veterinary care that it was possible to combine the different approaches to health and disease with preventative measures and the improvement of welfare. Next we outline the contemporary challenges set by the governance, management and regulation of animal diseases. The various stakeholders and responsibilities are considered as a background to the consideration of the most appropriate form of regulation in later chapters.[1] Viewed from an historical perspective, remarkably, changes in attitudes are apparent from the eighteenth-century view that animals are 'property' and, as economic commodities, susceptible to economic exploitation. Religious belief was also influential in viewing animals as a subordinate species to humans. Such attitudes slowly gave way to a more holistic approach that advances disease prevention and cure.

From cruelty and its prevention to developing animal health and welfare in response to disease

Animal welfare developed quite separately from animal health and, legally speaking, welfare can be understood from the perspective of preventing cruelty to animals. In contrast, animal health gradually developed in response to major disease outbreaks and the creation of a veterinary profession with scientific expertise. The development of appropriate approaches to animal welfare had to overcome several major obstacles. The early common law regarded animals as

---

1 The framework strategy is set out by Defra in 2004 in *Animal Health and Welfare Strategy for Great Britain*, London: Defra, 2004. In 2007, Defra published its influential *Responsibility and cost sharing for animal health and welfare: next steps Consultation Paper*, London: Defra, December 2007.

property, with limited safeguards for animal welfare either through legislation or its interpretation given in the courts. The courts viewed animals as private possessions enjoyed by owners rather than from the standpoint of the health and welfare of animals. Animal suffering went largely ignored, even on the rare occasions when prosecutions were taken. Philosophical constructions of rights and man considered human action as an individual fighting to survive in a hostile state of nature. At the same time, there was a sense that misusing animals reflected poorly on the owner. Property rights enjoyed by humans became a normative way of addressing animals.[2] Thomas Hobbes's[3] interpretation of man as an autonomous individual failed to distinguish anything else, such as a fish or a tree. Human rights philosophy failed to appreciate the world outside the human which was seen as coming within the ownership of the individual. Human mastery over other species further entrenched property ownership as part of the natural rights of man. The historical legacy from the eighteenth century is particularly unpromising as the period witnessed widespread cruelty to animals and disregard for their suffering. As Mike Radford expressed it, 'the mistreatment of other species was deeply entrenched in the social fabric and widely evidenced in daily life'.[4] John Lawrence, a prolific writer and farmer, in 1796 considered that 'the Rights of Beasts be formally acknowledged by the state and that a law be framed upon that principle'.[5] However, this was easier to express than to put into practice. State intervention to establish a framework in which animals ought to be treated humanely has been time-consuming and laborious, resulting in an estimated 3,500 provisions relating to animals over the past 200 years. The approach was often problem-driven and specific to a particular species. Animal suffering crossed religious as well as philosophical attitudes to Man. The traditional belief that Man followed a God-given right to treat animals as solely existing for Man's benefit, assumed Man's dominion over living creatures. Strongly entrenched property rights, particularly from the landed aristocracy, asserted ownership over animals that denied any interference over the treatment of animals, often by successfully claiming unassailable moral and legal property rights. Resistance to change was strongly encountered and difficult to overcome because of entrenched vested interests. Economic and social self-interest greatly influenced animal keepers, land owners and private enterprises engaged in the auction and sale of animals. A vibrant export market flourished. *Laissez faire* attitudes to animal market and sale were common. The relatively simple principle of owners owing

2 See Garner, R., 'Rawls, animal and justice: new literature, same response' (2012) *Res Publica* 159.
3 Thomas Hobbes (1558–1679). Educated at Magdalen College, Oxford, philosopher. See Linzey, A., *Why Animal Suffering Matters*, Oxford: Oxford University Press, 2009. Gearty, C., 'Do human rights help or hinder environmental protection?' (2010) *Journal of Human Rights and the Environment* 7–22.
4 Radford, M., *Animal Welfare Law in Britain*, Oxford: Oxford University Press, 2001, p. 3.
5 Lawrence, J. *On the Rights of Beasts in A Philosophical Treatise on Horses and on the Moral Duties of Man towards the Brute Creation*, London 1796. Nicholson, E.B., *The Rights of An Animal. A New Essay in Ethics*, London: C. Kegan Paul and Co., 1879.

direct and enforceable responsibilities to animals took a long time to become accepted. The latter part of the eighteenth century was also a time when, in general, society came under the influence of moral and political philosophers engaged in the study of political economy. Political economy addressed concerns about the role of the state in society, including a debate about the health and welfare of animals. The philosopher J.S. Mill[6] rejected the commonly held belief that legal intervention to tackle cruelty to 'defenceless creatures' was an unwarranted 'interference with domestic life'. Jeremy Bentham (1748–1832) was the original stimulus in re-assessing man's responsibility to animals.[7] He set the groundwork for considering that as sensitive beings, animals were linked to man's happiness, and that the interests of both man and animals were morally connected. Animals under the direction of human kind were important in assessing their interests and should not be overlooked in the assessment of man's happiness. Bentham rejected any moral distinction between humans and animals, and the obligations set on man's behaviour should include animals. This was a far-reaching prescription in terms of moral attitude. In Mill's view, the justification for laws for the prevention of harm to animals came from the perspective of the rights of animals rather than the interests of human life.[8] Legislation to protect animals from cruelty followed,[9] but struggled to be enforced through ineffective prosecutions and ambivalence over enforcement.

The Prevention of Cruelty to Animals Act 1849 introduced innovative strategies, such as broadening the scope of cruelty to include 'wantonness' and extending criminal liability to third parties, including employers and those responsible for condoning cruelty. Often, the suffering animal was a means of livelihood. Various attempts to regulate horses or farmed animals often failed when magistrates, sympathetic to the economic livelihood of the animal keepers, would not convict. Beyond cruelty, the legislation penalised 'unnecessary pain or suffering', which replaced a long catalogue of abusive actions with an overarching concept of pain and suffering. It also shifted the focus on the outcome rather than the cause and to the animal rather than the perpetrator. Animal protection was thereby linked to animal suffering and responsibility and social welfare provisions dealt with the animal's experience. This represented a seismic shift to animal protection that was linked to welfare and disease prevention. The Act also, for the first time, linked the carrying of an animal and its transportation to the regulation of an animal's health and safety, if there was unnecessary pain and suffering. The criminal law was used but this did not prove entirely successful

6 J.S. Mill (1806–1873), English philosopher and social reformer, J.S. Mill, *Principles of Political Economy*, 1848, London.
7 Bentham, J., *An Introduction to the Principles of Morals and Legislation*, London, c. 1789, Chapters 1 and 4.
8 Discussed by Radford, op. cit., n. 4, p. 61; see Mill, J.S., *The Principles of Political Economy*, 3rd edn, 1852, Vol II, Book V, chapter XI, section 9, pp. 546–547.
9 The Prevention of Cruelty to Animals Act 1849.

for prevention, and criminal prosecutions were often difficult. Debates about animal experimentation, or vivisection as the Victorians called it, engaged many views and divided opinions. Early campaigners against vivisection were pragmatic, but growing public debate by the 1860s led to constraints on animal experimentation involving cruelty.[10] Pressure groups and pamphlets kept up a steady pressure in favour of protecting animals.

Private initiatives on animal welfare and related good causes were also in evidence in the early part of the nineteenth century. The Royal Society for the Prevention of Cruelty to Animals (RSPCA) was established in 1824 and, under its auspices, private criminal prosecutions on animal cruelty were mounted. Supported by Royal patronage and endorsed by many landed proprietors, the RSPCA adopted several techniques to ensure a more effective response than in the past – it was able to investigate and prosecute animal owners and it was able to effectively lobby Parliament for support. Prohibiting excessive violence to animals became a popular cause and this culminated in further landmark legislation, the Protection of Animals Act 1911, in an attempt to control the export of live animals. The 1911 Act became the cornerstone of state regulation. It represented a growing public acceptance that state regulation could intrude into the private lives and property rights of animal owners. The combination of political pressure and prosecutions became a common feature of successful strategic policy making by the RSPCA.

The RSPCA's influence marked a further shift towards care for animals through measures to prevent and control animal neglect. Measures to improve animal health and welfare became inextricably linked to tackling animal cruelty. The regulatory arrangements fell short of tackling health, welfare and cruelty together and it took some time for this to happen.

Welfare issues began to take priority, especially concerns about animal neglect. The Temporary Home for Lost and Starving Dogs (now Battersea Dogs & Cats Home) was founded in 1860 to protect and care for stray dogs (cats were accepted from 1883). The public protection of stray dogs and the creation in 1867 of police responsibilities for taking unkempt and unwanted dogs off the streets of London was an important step in the criminalisation of neglect. The protection of animals and their health was intertwined in a matter of high moral concern – vivisection. Vivisection in England was widely practised in the latter part of the nineteenth century. Medical research involving animal experimentation advanced significantly through public health prevention and was used in the training of medical practitioners. There was also an element of scientific curiosity that contributed to advancing animal research. Human health and its understanding was greatly facilitated by research and experimentation on animals. The RSPCA gradually became concerned that voluntary self-regulation of animal experimentation was ineffective. Experimentation on animals in public meetings attracted

---

10 See Westacott, E., *A Century of Vivisection and Anti-Vivisection*, Rochford: CW Daniel Ltd., 1949.

large crowds but often brought considerable unrest and eventual outcry to the practices that were commonly used and became widely known. Manuals of voluntary conduct were produced to regulate experiments but appeared to be seldom adhered to, and the literature of former medical students and newspaper reports all spoke of cruel treatment. Public concern for animals and affection for pets spilled over in opposition to animal experimentation. In the 1870s, such concerns reached a crescendo of complaint and proposed private bill legislation was overtaken by weaker public legislation that followed the first *Royal Commission on the Practice of Subjecting Live Animals to Experiments for Scientific Purposes* in 1876. The Cruelty to Animals Act 1876, which remained in force for more than a century, linked cruelty and its prevention to the requirements of animal health, welfare and safety. A new Home Office Inspectorate was formed to impose sanctions and regulate restrictions on animal testing. It was an offence to perform an experiment calculated to give pain on any living animal unless with a view to advancing physiological knowledge, saving or prolonging life or alleviating suffering. The legislation reflected the hierarchy of norms that man's health and well being trumped that of animals. The Royal Commission had accepted the scientific case that the harm of animal experimentation was morally justified and outweighed by the public benefit. Excessive or undue cruelty was not acceptable but appropriate regulation would ensure that the worst case scenarios did not occur. However, the 1876 Act acknowledged that regulation was needed to control experiments and oversee the care of animals. Prosecutions were only to be taken by the written agreement of the Home Secretary and the various regulations might be waived in suitable cases, subject to the agreement of the medical profession.[11] Licences were another feature of the legislation with animal experimentation being subject to licence approval.

It is not surprising that the 1876 Act was not effective given its limited remit and considerable exceptions, added to which technical phrasing did not make it easy to interpret or enforce. Self-regulation was insufficient to satisfy public unease. Public outcry and effective pressure groups combined to make the case for tighter regulation. A second Royal Commission proved necessary in 1906 and it took six years to complete its report. The second Commission reached similar conclusions to the first Commission in 1876. Administrative and related regulatory adjustments were recommended over any substantial strengthening of the 1876 Act. Expansion of the inspectorate and more detailed rules on the conduct and oversight of animals in their slaughter and experimentation were introduced. Set within the narrow boundaries of the vivisection debate, the results were regarded as a disappointment to many who opposed animal experimentation of any sort.

11 The President of the Royal Society, the Royal College of Surgeons, the Royal College of Physicians, the General Medical Council, the Royal College of Veterinary Surgeons or the Royal Veterinary College.

We now turn to address how approaches to animal health developed. Animal health grew in parallel with and at times complementary to the development of animal welfare strategies. There was a distinct movement expressing concern for animal health and for improvements in the diagnosis and treatment of diseases. Poor animal husbandry had profound social, economic and political implications for human health and survival. Animal diseases and their treatment were the subject of veterinary care. The first veterinary school was established in 1791 in England at a private college in London, but at that time only rudimentary animal care was on offer devoid of any underpinning from science or research. This may have been the reflection of the poor knowledge of animals and their treatment; it may also have been because human health treatments did not work easily on animals. The primary purpose of the veterinary school was the education of students and it took considerable time for professional education and training to become fully established on a par with the medical profession. The importance of horses to the army and the role of the Royal College of Veterinary Surgeons (established by Royal Charter in 1844) should not be underestimated in advancing animal health and welfare strategies. Farm animals, particularly horses, received attention from a wide range of well wishers, quacks and charlatans. The advent of Agricultural Societies, including the English Agricultural Society in 1838 (renamed the Royal Agricultural Society of England in 1840), encouraged the development of veterinary education. Animal health had major economic consequences for farmers especially with disease outbreaks leading to poor stock. The Irish Famine in the later 1830s and 1840s demonstrated the vulnerability of a monoculture, the potato, with disastrous consequences. Animal diseases could result in failures in the food chain and animal feedstuffs were vulnerable to crop failure. Diseased animals did not thrive and were underproductive or died from illness. The FMD outbreak in 1842 led to the Royal Agricultural Society of England financing a professorship in cattle pathology at the London Veterinary College. Two years later a Royal Charter was added to the designation of the 'veterinary art' described in the foundation of the London Veterinary College. The standards of a professional society came soon after with the creation of a single body the Royal College of Veterinary Surgeons. This entailed registration and the setting of standards.[12] The Royal Charter took veterinary care to new heights as it removed the challenge of unregistered private commercial organisations being created as rivals for business. The *ad hoc* nature of veterinary qualifications of the past was replaced by common standards and the powers of expulsion granted to the Royal College of Veterinary Surgeons. Such powers were relatively weak and provided little support for setting and enforcing standards. Statutory powers under the Veterinary Surgeons Act 1881 strengthened the Royal College of Veterinary Surgeons considerably by making it a criminal offence to receive payment for falsely claiming to be veterinarian. Accompanying procedures and registration requirements gave

12   See the corresponding history of the Law Society.

the Royal College of Veterinary Surgeons considerable regulatory oversight of the profession.

Scientific advances and understanding gave rise to better diagnosis and cure. This included general anaesthesia, mechanical and surgical devices, including thermometers. These were important scientific developments that linked health and welfare, disease and its diagnosis to eventual treatment. Human health generally influenced many of the practices, including scientific examination and diagnostic techniques. We have already seen how legislation attempted to tackle cruelty, eventually leading to the setting of standards of animal welfare and care; now, legislation to prevent the spread of animal diseases linked animal health and welfare together. Animals imported from abroad and sold at Smithfield Market in London in September 1847 led to an outbreak of sheep pox. In 1848, the Contagious Disorders (Sheep) etc. Act 1848 was enacted to prevent the spread of contagious and infectious disorders amongst sheep, cattle and other animals. This was the first of its kind with a series of Acts following in quick succession and applying also to Ireland and Scotland. The legislation operated a new 'welfarism', namely state intervention in the private ownership of animals, which was partly motivated by economic necessity, the wider public interest over the national herd and also promoted by scientific advice and expertise. An 1857 cattle plague, rinderpest, killed 500,000 cattle and was brought under control by a general slaughter of infected cattle.

It is important to draw together the two strands in the development of animal health and welfare policy making. First, the transformation from the culture of a 'veterinary art' into a new veterinary science that possessed expert opinion based on scientific research. This gave authority, respect and influence to knowledge-based science that rapidly replaced religious belief or pre-determinism. This transformation coincided with a time when the Established church was losing many of its privileges and powers and its role was less influential.[13] The pre-eminence of science is well evidenced as the challenge of evolutionism took root, especially with the publication of Darwin's *On the Origin of Species* in 1859 and later disputes over the role of science and religion in the Metaphysical Society in 1869.[14]

The influence of science is also linked to the second strand of animal health and welfare, namely passing public legislation for the common good. Animal health in general was being dealt with at herd level and distinct from the health of an individual animal. Specific animal health concerns were considered within the general parameters of animal health in general. State paternalism and the emerging 'science' of political economy began to influence how the state regulated the individual who, if necessary, could be faced with limited but necessary interference over his property rights including animals. The eighteenth-century

---

13 In 1868 the Church of England lost its ability to tax through church rates being abolished and the Church's jurisdiction on divorce was also lost.
14 See Stott, R., *Darwin's Ghosts*, London: Bloomsbury, 2012.

free traders were influenced by Adam Smith's *Wealth of Nations* published in 1776, which adopted a *laissez faire* approach to the economy. By the middle of the nineteenth century, Smith's approach came under increasing pressure that supported state interventionist social policies centred around welfare support and wealth distribution. These twin pillars of economic progress – welfare support and wealth distribution – were tightly interconnected. There was a growing acceptance of a recapitulation of Smith's original *laissez faire* doctrine. An emerging capitalistic economic liberalism that gave rise to a new deal characterised much welfare legislation of the late nineteenth[15] century, and animal health fell under this influence.

Some of the greatest observations by naturalists, such as Gilbert White,[16] were also influential and it is possible to trace the mapping of 'nature' and the landscape, and attempts to influence their future through conservation to this period.[17] In fact, the beginning of the conservation movement dates from the eighteenth century and to the influence of Malthus.[18] The Romantic poets also engaged with the recognition and appreciation of nature. The nineteenth century, however, saw the growth of the conservation movement reflected in a proliferation of societies dedicated to lobbying for the protection of buildings, birds and nature often based on the observations of naturalists.[19] Notable among these societies were the Selborne Society for the Protection of Birds, Plants and Pleasant Places (1885) and the Commons Preservation Society (1865), which was a forerunner of the National Trust for Places of Historic Interest or Natural Beauty.[20] Wildlife protection legislation was championed by these societies and by individual naturalists. The first success came in the Sea Birds Preservation Act 1869 and was followed by others setting out the foundation for nature conservation and wildlife protection.

The next step in the development of animal health linked to welfare was the creation of a veterinary department first in the Privy Council Office and later transferred to the Board of Agriculture in 1889. In embryo, the foundations of a State Veterinary Service were begun resulting in a more holistic approach to animal diseases. Accompanying legislation on contagious diseases in animals, notably the 1869 Act, gave considerable force to the existing legislative structure.

---

15 The trend began earlier in the nineteenth century with limits on usury by the Usury Act 1837; the Bubble Act 1720 was modified by the Bankruptcy Act 1883.
16 White, G., *The Natural History of Selborne*, Mabey, R. (ed.), London: Penguin Books, 1977 (first published 1788–1789).
17 See Clapp, B.W., *An Environmental History of Britain*, London and New York, NY: Longman, 1994, p. 1. Clapp attributes the use of the term 'conservation' to Bertrand Russell in the 1950s. Gardner, H., *The Mind's New Science*, New York, NY: Basic Books, 1985.
18 Malthus, T.R., *Principles of Population*, London, 1798.
19 Lowe, P. and Goyder, J. (eds), *Environmental Groups in Politics*, London: Allen & Unwin, 1983.
20 Rootes, C., 'Nature Protection Organisations in England' in Markham, W.T. and van Koppen, C.S.A. (eds), *Protecting Nature: Networks and Organizations in Europe and the United States*, Cheltenham: Edward Elgar, 2007, pp. 34–62.

Thus began a focus on animal welfare, including animal transport and the provision of food and water. The emphasis also changed to one of a presumption of responsibility rather than the need to prove responsibility in the first place. Responsibilities and obligations followed, including the hours between feed and water and the conditions of journeys and transportation. From 1878 to 1910, legislation piled more responsibility upon the existing foundations of criminal liability. Ensuring that the animal feed was free from adulteration and that strict liability applied to any injurious substance to the health of animals also helped to create higher standards for the welfare of animals. The legislation adopted several assumptions that the spread of disease in animals was avoidable and that culpability should follow in the case of negligence.

The role of the RSPCA was instrumental in developing a proactive stance on animal health and welfare. The combination of Royal approval, close links to aristocratic and landed influences, popular lobbying and legally supported enforcement powers proved effective. The ability to stand back and take an holistic look gave the RSPCA access to information and influence. While supporting the transformation of veterinary care, the RSPCA took an independent stance. Its inspectors were often in conflict with veterinary advice when the criteria of animals able to work might be at odds with the view that work may cause unnecessary pain and suffering. The RSPCA was an active law enforcer and from 1890 to 1899 there were over 70,000 prosecutions, which was more than treble the number in the period 1830–1839.[21] Many criticisms of the RSPCA amounted to concerns about the Society's links with the establishment and a tendency to take an authoritarian attitude against individuals, often alienating sympathisers in its aloofness.

The various Acts preventing cruelty to animals had attempted to deal with cruelty in its various forms. The next step was to consolidate and clarify the law in the Protection of Animals Act 1911. The Act was a work of consolidation that brought England, Wales, Scotland and Ireland into alignment. It also addressed the steps needed to care for animals and ensure their welfare needs. Lobbying and public support had combined to result in a complex but quite comprehensive legislation that applied to most animals and required, through state supervision and regulation, standards of health and welfare. However, the legislation had many shortcomings – reliance on criminal prosecutions was not always effective; detection and enforcement were often random and individualistic; and the tasks of overseeing the complexity of duties and responsibilities was scattered throughout many agencies and inspection systems within different government and local government departments.

The rationalisation of animal health and welfare is an ongoing debate in contemporary society. The changing nature of agriculture and the spread of animal diseases create new challenges for the twenty-first century.

21 Radford, op, cit., n. 4, p. 83.

Historically, as outlined above, the framing of disease (including its categorisation) and disease control has been driven by public health and productivity. Since the 1960s, the health and welfare of the animals themselves has become an important component influencing disease control. Gunn *et al.*[22] draw attention to the way in which the EU agenda has changed to emphasise public goods provision, including animal welfare, and this creates a different context within which political definitions are constructed. In future, the question may not be 'Is this disease endemic or exotic?', but 'What harm does it cause to farm animal welfare?' This leads to a different political issue of what animal welfare is and how it can be improved. There are lobbying bodies which consider that animal welfare is different from animal health, i.e. the emotional and mental welfare of animals is different from physical health, although the two are related. Defra also makes a distinction;[23] for example lameness in dairy cows is a welfare disease, whilst mastitis (inflammation of the udder) is a production disease. Both diseases occur because of the way dairy cows are farmed, but the diseases have been labelled politically with the different categorisations welfare and production. The role of the EU and its implications in the agricultural market is important in developing future strategy for animal health and welfare. The principle that prevention is better than cure has become an important strategy in contemporary animal health and welfare policy making.

Animal Welfare Act 2006

The Animal Welfare Act 2006 extends to England and Wales and has limited application to Scotland. The Act addresses the main aspects of animal welfare, with only limited application to the welfare aspects regulated under the Animals (Scientific Procedures) Act 1986, and it also applies to wild animals. The main focus is on farmed and non-farmed animals, drawing on the past experience in the historical framework of the past century (see above). The Act brings together and generally updates legislation taking account of current scientific understanding. The Act went through an extensive consultation phase[24] before being introduced, including the use of pre-legislative scrutiny and a public consultation between January and April 2002. The Act effectively takes into a legal framework the five freedoms that provide how animals are housed, their behaviour patterns and their diet.

The five freedoms are as follows:

(1) *Freedom from hunger and thirst*: ensuring access to fresh water and a diet that maintains full health and well being.

---

22 Gun, G.F., and others, 'Measuring and comparing constraints to improved biosecurity amongst UK farmers, veterinarians and the auxillary industries' (2008) 84(3–4) *Preventative Medicine* 310–333. Radford, op, cit., n. 4, p. 83.

23 See Defra, 2004, op. cit., n. 1.

24 See Explanatory Notes for the Animal Welfare Act 2006. The draft Bill was published in July 2004 (Cm 6252).

(2) *Freedom from discomfort*: providing an appropriate living environment including a rest area, suitable bedding and shelter.

(3) *Freedom from pain, injury or disease*: implementing management protocols that are based on prevention and, in the event of a health issue, ensuring rapid diagnosis and treatment.

(4) *Freedom to express normal behaviour*: affording livestock the ability to exhibit normal behaviour by providing sufficient space, adequate facilities and interaction with the animal's own kind.

(5) *Freedom from fear and distress*: avoiding mental suffering through ensuring adequate conditions and stockmanship.

There is a wider scope given to the animals protected under the legislation. In the past, the notion of 'control' or 'custody' that gave rise to various responsibilities was very narrowly defined,[25] especially when there were ambiguous ideas about shared or temporary as opposed to permanent custody. The Animal Welfare Act 2006 adopts a clearer approach. Responsibility in section 4 of the Act is placed on animal keepers, and this may be assumed from the person who takes responsibility as part of his or her day-to-day tasks. There is also an updating of previous legislation whereby it is an offence to cause unnecessary suffering to any domestic or captive animal, which dates back to the Protection of Animals Act 1911.

The 2006 Act reflects modern practice in the legal protections provided. Section 4(1) makes it an offence to cause physical or mental suffering. This may be committed through acts of omission or commission, i.e. through a positive act as well as a failure to act. The test has an objective element where the person knew or is expected to know that the animal would suffer. The latter is based on objective standards and it is unnecessary to prove that a defendant knew his or her act or failure to act would cause suffering. Section 4(2) strengthens the law much further than in the past. Permitting a third party to cause unnecessary suffering is also an offence and this can be committed by the animal keeper as well as the person who causes the suffering.

The test of whether reasonable steps are taken to prevent the suffering sets the standard that the law expects to be applied in such cases. The question of whether the suffering is unnecessary is considered in section 4(3). The court must take into account all relevant considerations, including what is proportionate, necessary and competent within the conduct of the responsible person. There is a presumption of legality if the harm is permitted within a licence, for example a pest controller or where it is a legitimate use of the activities. Each case is likely to be decided on its particular facts but the court has a wide discretion in considering all the relevant factors in each case. The presumption of legality is capable of being rebutted by the court, based on the context and circumstances of the case. The law provides a major forum for the courts to adjudicate boundaries of

---

25 See *RSPCA v Miller* [1994] Crim LR 516.

what is expected from responsible animal keepers. This may also include the setting of standards of health and welfare. Also, the legislation addresses a number of related subjects such as mutilation and the docking of tails of dogs, the administration of poisons and provides a much tougher regime against fighting animals. Section 9 contains an extensive assortment of provisions in relation to non-farmed animals, which are already applicable to farmed animals. This part of the legislation supports the various regulations, such as the Welfare of Farmed Animals (England) Regulations 2000, SI 2000/1870, under Part 1 of the Agriculture (Miscellaneous Provisions) Act 1968. There is a general duty to ensure that the animal welfare provisions apply to all animals for which someone is responsible. Leaving an animal without making proper arrangements for its welfare is an offence, and reasonable steps are required for the welfare responsibilities to be addressed. The general welfare duty is a pre-existing part of the law that is updated by current good practice. This leaves the legal standards flexible in the sense that account may be taken of current scientific knowledge and good practice.

A further feature of the legislation is the provision of improvement notices on those responsible for animals. In many ways, this represents good practice and it leaves some discretion as to the application of legal rules to a set of circumstances where it may be necessary to take steps to ensure the animal's welfare. There are detailed provisions in section 10 of the Act for the inclusion of information on the notice and also for the use of prosecutions when required. The issuance of an improvement notice does not prevent a prosecution from being taken in the future or even at the same time.

There are additional supplementary powers in the hands of the relevant Secretary of State and the National Assembly for Wales relating to the making of regulations to promote the welfare of animals and applicable to responsible persons. This general power is a welcome addition and allows changes in the law to be speedily introduced. The terms of discretion for the use of such powers are widely defined. At the same time the legislation provides, in section 14, for a variety of Codes of Practice for the promotion of the welfare of farmed animals as well as non-farmed animals.

The Act contains a miscellany of powers and duties, including the licensing and registration of activities involving animals. Section 18 includes specific powers to address the problems when animals are clearly in distress. These powers may be exercised by an RSPCA inspector or a police constable. The Act has a detailed set of provisions for the prosecution of cases and the various powers open to police or RSPCA inspectors to enter and search premises and detain animals,[26] as well as arrest suspects.

---

26 Sections 22–29 set out enforcement powers; sections 30–31 address prosecution powers; and sections 32–45 consider post-conviction arrangements.

The Animal Health Act 2006 marks a new stage in the evolution of the legal regulation of animal health and welfare, and the impact of the Act has been considerable. The first animal protection legislation was passed in Britain in 1822 and since then the enhancement of animal health and welfare has continued, drawing on the foundations set by the 2006 Act. The allocation of a broad range of responsibilities comprises a general duty on anyone who takes responsibility for an animal. The past tradition of virtually unrestrained property rights has been replaced by responsibility sharing between the state through animal protection law and anyone who takes responsibility for animals. This is a changing relationship between animals and responsibility takers that is based on science and changing approaches to animal heath and welfare. There is recognition of the animal's interests and an enhanced vocabulary of health and safety. Delegating responsibility which in the past too often provided an excuse for inaction is no longer a feasible option. While the law has advanced considerably, there remains much to be done. In particular, the governance of animal diseases raises issues about how to manage the welfare and health of farmed animals. Specifically how animal health and welfare is best regulated and the principles that underline regulation need to be made clear. It is also clear that legislation alone is not sufficient to achieve all that is required. Legislation may provide the appropriate framework, but it is largely dependent on the various stakeholders to become effective. In many cases, such as in relation to companion animals, the effectiveness depends on the responsive individual.

Food standards and agriculture

The setting up of the Food Standards Agency (FSA) under the Food Standards Act 1999 is also significant in ensuring that attention is given to the standards and quality of food in the context of food hygiene and safety. This includes monitoring of UK meat plants, food labelling and nutrition policy. The FSA operates throughout the UK with offices in Wales, Scotland and Northern Ireland. It is focused on improving public health and operates under risk-based and proportionate regulation. The implications of animal health and welfare are important to the FSA. There is an Advisory Committee on Animal Feedstuffs (ACAF) with stakeholders meetings on animal feed issues. There is also important research on dangerous pathogens, work on pesticides and on the standards of veterinary products through the work of the Veterinary Products Committee. As an organisation the FSA helps to monitor the food chain and the consequences of animal diseases on human health by drawing on information from the ACAF and the Veterinary Products Committee.[27]

---

27 See House of Commons Library, *The Food Standards Bill: Bill 117 of 1998–99*, Research Paper 99/65, 18 June 1999.

Governance of animal disease: how diseases are currently managed and how management has arisen

In broad terms, it is possible to distinguish between three forms of governance of animal diseases. This is important as we proceed in later chapters to consider the appropriate regulatory strategy.

Action taken by the individual livestock keeper

This action depends on a number of factors, of which the most significant might be: whether the farmer can readily detect the disease in the animal/herd; whether the disease has obvious economic impact relative to the value of the animal/herd and its products; the likelihood of re-infection into the herd (although this often ignores the fact that new strains introduced might be more virulent than existing strains); whether a treatment is readily available; and whether it is affordable. In practice, the livestock keeper's decision will also be influenced by the advice that is available. It will also depend on the livestock keeper's own qualifications and state of knowledge as well as economic circumstances.

Veterinary surgeons are presumed to be an important source of such advice, but other sources might be other farmers, breed societies and farming organisations.[28] The interviews undertaken for the research are relevant here, showing that in some cases veterinarians are fully integrated into the farm management team.

Particular to infectious disease is that farmers are not independent in terms of the risk of disease and the impact of interventions. One farmer's management (or mis-management) of an infectious disease affects other farmer's livestock by reducing (or increasing) their risk of exposure to the pathogen. This is not only a farm-to-farm issue; the risk of infectious disease transmission is influenced by hauliers of food, livestock and livestock products, humans who move between farms, and the use of markets that disseminate animals and potentially their pathogens. That is, there are many actors to consider when attempting control of infectious diseases.

Self-regulation by a group of farmers but without government intervention

Action taken by the individual livestock keeper might be undermined by inaction or actions by other farmers. Hence, there is a classic collective action and free riding situation (i.e. the best action for a farmer depends on what other farmers

28 Gunn, G.J., Hefferman, C., Hall, M., McLeod, A. and Hovi, M., 'Measuring and comparing constraints to improved biosecurity amongst United Kingdom farmers, veterinarians and the auxillary industries' (2008) 84(3–4) *Preventative Veterinary Medicine* 310–323. Ellis-Iversen, J. and Hoegeveen, H., 'Barriers and motivators for zoonotic control on cattle farms', Society for Veterinary Epidemiology and Preventative Medicine, London, 1–3 April 2009, pp. 177–187.

are doing). For example, if all farmers are vaccinating against BVD, then the rational action for any individual farmer is to cease vaccination since he is protected by the action of the others. There is also a clear ethical component in relation to farmers who take actions (at a cost to themselves) from which other farmers benefit (so-called 'first movers'). Farmers might attempt to overcome this by banding together voluntarily to regulate a disease in a defined geographical area. This may be easiest to achieve in a geographically isolated area such as an island. These activities may be facilitated and in part organised by veterinarians (either in practice or in academic institutions). Government may encourage such actions, while offering no tangible support.

Interestingly, we know of no examples where such governance has developed spontaneously amongst dairy farmers, and several examples where attempts to develop such governance – through industry or veterinary leadership – have had, at best, muted success (e.g. BVD in Orkney, the UK and the EU).[29] Understanding why collective action to control endemic cattle disease in the UK is rare would be a major step forward in developing governance of endemic cattle disease. The question of coordination between farmers is discussed further below.

Government intervention

A range of policy instruments have been used at different times to manage and assist control of some diseases at a national level. These include: culling of affected animals with compensation to the owner or of affected wildlife considered to be a disease reservoir; control of animal movements; research into the transmission of diseases and their treatment; provision of vaccines below cost price; and creation of bodies to provide advice and mediate between conflicting interests and perspectives. In the case where a pathogen has a wildlife reservoir, some form of public (government) control is likely to be critical, especially if the reservoir species has legal protection, as in the case of badgers and bTB.

Motivations for government-led control arise from the impact of the disease on humans and animals and the nature of the pathogen. Public health was a major driver for action on bTB in the 1930s. A Medical Research Council reported stated, '2,000 human deaths each year may be ascribed to bovine tuberculosis derived from cows' milk, and at least 4,000 (a most conservative estimate) fresh human cases infected with bovine tuberculosis probably occur'.[30] This particular route of infection is largely overcome by pasteurisation, although transmission could occur through an aerosol or consumption of raw milk from an infectious animal. Also, as milk from infected herds is taken out of the system, bTB is therefore no longer a major zoonosis, but this has not diminished political interest in the disease. This may, in part, suggest the importance of 'path dependency'

---

29 Gunn, *et al.*, ibid.
30 Jordan, L., *The Eradication of Bovine Tuberculosis*, London: HMSO, 1933.

effects resulting from the initial classification of a disease, and in the case of bTB the role of international legislation. It would also, of course, be a serious animal disease if it returned to its early twentieth-century levels when around 30 per cent of cattle died from bTB. This is arguably highly disruptive and has psychological effects on farmers.

Other factors include the political costs of taking or not taking action on the disease; in particular, whether key stakeholder groups hold positions for or against intervention. The economic impact of the disease, including its impact on international trade, is also a major driver. As is outlined in Chapters 3 and 4, this seems to have been important in relation to FMD[31] but less so for Johne's disease or BVD. Johne's disease was one of the four diseases included in the wartime scheme known as the Panel Scheme or Four Diseases Scheme,[32] and it was recognised as a disease that 'has presented a serious problem in our cattle herds for many years leading to considerable loss. This may suggest that the disease ought to have been tackled earlier. The fact is, however, that it has no public health significance.'[33] The prevalence of the disease is now much lower, but this probably has more to do with changes in cattle demography (especially reduced life expectancy) than concerted action.

It is important to have a readily usable and reliable diagnostic test for a disease and some strategy for treatment, for example through vaccination. In the case of bTB, an effective vaccine has been promised for a long time, but is yet to be achieved because of the nature of the pathogen/host interaction. We also lack uncontested knowledge about the reservoirs for transmission of bTB and persistence in the environment. The distinction between vaccinating badgers and cattle needs to be made clear, with the economic consequences of each strategy fully considered.

Johne's disease presents several problems: carriers are difficult to identify; much effort may be required to reduce the spread of disease; and there is no effective treatment or wholly effective vaccine.[34] In the case of BVD the technical tools and knowledge for elimination are available, but it has not been accorded a high priority in England.

The political costs of controlling a disease include the public expenditure costs of the measures taken; the time taken by decision makers (ministers and civil servants) in reaching decisions; personal abuse or threats to those taking the decisions; and the political costs in terms of unfavourable publicity and criticism

---

31 Woods, A., *A Manufactured Plague: The History of Foot and Mouth Disease in Britain*, London: Earthscan, 2004.
32 Ministry of Agriculture, Fisheries and Food, *Animal Health: A Centenary 1865–1965*, London: HMSO, 1965 p. 97.
33 Ritchie, J.N., 13 December 1963, National Archives, MAF 287/184.
34 Stott, A.W., Jones, G.M., Humphry, R.W. and Gunn, G.J., 'Financial incentive to control para-tuberculosis (Johne's disease) on dairy farms in the United Kingdom' (2005) 156 *Veterinary Record* 825–831.

by stakeholder groups. All these elements have been present in the case of bTB.[35] The public expenditure costs of attempting to manage the disease over a 70-year period have been, and remain, considerable. It is estimated to cost approximately £1 billion between 2008 and 2013 and 'takes up 40 per cent of the Animal Health Agency's resources'.[36] Considerable ministerial time, up to prime ministerial level, has been taken up with the issue and special working groups have had to be formed by the civil service. Those involved in reports and other studies have been subjected to considerable hostility and personal abuse, including threats against them. Media treatment of policy has been generally highly critical and there has also been outspoken criticism by stakeholder groups, including a private prosecution launched against a minister. The whole topic is highly politicised in an emotional fashion because measures to control the disease have involved the killing of badgers, a highly valued wild animal. The management of bTB may be characterised as one of policy failure.[37] The high political profile has also influenced research into bTB hugely, with many years of work, after the 1970 discovery of TB in a badger carcase, funded only on badgers and a strong belief that this was the area where research was needed. Only since the Krebs Report in 1996[38] has research into cattle been highlighted to obtain a more rounded portfolio of research (the Independent Scientific Group (ISG) on Cattle TB,[39] etc.) and provide scientific evaluation. In contrast, Johne's disease and BVD have had a very low political profile.

It might be expected that a cost–benefit analysis could be conducted to determine the economically optimum level of control for any disease, as is done for human disease by the National Institute for Health and Clinical Excellence (NICE). In the light of such an analysis, a social planner might decide to live with the disease if the cost of elimination outweighs its benefit.[40] However, the impact of any intervention is unknown at the outset (although the probabilities of its possible outcomes can be predicted), so that stating an objective to eliminate, especially by a particular date, has a clear risk of failure, which will have political

---

35 See the Bovine TB Advisory Panels at Defra, the Consultative Panel on Badgers and Tuberculosis, the Independent Scientific Group on Cattle TB, the Bovine TB Advisory Group and the Bovine TB Eradication Group for England.

36 Hansard, House of Commons Debates, Bovine TB, cols 1153–1158, 7 July 2008.

37 Grant, W., 'Intractable policy failure: The case of bovine TB and badgers' (2009) 11(4) *British Journal of Politics & International Relations* 557–573.

38 Krebs, J. and the Independent Scientific Review Group, *Bovine Tuberculosis in Cattle and Badgers: Report by the Independent Scientific Review Group*, London: Ministry of Agriculture Fisheries and Food, 1997; HC Deb, Vol. 303, cols 136–137, 16 December 1997.

39 House of Commons Environment, Food and Rural Affairs Committee, *Badgers and cattle TB: the final report of the Independent Scientific Group on Cattle TB*, Fourth Report of Session 2007–08, HC 130-1, London: The Stationery Office, 2008.

40 Sumner, D.A., Bervejillo, J.E. and Jarvis, L.S., 'Public policy, invasive species and animal disease management' (2005) 8(1) *International Food and Agribusiness Management Review* 78–97.

and economic consequences. On the other hand, a clear, politically articulated, date-stamped intention has been suggested to be critical for the success of the eradication of human disease, despite the fact that the date for eradication is continually moved.[41] This forms the politics of expertise, epistemic communities and the rise in veterinary epidemiology.

What is evident is that decisions about animal disease management are highly political, although more so in relation to some diseases than others. Although technical advice from veterinarians and other scientists is an important component of the decision-making process, that advice is viewed through a political lens which involves a calculation of the costs and benefits to decision makers of action or inaction.

Once a disease is eliminated, i.e. removed from a defined region, resources are required to prevent its re-introduction into the region. Once a pathogen is eliminated, the perceived threat to productivity and welfare is lower, but may be actually greater since immunity to infection will be lost. Such prevention measures are required until the pathogen is eradicated from the globe. These resources include border control and trade barriers that may control any likely source of animal, animal product or human traffic that could lead to accidental or deliberate re-introduction. The use of trade barriers that are likely to control animals, animal products or even human traffic are problematical. Trade barriers between countries may limit the markets addressed by farmers and consequently reduce their bio-security incentives.[42]

Consequently, excellent monitoring and accurate testing are required to prevent re-entry of a pathogen, and rapid response is required if a re-introduction occurs to prevent the pathogen becoming endemic again. There is a critical timeframe within which this response must occur and be successful before the pathogen's mechanisms for persistence occur and elimination becomes much more difficult.

---

41 Dowdle, W.R. and Hopkins, D.R. (eds), *The Eradication of Infectious Diseases, Dahlem Workshop Report*, Chichester: John Wiley & Sons, 1998. See, for example, *Progress report on rinderpest eradication: Success stories and actions leading to the June 2011 Global Declaration*, at www.fao.org/ag/againfo/resources/documents/AH/GREP_flyer.pdf, and Mariner *et al.*, 'Rinderpest eradication: Appropriate technology and social innovations' (2012) 337 *Science* 1309–1312. The Dahlem Workshop, Frei Universitat Berlin, 97th International Conference.

42 A barrier to trade between non-infected countries can lead one of them to trade with an infected country especially if the barrier raises prices above the implicit price of disease risk. If the barrier prevents traffic with all infected countries, the incentives for specific precautions and screening are sure to fall as the perceived and actual risk falls. This may delay the detection of any accidental reintroduction of disease and may slow the response time to take action.

Challenges and strategies: coordination success and failure

Disease elimination results in a public good.[43] However, it involves commitments by producers that are difficult to monitor even in the presence of regular monitoring and financial incentives provided by the public veterinary service. For instance, Great Britain has been following a policy of paying compensation to farmers who report certain types of disease occurrence in their stock (see, e.g., the Sheep Veterinary Society, 2006, for sheep scrapie-related payments). However, such compensation has not resulted in total elimination of the diseases for which the scheme works. Kuchler and Hamm[44] make a similar observation in relation to compensation payment to encourage elimination of sheep scrapie in the USA for the period 1952–1992. It is not that farmers do not respond to such incentives; they do, but there are other incentive structures at work which counter the effect of such compensation schemes. In particular, it should be noted that such schemes incentivise reporting, but not elimination – without other measures, the infected animal has a protected value. There are also perverse incentives which may have an opposite effect to that intended.

Hennessy makes the point that farmers have the incentive to make commitments that, if implemented simultaneously by a critical mass, have the potential to eliminate a disease from a country, but only if they believe that others also have the incentive to act. In a market where such a belief is missing, however, an individual farmer might not foresee benefit, but only a cost, from a private action to eliminate disease from his or her own farm. This produces a situation where the disease remains endemic, and some farmers must contend with a risk of herd infection from neighbours' herds. This points to the importance of signals which indicate the level of commitment among farmers to eradicate disease. According to Hennessy,[45] one way of making such signals available to farmers is through coordination of their efforts, which can be achieved if, for instance, the

---

43 Animal welfare is defined in many ways but one of the most common definitions is that proposed by the Farm Animal Welfare Council, in terms of the five freedoms. Disease directly reduces welfare under freedom 3, but may result from poor welfare under the other four freedoms. The five freedoms are: (1) freedom from hunger and thirst – ensuring access to fresh water and a diet that maintains full health and well-being; (2) freedom from discomfort – by providing an appropriate living environment including a rest area, suitable bedding and shelter; (3) freedom from pain, injury or disease – implementing management protocols that are based on prevention and in the event of a health issue, ensure rapid diagnosis and treatment; (4) freedom to express normal behaviour – affording livestock the ability to exhibit normal behaviour by providing sufficient space, adequate facilities and interaction with animal's own kind; (5) freedom from fear and distress – avoiding mental suffering through ensuring adequate conditions and stockmanship.

44 Kuchler, F. and Hamm, S., 'Animal disease incidence and indemnity eradication programs' (2000) 22 *Agricultural Economics* 299–308.

45 Hennessy, D., 'Coordinating to eradicate animal disease and the role of insurance markets', Working paper 07-WP 45, Iowa State University, Iowa, 2007.

level of effort expended by individual farmers on disease control is monitored over time and made publicly available.

Thus, farmers face a coordination problem; both elimination and non-elimination could exist as equilibrium behavioural *conventions* but the efficient outcome may emerge only if it is possible for farmers to commit to contingent (or matching) behaviour or if elimination is not only efficient but *risk-dominant* – in other words, if it takes more simultaneous errors or shocks to undermine the elimination regime than the non-elimination regime. This, in turn, may depend on the (social) network structure linking farmers (which, e.g., reinforces 'good' behaviour) *and* the epidemiological network linking their herds (which determines the fragility or otherwise of progress towards elimination in local areas). Additionally, robustness depends on the correlation of these two networks; a favourable local epidemiological situation may produce demonstrable success, which encourages the diffusion of elimination behaviour (or ambitions) through social networks. Conversely, a favourable social climate (e.g. a cluster that lies also at the heart of the epidemiological network) can change underlying infectivity and thus encourage other parts of the social network to evolve towards elimination.

Hennessy[46] argues that farmers in close geographical contact are more likely to believe in (and implement) effective coordination than farmers with small farms that are dispersed as they stand to gain more – both from improved market access and from enhanced productivity as a result of disease eradication. As the above makes evident, one explanation for why a certain disease will exist in one country as endemic emanates from failure to coordinate farmers' and government's efforts to eradicate the disease. Some evidence of these processes can be found by comparing livestock species. The pig and poultry industries in the UK are configured very differently from the sheep and cattle sectors, with the consequence, we argue, that disease control is significantly more coordinated in pig and poultry sectors.

Diseases differ between countries in terms of presence, prevalence and impact. Countries which have eliminated a disease (or in which it was never endemic) have a comparative advantage in international trade because, all else being equal, they can trade a larger volume of animal products and have a smaller excess burden associated with the disease.[47] Given the economic alignment in international trade, those countries which have not yet eliminated the disease have a relatively lower incentive to avoid engaging in animal trade that facilitates the re-entry of the disease to countries with disease-free status. In this particular case, unless countries with disease-freedom coordinate with those which have not declared such a freedom, they will find it difficult to maintain freedom indefinitely. Therefore, in the same way that coordination of farmers' efforts plays a

---

46   Ibid.
47   'Excess burden' is defined as a burden beyond the case reports of disease incidence collected by the public health authority if costly disease prevention occurs (Philipson, T., 'The welfare loss of disease and the theory of taxation' (1995) 14 *Journal of Health Economics* 387–395).

significant role in ensuring disease elimination at the local level, so coordination of countries' efforts plays a role in ensuring regional elimination and global eradication. Such a global coordination is difficult to achieve unless there are international organisations which set disease control standards and enforce them.[48] The formation of the OIE was a result of such calls for standards and enforcement, and, as a consequence of this coordination, the global eradication of rindepest has been achieved.

EU and international context

There is an international and EU dimension to the national regulation of animal health and welfare. The UK is a member of the OIE, represented by Defra. One of the conditions of OIE is any member country's veterinary authority must report any new incidence of animal disease within the Member Country. The OIE is critical in developing updates and standards for animal health services, including the terrestrial Animal Health Code. The Code contains over 80 types of animal disease and there are mandatory reporting obligations on Member States. This has assisted in building up an animal health strategy based today around the various EU requirements.

One of the main challenges that was identified in 2006 by the Food and Agriculture Organisation in its Report *Livestock's Long Shadow: Environmental Issues and Options*, in which it noted that the livestock sector is responsible for 18 per cent of greenhouse gas emissions measured in carbon dioxide emissions (CO_2). This is a higher proportion than transport and, although the amount is contested, there is growing acceptance that tackling climate change through reductions in emissions is a critical part of the overall strategy. In planning to reduce emissions it is clear that agriculture is susceptible to other aspects of climate change. These include increases completion for water resources and the spread of new pests and diseases.

Conclusions

The history and development of animal health and welfare is indicative of the changing nature of and culture surrounding animal health and welfare. Animal health and welfare is about human responsibilities. Societal influences and changing approaches to welfare issues are a key factor in public culture and in influencing public opinion. As Marian Dawkins has shown, the past was influenced by the human dominance over animals based on exploitation and gain rather than by concern over animal health and welfare.[49] Moral and philosophical

---

48 Barrett, S., *Why Cooperate? The Incentive to Supply Global Public Goods*, Oxford: Oxford University Press, 2007.
49 Dawkins, M.S., *Animal Suffering. The Science of Animal Welfare*, London: Chapman & Hall, 1980.

doctrines tended to support human endeavour even at the cost of animal well being. Changing perceptions about animals through better informed veterinary knowledge and understanding of animal health have provided a new basis for evaluating animal health and welfare. As human health has improved and social welfare strategies influenced society as a whole, animal health has followed in the general consideration of welfare ethics.[50] Over time and with the influence of the EU, the strategy for protecting animal health and welfare has developed considerably. The challenge is to provide the best regulatory regime to implement different ideas about cost sharing and responsibility. In considering the design and remit of a suitable regulatory structure, account must be taken of defining its role and clarifying its objectives. A good regulatory system must set high standards but also must be designed to secure particular objectives. The regulatory structure ought to be able to detect undesirable behaviour, encourage good practice and develop adequate responses including enforcement tools. At its base, it needs to ensure that there are strategies to engage with relevant stakeholders. The interests of the public and the interests of animals should coalesce in animal health and welfare policy that protects human health and sets standards for animal health and welfare.[51] It may be necessary for an animal perspective to be part of the regulator's role. The robustness of the regulatory design must take account of tensions between stakeholders and respond flexibly. As Mike Radford explains:

> The law is the means by which society expresses its collective choice. Any shortcomings are those of society itself. In the present state of public opinion, however, it is submitted that the most effective way of advancing the interests of animals is by the formal imposition of human responsibilities through legal regulation.[52]

50 Francione, G.L., *Animals, Property and the Law*, Philadelphia, PA: Temple University, 1995.
51 See Bishop, P., 'Badgers and bovine tuberculosis: the relationship between law, policy and science' (2012) 24(1) *Journal of Environmental Law* 145–154.
52 Radford, op. cit. n. 4, p. 11.

3   Combining disciplines

The RELU programme was built around the idea of interdisciplinarity. This was seen as something more than multidisciplinarity where distinct disciplines contributed to the analysis of a common problem requiring 'scholars to be aware of salient contributions from other disciplines and to draw on them in useful and limited ways'.[1] 'It involves the joining together of two disciplines with little or no integration.'[2] In later work emerging from RELU, it is described as a cross-disciplinary research programme which is not defined but is described as a 'neutral term'.[3] It does seem to be less demanding in the sense that it refers to collaborative 'endeavours'.[4] This may simply have been expedient for the particular article, but it may also involve a recognition that getting disciplines to collaborate on any basis is itself an achievement. Disciplines are 'stable communities within which researchers concentrate their experience into a particular worldview. This puts limits on the kinds of questions they can ask about their material, the methods and concepts they use, the answers they believe and their criteria for truth and validity.'[5] At the other end of the spectrum, we have not aspired to or achieved transdisciplinarity where the identities of individual disciplines would disappear by 'adding an overarching common meta-theoretical perspective to the common definition of the problem and methods'.[6] Indeed, the authors of this book would not subscribe to such a radical position. We need academic disciplines if interdisciplinarity is to be possible.

1 Warleigh-Lack, A. and Cini, M., 'Interdisciplinarity and the study of politics' (2009) 8(1) *European Political Science* 4–15, 8.
2 Greaves J. and Grant, W., 'Crossing the interdisciplinary divide: political science and biological science' (2010) 58(2) *Political Studies* 320–339.
3 Lowe, P., Whitman, G. and Phillipson, J., 'Ecology and the social sciences' (2009) 46 (2) *Journal of Applied Ecology* 297–305, 298.
4 Ibid., p. 297.
5 Lyall, C., Bruce, A., Tait, J. and Meagher, L., *Interdisciplinary Research Journeys*, London: Bloomsbury Academic, 2010, p. 11.
6 Warleigh-Lack and Cini, op. cit., n. 1, p. 9.

What do we mean by interdisciplinarity? As Harvey[7] puts it, 'There are nearly as many definitions of the term as there are researchers trying to do it'. Lowe and Phillipson[8] claim, 'Interdisciplinarity differs from disciplinarity and multidisciplinarity in the emphasis it places on interaction and joint working, which brings the knowledge claims and conventions of different disciplines into a dialogue with each other, yielding new framings of research problems'. McNeill[9] goes even further when he argues that interdisciplinarity involves 'the formulation of a uniform, discipline like terminology or common methodology' as well as 'co-operation within a common framework shared by the disciplines involved'. 'In short', argues Harvey,[10] 'interdisciplinarity requires a common language'.

That requirement brings with it particular challenges as terminology is one way in which a discipline constitutes itself. A shared and specific jargon allows the practitioners of the discipline to talk to each other and distinguish themselves from those in other disciplines. The phrase 'trading zone' is sometimes used to denote an interdisciplinary partnership in which two or more perspectives are combined and a new, shared, language develops.[11] The risk associated with a common language is that it would result in the dumbing down of disciplinary knowledge and expertise.[12] What is needed is a means for disciplines to converse with each other while retaining their own distinctive contributions. We would argue that successful interdisciplinarity requires all the parties to learn the language of the other disciplines but retain the ability to speak their own.

The authors have been able to have a meaningful conversation, but converting dialogue into the written word is one of the biggest challenges in interdisciplinary work. This is as much because of the readership as our own difficulty in writing. The reader requires some fluency in all of the 'languages' in which the work is written. The conventions under which one writes are very different. Most economics articles use notation or graphs and articles in legal journals commonly cite cases. Articles in life sciences journals are typically a few pages, while political sciences articles can be ten times as long. There is no doubt that social scientists write more discursively, in part, because they are often engaged in a process of contention rather than presenting experimental evidence. Science articles are

7   Harvey, D., 'RELU special issue: Editorial reflections' (2009) 27(2) *Journal of Agricultural Economics* 329–336, 331.

8   Lowe, P. and Phillipson, J., 'Reflexive interdisciplinary research: the making of a research programme on the rural economy and land use' (2006) 57(2) *Journal of Agricultural Economics* 165–184.

9   McNeill, D., 'On interdisciplinary research: with particular reference to the field of environment and development' (1999) 53(4) *Higher Education Quarterly* 312–332, 313.

10   Harvey, op. cit., n. 7, p. 331.

11   Collins, H., Evans, R. and Gorman, M., 'Trading zones and interactional expertise' (2007) 38(4) *Studies in History and Philosophy of Science Part A* 657–666.

12   Bracken, J.I. and Oughton, E.A., '"What do you mean?" The importance of language in interdisciplinary research' (2006) 31(3) *Transactions of the Institute of British Geographers* 371–382.

typically multi-authored, and significance attaches to the ordering of names, such as who appears first or last. Nevertheless, we have succeeded in writing together in science journals.[13]

One of the ways in which direction can be lost is that the absence of a common language leads to a lack of common understanding, and one test of a genuinely interdisciplinary project is its ability to create language that describes shared meanings. We would not claim that we have created such a language in this project, although certain terms, such as 'governance', 'regulation', 'animal welfare' and 'animal health', were commonly used and central to the project as a whole. A determined effort was made, however, to understand each other's disciplinary terminology and to avoid confusion in the use of language. An example would be the exploration of the term 'public good' in economics. A procedure that was followed was to read articles from other disciplines and then discuss them in team meetings to secure a better understanding of the terminology, methodology and substantive findings. We may not have evolved a common methodology, but we have worked effectively together across the interdisciplinary divide.

Why RELU was needed

RELU does not represent the first attempt to establish an interdisciplinary programme on rural policy issues. The Joint Agricultural and Environment Programme (JAEP) was sponsored in the late 1980s by the same three Research Councils as sponsored RELU. 'JAEP is widely regarded as having failed to meet its ambitious objectives, in particular by failure to foster genuine interdisciplinarity and by failing to generate any substantial advances in problem-oriented solutions and answers to practical challenges.'[14] It was certainly viewed as a warning about what should be avoided by the coordinators of RELU.

Why, then, was a new attempt made to instigate a substantially funded interdisciplinary programme on rural issues? This is a question that can be answered at a number of levels. At a meta-level it can be seen 'as part of a broader transformation in the nature of scientific knowledge and its relationship with society. A shift in the development of knowledge is discerned from being linear, hierarchical, compartmentalised and distinct from society to being open, networked and permeable and without rigid government'.[15] Interdisciplinarity can be seen as representing 'the resurgence of interest in a larger view of things'.[16] Interdisciplinary working can offer more complete ways of defining problems and hence illuminate the policy agenda. It permits technological innovation

---

13 Carslake, D., Grant, W., Green, L.E., Cave, J., Greaves, J., Keeling, M., McEldowney, J., Weldgebriel, J.H. and Medley, G.F., 'Endemic cattle diseases: comparative epidemiology and governance' (2011) 366 (1573) *Philosophical Transactions of the Royal Society B* 1933–1942.
14 Harvey, op. cit., n. 7, p. 330.
15 Lowe and Phillipson, op. cit., n. 8, p. 166.
16 Froderman, R., 'Introduction' in Froderman, R., Klein, J.T. and Mitcham, C. (eds), *The Oxford Handbook of Interdisciplinarity*, Oxford: Oxford University Press, xxix–xxxix, xxxi.

that facilitates and works with the grain of social change and social and environmental adaptation which creatively exploits technological opportunities. The complex requirements of sustainable development mean that technological solutions on their own will not suffice – they must be responsive to consumer demands and sensitive to the social and economic contexts in which they are to be applied.[17]

Effective stakeholder engagement is also a need of modern governance as the number of organised cause groups proliferates. Interdisciplinary research can offer new mechanisms for engaging with affected publics. An example from within RELU is the work on competency groups undertaken by Whatmore, Ward and Lane[18] in a project on the contested production and circulation of environmental knowledge in relation to flood risk management. This represented an attempt to develop a 'radical' mode of interdisciplinarity that draws on the working principles of the philosopher of science, Isabelle Strengers.[19] It utilises an interactive mode of public engagement that involves non-scientists in a collaborative research process from the outset. The participating scientists are required to engage constructively with the different environmental knowledge claims and practices of concerned publics, building these perspectives into the research process.

At another level, interdisciplinarity addressed real needs felt by policy makers. From an era in which the development and deployment of technology and knowledge of use to producers had been seen as the optimal means of maximising production, a more complex set of objectives came into play. A politics of production was replaced by a politics of collective consumption, with a new emphasis on negative externalities resulting from the way in which production was organised and undertaken.[20] These pressures were felt in relation to environmental policy generally, but were particularly acute in the food chain, where they were inextricably tied up with constructions of national and personal identity as reflected in the phrase 'you are what you eat'. 'These changes in perception, in turn, required research and innovation to be more closely attuned to the consumption-centred and socially constructed character of contemporary food chains.'[21]

17 Phillipson, J. and Lowe, P., 'Towards sustainable food chains: harnessing the social and natural sciences' (2009) 19 *Trends in Food Science and Technology* 224–225, 224.
18 Whatmore, S., Ward, N. and Lane, S.N., 'Environmental knowledge controversies: competency groups as an experimental methodology', paper presented at the British Association for the Advancement of Science, University of Newcastle, meeting panel, 'Working together Across Disciplines: challenges for the natural and social sciences', York 2007.
19 Whatmore, S., 'Generating Materials' in Pryke, M., Rose, G. and Whatmore, S. (eds), *Using Social Theory: Thinking Through Research*, London: Sage, 2003, pp. 89–104.
20 Grant, W., *Pressure Groups and British Politics*, Basingstoke: Palgrave Macmillan, 2000.
21 Lowe, P., Phillipson, J. and Lee, R.P., 'Socio-technical innovation for sustainable food chains: roles for social science' (2008) 19 *Trends in Food Science and Technology* 226–233, 230.

The 1997 Labour Government attempted to develop 'a distinctly New Labour agenda for the countryside'.[22] Challenges like climate change required a multi-faceted approach that took account not only of the relevant scientific knowledge but also of patterns of human behaviour. Efforts to enhance the environmental dimension of the Common Agricultural Policy and to develop government policy to the contested issue of genetically modified crops all also required new ways of organising knowledge and understanding.

A loss of public trust in an increasingly complex food chain with a greater distance between farm and fork created a particular need for interdisciplinary research which could challenge conventional ways of thinking. As Phillipson and Lowe pointed out:[23]

> It is clear that farming crises, chronic health risks, food safety scares, and resource and habitat depletion have evoked considerable mistrust of the science and technology underpinning food chains and have been an associated with an assertion of consumer/public interest not only in what food is produced but also how it is produced, stretching along the food chain.

Animal health and cattle diseases in particular faced particular challenges which created a special need for new ways of thinking. '[W]hen the first cases of bovine spongiform encephalopathy (BSE) in UK cattle arose, former unquestioned assumptions were broken by the emergence of a new paradigm by which infectious diseases could be spread in the food chain independently of viruses, bacteria or parasites.'[24]

FMD outbreaks occurred from time to time, but the last major outbreak before the 2001 episode was in 1967–1968. As a consequence, 'Not only did the visibility of the disease within political, public and expert discourses tacitly wane, but institutions and society "forgot" the necessary skills and capacities needed to cope with a future outbreak'.[25] (As a consequence, the response to the FMD outbreak, in which 10 million livestock were killed and rural tourism severely impaired in the affected areas, bore all the hallmarks of a 'policy disaster'.[26]) One response was to replace MAFF with Defra which, of itself, created a context in which there was potentially greater receptivity to innovative ways of thinking about policy challenges.

22 Lowe, P. and Ward, N., 'New Labour, new rural vision? Labour's rural white paper' (2002) 72(3) *Political Quarterly* 386–390, 386.

23 Phillipson and Lowe, op. cit., n. 17, p. 225.

24 Fish, R., Austin, Z., Christley, R., Haygarth, P.M., Heathwaite, L.A., Latham, S., Medd, W., Mort, M., Oliver, D.M., Pickup, R., Wastling, J.M. and Wynne, B., 'Uncertainties in the governance of animal disease: an interdisciplinary framework for analysis' (2011) 366 (1573) *Philosophical Transactions of the Royal Society B* 2023–2034, 2025.

25 Fish *et al.*, ibid., pp. 2029–2030.

26 Dunleavy, P., 'Policy disasters: explaining the UK's record' (1995) 10(2) *Public Policy and Administration* 52–70.

The third element in the policy mix as far as cattle diseases were concerned was bTB. At one time it appeared that bTB had been brought under control, but it reappeared and the incidence of the disease worsened over time with an increase in the public expenditure burden. Not only was the science contested, but the whole question of how to tackle the disease was affected by the fact that it involved a cherished wildlife species, the badger. In the case of this disease, there was a particular imperative to explore how understandings of the disease were framed by policy makers and the wider public.[27]

Challenges of interdisciplinarity

'It is difficult to do interdisciplinary research ... If it were easy, we would have already done more and better.'[28] It can be 'difficult simply for social scientists to collaborate amongst themselves across disciplines'.[29] At one level, this is simply because social scientists are asking different questions about the same set of problems and answering them in different ways. It could be that collaborating between the social sciences presents as many challenges as collaboration between the natural and social sciences.

Consider the example of international trade policy which has relevance to cattle diseases as its regulation can be utilised as an effort to stop the spread of disease. Economists start from a presumption in favour of international trade as it can be shown to generate higher levels of prosperity than would exist in its absence. Although there may be losers from freer trade, there is a net welfare (but not animal welfare) gain. A key concern, then, is how protectionist barriers can be reduced and whether particular types of trade arrangements, for example regional trade agreements, are trade facilitating or trade diverting.

For a lawyer, a central concern is the provisions of particular treaties relating to trade and how these are interpreted by quasi-judicial procedures such as the Dispute Settlement Mechanism of the WTO, the European Court of Justice and national courts or quasi-judicial bodies. As far as animal health is concerned, the lawyer may be interested in the relationship between the WTO and the OIE. The WTO's Sanitary and Phytosanitary Agreement states that 'to harmonize sanitary and phytosanitary measures on as wide a basis as possible, Members shall base their sanitary or phytosanitary measures on international standards, guidelines or recommendations'. The Agreement names the OIE as the relevant organisation for animal health.

A political scientist, or more specifically someone working in the sub-discipline of international political economy, is likely to focus on the construction of the

27 Grant, W., 'Intractable policy failure: the case of bovine TB and badgers' (2009) 11(4) *British Journal of Politics & International Relations* 557–573.
28 Harvey, op. cit., n. 7, p. 331.
29 Phillipson, J., Lowe, P. and Bullock, M., 'Navigating the social sciences: interdisciplinarity and ecology' (2009) 46 *Journal of Applied Ecology* 261–264, 261.

interests of various members of the WTO in relation to agricultural trade, how this relates to their stances in negotiations and how they might form more or less formal coalitions with each other to advance their views. A central concern will be who exercises power in this process, for example how the hegemony of the USA and the EU in international trade negotiations has been challenged by emerging countries, notably India and Brazil.

Answering each of these sets of questions requires different sets of techniques. Economists have a variety of modes they can apply to patterns of international trade using quantitative analysis and statistical tests, for example gravity trade flow models. Lawyers will necessarily engage in the detailed analysis of texts, for example treaty provisions and court judgments or rulings of quasi-judicial bodies. Political scientists will use a variety of techniques, but a classic one is semi-structured interviewing with actors involved in the decision-making process. Epidemiologists will undertake quantitative risk analyses for specific diseases and trade routes, and so their approach is automatically more particular and less general than the others.

Of course, in some respects, these approaches are complementary. An economist might be able to quantify the net benefits of freer agricultural trade. The lawyer might be able to specify how current treaty provisions needed to be modified or reinterpreted to facilitate such an outcome. The political scientist should be able to identify where the opposition to such changes might come from and how one could move towards a position that represented an improvement on the status quo. An epidemiologist can quantify the risks of disease and advise on their reduction and mitigation.

However, the challenges are more fundamental than simply respecting the validity of complementary contributions to problem resolution. There are more fundamental differences within the social sciences about epistemology, how knowledge is constituted and how it might be obtained. In broad terms, there is a distinction between naturalists or positivists and constructivists. Naturalists consider that 'There exist regularities or patterns in nature that can be observed and described. Statements based on these principles can be tested empirically according to a falsification principle'.[30] Constructivists 'see the world as socially constructed ... they do not expect to see objective (and verifiable) patterns of social phenomena existing naturally in the social world'.[31]

This difference of approach might seem to stop interdisciplinary research in its tracks even before it has begun in the social sciences, let alone before one attempts to cross the interdisciplinary divide between the natural and social sciences. How can one reconcile the experimental method or statistical analysis seen as superior by naturalists with the use of discourse analysis or participant observation by constructivists? Participant observation, which was used in this

---

30 Moses, J. and Knutsen, T., *Ways of Knowing: Competing Methodologies in Social and Political Research*, Basingstoke: Palgrave Macmillan, 2007, p. 9.

31 Ibid., p. 16.

research, involves taking part in the life of the research object, in this case Defra. It involves interpretation of meanings and perceptions of research objects and two different observers could easily come to different conclusions.

In attempting a reconciliation, one first has to recognise 'that good science should be driven by questions or problems, not by methods'.[32] This proposition is a central one of scientific realism which is claimed to offer 'a new universal approach – one can that straddle the natural and social sciences, as well as the naturalist and constructivist traditions'.[33] In this sense it is inherently interdisciplinary. 'Scientific realists recognize that there is a Real World independent of our existence. At the same time, they embrace Weber's famous constructivist maxim, that man is an animal suspended in webs of meaning that he himself has spun.'[34] It then becomes possible to deploy 'a "Swiss Army Knife", representing the multifunctional toolbox of interdisciplinarity'.[35]

There may thus be particular problems within the social sciences 'where competing methodologies are brought to bear on the same research topic'.[36] For example, methodological individualism is a core element of modern classic economics, whereas sociologists and political scientists are more interested in collective behaviour and rational choice institutionalism is not necessarily accepted as a way of bridging that divide. For economists, policy instruments are essentially second order means of achieving the ends, whereas for political scientists they may be seen as constitutive of policy itself. Science requires competing hypotheses to develop, but hypotheses often differ in terms of measurement or context rather than genuine theoretical underpinning, and natural science is complex enough that no two people need be studying exactly the same thing. However, when it comes to intervening against disease, there can also be different perspectives within the natural sciences, for example between veterinary specialists and epidemiologists over the handling of the FMD outbreak. This difference might partly be explained by the difference between a medical training and a science training, but was also due to misunderstanding of the role of predictive modelling.[37]

What about the challenges of bringing the natural and social sciences together? There is a view amongst some natural scientists that their discipline can provide proof or a higher degree of certainty than the social sciences. Furthermore (and this is a related but subtly different point), they may feel that social scientists hold beliefs/make statements which are not backed by sufficient evidence to justify the

32   Moses and Knutsen, op. cit., n. 30, p. 14.
33   Moses and Knutsen, op. cit., n. 30, p. 15.
34   Moses and Knutsen, op. cit., n. 30, p. 13.
35   Marzano, M., Carss, D.N. and Bell, S., 'Working to make interdisciplinarity work: investing in communication and interpersonal relationships' (2006) 57(2) *Journal of Agricultural Economics* 185–197, 194.
36   Greaves and Grant, op. cit., n. 2, p. 334.
37   Green, L.E. and Medley, G.F., 'Mathematical modelling of the foot and mouth disease outbreak of 2001: strengths and weaknesses' (2002) 73(3) *Research in Veterinary Science* 201–205.

confidence to which that belief is held/statement is asserted. Although this was not an issue in our research, where it does occur it could undermine the mutual respect necessary for interdisciplinary research to proceed. 'A key qualitative difference between the social and physical sciences is that the former deal with conscious and reflective subjects, capable of acting differently under the same stimuli, while the units comprising the latter can be assumed to be inanimate, unreflexive and predictable in response to external stimuli.'[38] Applying these assumptions to animals, of course, raises some difficult normative and analytical issues once one accepts that they are sentient beings. Nevertheless, 'Agency injects indeterminancy and contingency into human affairs and there is no analogy for this in the physical sciences'.[39]

It is possible that the sheer distance between the natural and social sciences induce mutual respect and a willingness to learn from each other.[40] This possibility may be enhanced if two conditions are met – an acceptance of the naivety problem and a repudiation of an 'end of pipe' role for social science, i.e. in which social science brought in at a late stage to try and tackle problems that have arisen from the limited character of the earlier decision-making framework. Both sets of disciplines have in common a naivety problem: interdisciplinary research helps to overcome 'the partiality that can arise when natural scientists make naïve assumptions about the social world or social scientists make naïve assumptions about the natural world'.[41]

Understandably, natural scientists may have a simplistic or formalistic view of how the policy process works. Even if they are involved in that policy process themselves, they may assume that their expert advice should shape policy outcomes and that if politicians refuse to listen to this advice, they are simply perverse. Some natural scientists have tended to adopt a '"deficit model" of turning science into policy, the view that if only politicians are told what the science reveals, "correct" policies will automatically follow'.[42] This approach implies that all that is needed is better communication to decision makers of the scientific message.

The RELU programme paid considerable attention to how knowledge transfer occurred and how new paradigms might be developed and applied. The existing definitions of knowledge transfer were often preoccupied with classic notions of technological development and the commercial application of scientific knowledge. This was reinforced by the knowledge-driven economy agenda which gained purchase under New Labour.[43] These kind of approaches did not always fit comfortably with the often critical character of social science knowledge.

38 Greaves and Grant, op. cit., n. 2, p. 325.
39 Greaves and Grant, op. cit., n. 2, p. 325.
40 Greaves and Grant, op. cit., n. 2, p. 334.
41 Lowe and Phillipson, op. cit., n. 17, p. 224.
42 Lawton, J.H., 'Ecology, politics and policy' (2007) 44(3) *Journal of Applied Ecology* 465–474.
43 Lowe and Phillipson, op. cit., n. 8, pp. 167–168.

What is needed is a more sophisticated appreciation of the contribution of social science to the development and application of knowledge going beyond the 'end of pipe' models which used to prevail. Under this approach, the role of natural science was to develop new technologies for food production, and the task of social scientists was to ensure that there were no blockages preventing their speedy application by 'facilitating social acceptance of novel products or processes'.[44] For example, agricultural economists and rural sociologists were expected to provide understandings of the diffusion of innovation, identifying the characteristics of farmers who might be 'early adopters' of new technologies. A 2006 report from Defra's Science Advisory Council argued against an 'end of pipe' role for social science, validating its removal as an orthodoxy of the relationship between research and policy.[45]

The social scientists in the project were reliant on the natural scientists for technical knowledge about the diseases being studied. At a basic level, they needed to avoid naïve errors, for example confusing a prion with a virus. More generally, they needed to know whether a given cattle disease could be readily diagnosed, what the transmission mechanism was, whether it affected animals other than cattle and whether it was a zoonosis. All of these and other considerations affected the policy responses that might be appropriate. However, this was not simply a matter of the natural scientists providing an 'idiot's guide' to cattle diseases. The social scientists needed to understand how their natural science colleagues collected data and the procedures they used to analyse it. They also needed to uncover the 'hidden knowledge' that the natural scientists had about structures of power and operation of policy networks of different actors inside and outside government in relation to cattle diseases, and place that knowledge within the context of social science theories. For example, they had an understanding of the profound changes in structure, personnel and relationship with the state that have taken place in the veterinary profession, leading to reflection on their implications for policy making and implementation. [46]

From an epidemiological viewpoint, transfer of livestock clearly poses risks of transfer of disease. Introduction of new diseases and new types of existing diseases create the possibility of epidemics that can be very damaging to productivity and welfare, the FMD outbreak in the UK in 2001 being the prime example. The key concerns for an epidemiologist will be the presence of 'exotic' diseases, and the ability to diagnose and control them. The viewpoint of the epidemiologist is necessarily a quantitative one with the numbers providing guides to the actions that need to be taken. There was thus an ongoing process of knowledge exchange

44   Lowe, Phillipson and Lee, op. cit., n. 21, p. 230.
45   Science Advisory Council, 'Increasing the capacity and uptake of social research in Defra', paper SAC (06) 42, London: Defra, 2006.
46   Grant, op. cit., n. 27; Enticott, G., Donaldson, A., Lowe, P., Power, M., Proctor, A. and Wilkinson, K., 'The changing role of veterinary expertise in the food chain' (2011) 366 (1573) *Philosophical Transactions of the Royal Society B* 1955–1965.

between the natural and social scientists and also with stakeholders and knowledge users (e.g. through work shadowing and workshops), which was as much about methodology as it was about substantive information. There was a partial immersion in the perspectives of other disciplines, exemplified by the attendance of social science project members at research lectures and seminars in biological sciences. One project member from the social sciences started to teach on a new second-year life sciences course concerned with the relationship between biosciences and society. One of the biggest surprises for the natural scientists was the process by which social scientists work. The natural scientists would enjoy a chat with the social scientists over coffee, and then be surprised that it was considered work – to most natural scientists, work must involve a computer or laboratory equipment.

However broad and deep the gap between two or more disciplines is perceived to be, that distance must be bridged in some fashion that allows meaningful interdisciplinary work to proceed. This could be by a rope bridge or a suspension bridge, to use the analogies of Marzano *et al.* To extend that analogy, either means of crossing is likely to wobble under stress, but this would not prevent it being used as long as there is a confidence in the underlying project, i.e. that the questions being asked are relevant, important and in some sense answerable, at least in an interim way, which was a shared understanding we had in our project. There is some evidence that researchers find 'it more straightforward to explain and explore differences in *how* they know (i.e. methodological approaches) than in *what* they know, and thus found a basis of mutual respect in admitting the provisionality and exercise of judgement in their own knowledge processes'.[47] As one of the natural scientists in the project commented, he proceeded from the assumption that everything that he knew was potentially wrong.

Framing

On one level it is the policy makers who have the problems and they expect academics to have the methods to suggest how they might be resolved. However, we would suggest that one of the important contributions that academics can make is to suggest new ways of thinking about what the problem is. For example, what is animal welfare, how can we maximise it and what is the relationship between animal disease and animal health? 'Is bovine-TB a veterinary problem, a conservation problem, an animal welfare problem, or a public health problem?',[48] or is it even an historical cul de sac that has become ossified in EU legislation from which the UK cannot escape?

---

47 Marzano *et al.*, op. cit., n. 35, p. 195.
48 Phillipson and Lowe, op. cit., n. 8, p. 231.

Intractable policy controversies surround issues like bTB. 'Frame analysis helps us to account for their origin and stubborn survival.'[49] Different forms of expertise may 'frame' a problem in different ways. In the case of bTB, a belief in the existence of the 'old rogue badger' had an influence on the debate about the way in which the disease should be tackled, even though there was no scientific evidence of the existence of such a creature.[50]

'The labelling of a disease as exotic or endemic is essentially a political decision to "frame" or label a disease in a particular way.'[51] Diseases do not have an enduring status as endemic or exotic, and political decisions and a commitment of substantial resources must be made to try to eliminate them. Thus, *Brucella abortus* was recognised as having been eliminated from Britain in 1985 and government has sought to eliminate FMD, thus maintaining its exotic status. The labelling of a disease as endemic or exotic has a considerable impact on the resources devoted to it or, indeed, whether government is involved at all. Diseases which may have considerable implications for animal welfare and production may be left to farmers to deal with as best they can. The way in which something is labelled is charged with political meaning shapes the contours of policy and has implications for the conduct of governance.

Conclusions: climbing the mountain together

Marzano *et al.*[52] using the analogy of the 'mountain to climb' to represent:

> the ultimate goal of novel, shared understandings. Researchers have to assemble at the foot of the mountain and at first the climb is easy, but as the ascent becomes more demanding, there is a greater need for people to assist one another. This mutual assistance should create shared learning and support, but the group must be resilient as the journey may be like the game of 'snakes and ladders'.

Mists may descend which cause those ascending to lose their way and a compass of shared understandings is needed to navigate out of them.

One of our central contentions is that cattle pathogens can be analysed in both their socioeconomic and epidemiological environment. Given that both natural and social processes are at work and interact with each other, we constructed a classification of cattle diseases combining political and epidemiological dimensions.[53] This can be considered as a dynamic system and could serve as part of a

49   Schön, D.A. and Rhein, M., *Frame Reflection: Toward the Resolution of Intractable Policy Controversies*, New York, NY: Basic Books, 1994.
50   Grant, op. cit., n. 27.
51   Carslake *et al.*, op. cit., n. 13.
52   Marzano *et al.*, op. cit., n. 35, p. 193.
53   Carslake *et al.*, op. cit., n. 13.

policy toolkit contributing to the development of decision making, facilitating interventions that are proportionate and governance that is appropriate to each pathogen. Such a methodology offers a theoretical and empirical application of the interdisciplinary approach, yielding results that could not be obtained by a discipline working on its own.

4 Understanding and assessing the risk management of animal health and welfare

In this chapter we introduce the current 'natural science' approach to endemic livestock disease and welfare. It is widely held by natural scientists that there is a real world and fundamental truths about it can be deduced from observation and experiment. However, natural science (and natural scientists) cannot be divorced from a social context, and this frames much of what is studied and the way in which it is studied. For example, the existence of (human) medicine and veterinary medicine as two distinct disciplines is a 'social construct'. It is not, therefore, surprising that we find that social perspectives have a great influence on the way that diseases of livestock are researched and understood.

In this chapter we start with definitions and classifications, since these frame current understanding. We then describe the current understanding of the causes and consequences of the epidemiology of infectious disease in livestock, which involves both natural and social science perspectives. Next, we consider that the epidemiology or state of a disease can only be described accurately if the description includes economic and political perspectives combined with the biological aspects, and this is this state that determines what control is applied. Lastly, we address the question of how farmers interpret endemic disease and make decisions about interventions to apply.

Definitions and classifications

Disease in farmed livestock can be considered as anything that affects an animal's well being and welfare. Diseases in animals are defined in terms of *signs* – physiological or behavioural anomalies – and diseases often have common names which emphasise particular signs or conditions under which the disease is frequently seen, for example black leg, louping ill and shipping fever.[1] An agreed definition of a disease is critical because it enables surveillance data

---

1 Black leg is caused by infection with *Clostridium* bacteria in cattle and sheep, louping ill is caused by a tick-borne virus of sheep and shipping fever is a respiratory infection caused principally by *Mannheimia* bacteria. See Carter, G.R. and Wise, D.J., *Essentials of Veterinary Bacteriology and Mycology*, 6th edn, Chichester: John Wiley & Sons, 1993.

(i.e. reporting trends in incidence and prevalence of disease) and development of treatments that can be demonstrated to be effective. For infectious disease, a necessary part of a definition is the presence of the pathogen associated with it, and diagnosis requires identification of the pathogen and/or some physiological consequence of its presence (e.g. antibodies). Without definitions of disease and a good understanding of their causality, governance is impossible, although the definitions and understanding of causality do not have to be perfect in order to be able to implement effective control.

Development of an agreed definition of a disease and its diagnosis are not straightforward since signs are rarely uniquely associated with particular diseases; for example, pyrexia (raised temperature) is associated with most acute infections, and anorexia (reduced eating) is associated with many diseases. When new diseases are recognised and classified, there is usually a period of considerable debate before a cause, or set of causes, is agreed and a set of signs agreed as a definition, and the finally agreed name usually reflect this debate. Recent human examples include AIDS (acquired immunodeficiency syndrome) and SARS (severe, acute respiratory syndrome), and a recent veterinary example is PMWS (post-weaning, multi-systemic wasting syndrome).[2]

There are considerable differences between infectious diseases and non-infectious diseases. Infectious diseases are caused by a pathogen, a transmissible organism; examples include bovine tuberculosis, Johne's disease, BVD, mastitis in cattle, swine fever, swine vesicular disease and porcine reproductive and respiratory disease (PRRS) in pigs, bluetongue and foot rot in sheep. Pathogens may be specific to one livestock species or may affect many species. Non-infectious diseases are caused by the management of the animal, for example poor physical resources, such as lying on hard concrete surfaces, which causes foot and limb injuries in all livestock species kept in such conditions, or poor diet, leading to deficiencies that cause metabolic disease. Attempts to eliminate disease from a population target known causes. For non-infectious disease this equates to changes in management. For example, a 2008 EU Directive described minimum standards for, amongst other things, pig flooring to reduce lameness,[3] and a 1999 EU Directive laid down minimum standards for commercial egg production, including the phasing out of conventional ('battery') cages.[4] For infectious disease the pathogen responsible is targeted, i.e. elimination of infection automatically eliminates the associated disease. However, note that (depending on definition) most diseases have multiple causes. For example, mastitis in cattle is caused by bacterial infection with any one of a large number of species, such as

2   See Baekbo, P., Kristensen, C.S. and Larsen, L.E., 'Porcine circovirus diseases: a review of PMWS' (2012) 59 *Transboundary and Emerging Diseases* 1865–1682.
3   Council Directive 2008/120/EC (Laying down minimum standards for the protection of pigs).
4   Council Directive 1999/74/EC (The Welfare of Laying Hens Directive).

E. coli and *Streptococcus uberis*, so eliminating *S. uberis* will eliminate *S. uberis* mastitis, but might not reduce the total amount of mastitis.[5]

The important point is that physiological and psychological states are, in reality, a collection of very complicated, interconnected phenomena, including genetics, nutrition, environment and presence of other species (including pathogens). Science and medicine have imposed a simplified structure, developed over time with the accumulation of experience and evidence that enables us to explain some of these phenomena. Consequently, diseases (infectious and non-infectious) are not fixed, but come and go in importance according to changes in definition and evolution (e.g. antibiotic resistance), and changes in livestock management and environment. Examples here include the invasion of bluetongue into the UK in 2008 and the emergence of the Schmallenberg virus in 2012. Consequently, any governance framework must be sufficiently flexible to cope with such changes.

Classifications of disease

The incidence and prevalence[6] of infection and disease vary over time and space, often dramatically. This has led to two main classifications of disease – endemic and non-endemic. This classification is recognised both in epidemiological terms, but also reflected by government structures and approaches to regulation and management. Endemic diseases are those which are continuously present in a nation or region, although their prevalence can vary considerably (e.g. due to seasonal effects). From a risk perspective, an endemic disease poses very few risks to governments (because it is there all the time), but continuously poses risks to individual farmers.[7] (Note that an endemic disease can cause epidemics on individual farms.) A disease which is not endemic is one which, from a UK perspective, is absent but is endemic elsewhere, but if introduced to the UK would potentially cause an epidemic, i.e. a rapid and dramatic increase in

---

5   Although that might not be the case, or it might result in an increase in mastitis of a different cause, since the presence of one bacterial species might be protective against infection with others – see, for example, Reyher, K.K, Haine, D., Dohoo, I.R. and Revie C.W., 'Examining the effect of intramammary infections with minor mastitis pathogens on the acquisition of new intramammary infections with major mastitis pathogens – a systematic review and meta-analysis' (2012) 95(11) *Journal of Dairy Science* 6483–6502.

6   The two basic measures of disease abundance are incidence and prevalence. Incidence is the rate at which cases arise in the population. Prevalence is the proportion of the population that is afflicted by the disease at a single point in time, expressed as a percentage of the total population, and is a product of the incidence and duration of the disease. If the risk of an individual developing a disease is 2 per cent per day, and there are 1,000 individuals, then the incidence will be $0.02 \times 1,000 = 20$ per day, and if the disease lasts two weeks, then the prevalence is $20*14/1,000 = 28$ per cent.

7   We use the term 'farmer' as a collective term to indicate the individuals and/or organisations that own the animals, are responsible for the welfare of the animals and who gain a profit from ownership.

prevalence. Consequently, non-endemic diseases are referred to as exotic (because they exist outside the UK), epidemic (because they cause large-scale epidemics) and absent (because they are not in the UK). Although these labels change with infection and disease prevalence (so that FMD is now absent/exotic, but in 2001 was epidemic/exotic), it is the non-endemic status that is important for this book. From a risk perspective, an exotic/epidemic/absent disease poses few risks to individual farmers (because it is not here), but poses continuous risks to government (because it might be introduced).

This classification of disease is reinforced by societal perspectives and government structure. The creation of the EU has meant that diseases are now considered as endemic or epidemic from an EU perspective (and controlled as such). For example, the devolved Scottish government has attempted to create a divide within the UK by being declared a region 'free' of bTB.[8] This enables, indeed requires, that Scotland institutes controls and restrictions on trade of cattle with the rest of the UK and Ireland, which are not required for the other EU States that are also declared officially bTB free. The controls include requirements for testing and quarantine.[9] Note that this declaration of *official* bTB freedom does not mean that Scotland is free of bTB, but rather enables development of a political stance and access to legal avenues. Epidemiologically, Scotland is little different from some regions of England, which do not have the status to apply to the EU for declaration of official freedom. Scotland is also attempting to eliminate BVD (see Chapter 5), presumably with a view for declaration of freedom.

The classification status can arise through intervention, so that diseases that have been historically endemic in the UK (e.g. contagious abortion of cattle or brucellosis caused by *Brucella abortus*) have been eliminated. Epidemiologically, this effectively moves the disease from endemic to absent/epidemic and, in terms of management, brucellosis is now considered exotic by Defra. However, the incursion of bluetongue[10] into the UK in 2007 did not change its status from exotic to endemic, perhaps because the incursion was rebuffed. Indeed, the considerable economic effort expended in removing bluetongue and FMD from the UK was because of their status as exotic infections. If, however, attempts to remove bluetongue had failed and it had become endemic, then its status, and responsibility for control within Defra structures, would presumably have had to change.

Some diseases are notifiable, i.e. 'any person having in their possession or under their charge an animal affected or suspected of having one of these diseases must, with all practicable speed, notify that fact to a police constable'.[11] The list

8   Scotland became officially tuberculosis free as recognised by Commission Decision 2009/761 (September 2009) in recognition of the low and stable incidence of bTB in Scottish herds.
9   For the current situation, see www.scotland.gov.uk/Topics/farmingrural/Agriculture/animal-welfare/Diseases/disease/tuberculosis.
10 Szmaragd, C., Wilson, A., Carpenter, S., Mertens, P.P.C., Mellor, P.S., *et al.*, 'Mortality and case fatality during the recurrence of BTV-8 in northern Europe in 2007' (2007) 161 *Veterinary Record* 571–572.
11 Section 15(1) of the Animal Health Act 1981 or an Order made under that Act.

of notifiable diseases[12] in the UK comprises primarily exotic (i.e. absent/ epidemic) diseases, with the notable exceptions of bTB, BSE and scrapie. Individual country lists and the EU list of notifiable disease are closely related to the OIE list. The OIE also determines recognition of animal disease statuses of OIE Members and territories, which determines disease and pest-free areas for trade purposes, in the context of the WTO Agreement on the Application of Sanitary and Phytosanitary Measures.

Animal diseases can also be classified as zoonotic, i.e. they are known to cause disease in humans, and consequently are subject to more attention than non-zoonotic diseases.[13] Many endemic diseases are zoonotic (e.g. *E. coli* and *Campylobacter*) and not notifiable, although the UK classifies some diseases as reportable, i.e. there is a statutory requirement for laboratories to report laboratory confirmed isolation of organisms.[14] An endemic zoonotic infection poses more risks to government in that increases in prevalence of human disease (e.g. recent outbreaks of *E. coli* O157) can become politically important. Legislation for human diseases runs parallel to the animal disease legislation regarding notification and reporting, so that, for example, anthrax is notifiable in livestock and humans, but Rift Valley fever (an exotic, zoonotic infection) is notifiable in animals but not in humans and food poisoning (for example by *Campylobacter*) is notifiable in humans but not in animals. Additional to this complication is that the different administrations in the UK have slightly different lists for animal disease.

Consequences of classification

The classification of zoonotic or non-zoonotic is largely based on the biomedical issue of whether the disease can be naturally transmitted from animals to humans. However, the other classifications are almost entirely man-made. Once a disease has been declared as either endemic or exotic, then it is managed in a way that reinforces that classification. Epidemic diseases such as FMD typically provoke legislation, requiring government to act to eliminate them. The legislation often derives from international trade agreements and international law that force government intervention. Notifiable diseases, which are mostly epidemic/exotic, are required to be reported so that there is much higher quality of data for epidemiological research and control purposes than for non-notifiable diseases. This leads to greater impetus for research to find interventions (e.g. vaccines) in the private sector, since the pharmaceutical industry can see the need and has the necessary information for marketing. Epidemic disease attracts considerable central government funding, with the consequent development of scientific

---

12 See www.defra.gov.uk/animal-diseases/notifiable (accessed 27 March 2013).
13 Defra, *Zoonoses Report: UK 2010*, www.defra.gov.uk/publications/files/pb13627-zoonoses-report2010.pdf (accessed 27 March 2013).
14 Zoonoses Order 1989, SI 1989/285.

understanding and techniques that make it possible to remove the disease should it invade.

The involvement of government in a disease is determined by its political profile which is closely linked to the classification of diseases described above, although not exclusively. Before its incursion, bluetongue had the same classifications as FMD but almost no political profile. Carslake *et al.* (2011) developed a framework for assessing the strength of different factors that contribute to a profile. The list of factors resembles the criteria used in Defra's Prioritisation project[15] and includes the zoonotic potential, the general awareness of the disease, whether there are usable interventions, the economic impact and the international perspectives. Thus a disease such as rabies would be expected to have a high political profile since it is highly zoonotic and well known with proven interventions and important internationally (from which the economic impact would be felt). Higher-profile diseases are more likely to be eliminated, but may persist if there are technical and political barriers to elimination (e.g. bTB). Lower-profile diseases may be eliminated if there are strong economic incentives. An example is warble fly, a parasitic infection of cattle. This infection was eliminated from the UK in response to concerns about damage caused to hides. In 1978, the MAFF Parliamentary Secretary announced a plan for elimination that used legislation (e.g. making the infection notifiable) and movement controls to eventually eliminate the infection in 1990.[16]

In contrast, an endemic disease is not regarded as problematic for government, since it poses few risks, and farmers are expected to manage it and mitigate against the production losses associated with it. Non-zoonotic endemic diseases are not notifiable, and consequently there is relatively poor surveillance data, so that the prevalence of disease and impact on (national) productivity are largely unknown. There is relatively little central government money spent on development of diagnostics and control. Endemic diseases, such as mastitis or infectious bovine rhinotracheitis, receive relatively little government attention or funding, as they are typically considered 'production diseases' or 'industry problems'. This reinforces the status as endemic since there is a smaller chance of being able to eliminate it without the necessary technical tools for intervention. Consequently, endemic diseases must become accepted as part of the farming landscape and be viewed as an inevitable constraint or friction reducing productivity.

Consequently, the classification of a disease as endemic or exotic creates a 'path dependency', meaning that the initial classification is self-reinforcing. The difference in government funding, public profile and legal position locks each disease into a public or private status that may bear little relationship to its actual impact on production, health and welfare. It is possible for disease to switch categories, for example brucellosis, but this is uncommon. Brucellosis was

---

15   http://archive.defra.gov.uk/foodfarm/farmanimal/diseases/vetsurveillance/documents/dst_summary.pdf.

16   http://archive.defra.gov.uk/foodfarm/farmanimal/diseases/atoz/warblefly/index.htm.

endemic[17] but, motivated by its zoonotic potential and trade benefits of official free status, was eliminated in 1979. Surveillance and statutory measures required to maintain disease freedom and official free status is estimated to have cost around £6 million in 2003/2004.[18] The elimination programme was begun in 1962, including vaccination and a voluntary attested herds scheme to establish a nucleus of disease free herds, and switching to a compulsory area eradication policy in 1971. We are unaware of any disease that has moved in the opposite direction.

The classification and path dependency produce the apparently rather perverse situation that there is more data, research money and government time spent on diseases which do not (currently) reduce the productivity and welfare of UK livestock than on diseases which impose a burden on both. Further, given the differences in surveillance between the differently classified diseases, the impetus to change the classification cannot arise from within the national agricultural industry, but generally comes from the zoonotic potential (i.e. as dictated by the human health agenda) and the need to comply with international trade standards.

Goals for intervention programmes

Given that a disease is recognised as being of sufficient impact for intervention to be necessary, there are three general targets: control of the disease (i.e. reduction of its incidence and prevalence), elimination (removal of the disease from a defined region) and eradication (removal of disease from all livestock globally).[19] Only one animal disease has been eradicated – rinderpest.[20] Elimination of diseases in the UK commenced during the eighteenth century with CBPP and rinderpest. Elimination was possible because these diseases only occurred in cattle, so culling animals diseased with CBPP and rinderpest also destroys the pathogen. With the development of germ theory and the introduction of vaccines, other diseases, such as brucellosis, have been successfully eliminated. Elimination of a disease means that the hosts do not develop natural immunity, so that reintroduction of the disease will result in an epidemic. Consequently, elimination from the UK (or any other region) requires measures to keep the disease out (e.g. legislation to prevent the movement of livestock or their products, such as milk, cheese, meat or hides). If vaccination is available it could, theoretically, be used to maintain immunity in the livestock population; this is the

---

17 Woods, A., '"Partnership" in action: contagious abortion and the governance of livestock disease in Britain, 1885–1921' (2009) 47(2) *Minerva* 195–216.

18 Above, n. 16.

19 Dowdle, W.R. and Hopkins, D.R. (eds), *The Eradication of Infectious Diseases*, Dahlem Workshop Report, Chichester: John Wiley & Sons, 1998.

20 See, for example, *Progress report on rinderpest eradication: Success stories and actions leading to* the June 2011 Global Declaration, www.fao.org/ag/againfo/resources/documents/AH/GREP_flyer.pdf (accessed 27 March 2013), and Mariner, J.C. et al., 'Rinderpest eradication: appropriate technology and social innovations' (2012) 337(6100) *Science* 1309–1312.

strategy to maintain elimination of human diseases such as polio, where all children in the UK are vaccinated even though the disease no longer occurs naturally in Europe. The disadvantage of continual vaccination against a disease that is no longer present is that the costs of control are of the same order of magnitude as the loss of production from the disease – the economic and welfare benefit of elimination is that the disease no longer requires control. There are also surveillance issues with using a vaccine, since it might not be possible to differentiate accurately between an animal that has had the natural disease and an animal that has been vaccinated. This was one of the aspects of the argument against vaccination to eliminate FMD in 2001, and certainly why vaccination is not permitted within the EU unless under particular unusual circumstances.[21]

The key concept is that elimination and eradication of disease (i.e. complete removal from specific spatial regions) requires both the diagnostic and intervention tools and the political will. Without this concerted action, then disease remains endemic and must be controlled or its effects mitigated. It is this situation in which the majority of livestock disease pathogens exist.

Epidemiology of disease

Diseases are manifest within individual animals, but it is at the population level that many of the causes and consequences of disease impact. At a very simplistic level, the incidence of disease in a population is a product of the risk of each individual and the size of the population. A key concept is that the risks of development of disease are not equally distributed, but tend to be highly clustered. For infectious diseases, the risk of infection is largely determined by the numbers of other animals that have the disease. Farmed livestock are typically kept in distinct populations (herds or flocks), and the risk to the individual is highly dependent on the state of the herd; for example, if there is no PRRS in a herd of pigs, then there is no risk of infection for the members of the herd. Similarly, for non-infectious disease, herd members will be subject to the same management (diet, flooring, etc.) and will be more similar to each other in terms of risks of specific diseases than they are to animals in other herds. The consequence is that diseases tend to be highly clustered within herds, i.e. most herds have zero or low levels of a disease, but the minority of herds will have the majority of disease.

There is also considerable structure between herds. The distribution of herd sizes is skewed, with the majority being very small populations (backyard and small holders) and a relatively few very large populations with sizes, in the UK, of several hundred cattle, several thousand pigs or sheep or hundreds of thousands of poultry. These populations have some contact with each other forming a meta-population, i.e. population of populations, which is referred to as a meta-herd.

---

21   Council Directive 2003/85/EC of 29 September 2003 on Community measures for the control of foot-and-mouth disease.

The presence of a non-infectious disease in a herd does not pose a risk to other herds, but the presence of an infectious disease does, since it can be transferred through contact (e.g. movement of animals, personnel and equipment) or via environmental contamination (e.g. air plumes or wildlife).

How a pathogen invades and persists in the meta-herd, not just the individual herd, is of great importance for regulation and management. The pattern of incidence and prevalence in the meta-herd largely determines the economic and political importance of a disease within different sectors of the agriculture industry. A consequence of the skewed distribution of disease between herds is that most farmers do not experience the disease and do not lose money from it, whilst a few perceive it as a major impediment. For example, Johne's disease is found predominantly in large dairy farms because of the movement of animals and their management, but is much less prevalent in beef farms: a recent study of 114 farms showed that approximately 98 per cent and 80 per cent of dairy and suckler herds harbour at least one infected animal.[22] Note that the infection is equally able to infect all cattle, but it is the manner in which they are traded and kept which determines the difference. Consequently, Johne's disease might be a high priority for the diary sector, but support for government intervention might be less easily gained from the beef sector. Although many farmers will be involved in both enterprises, the sectors are relatively distinct in terms of political organisation.[23] Since farm size, livestock species and enterprise purpose tend to be clustered by geographical area (e.g. the great majority of English pigs are kept in Norfolk and Yorkshire), perceptions of disease impact are similarly clustered. Clustering extends throughout all spatial scales, up to global, where the presence/absence of different infections in different nation states has an important impact on international trade.

Consequently, economic and political perceptions of disease are shaped by the epidemiology, and there is rarely consensus about the most important endemic diseases and appropriate interventions. bTB is currently an exception and is complicated by the involvement of non-farming (i.e. conservation) considerations. In Chapter 5 we return to the political perceptions of bTB in contrast to other infections.

Determinants and consequences of disease epidemiology

In this section we consider what determines the patterns of disease in time and space, i.e. its epidemiology. We take a broad-brush approach, considering the

---

22 Woodbine, K.A. *et al.*, 'Seroprevalence and epidemiological characteristics of *Mycobacterium avium* subsp. *paratuberculosis* on 114 cattle farms in south west England' (2009) 89 *Preventive Veterinary Medicine* 102–109.

23 For example, the National Farmers Union has separate arms for dairy and beef. The strongest organisations are bodies such as the National Beef Association, the National Dairy Council and the Royal Association of British Dairy Farmers.

general influences. For some diseases, especially those not achieving any special classification, there is very little scientific evidence on which to base understanding; but for others there is a huge literature devoted to the epidemiology and effects of different interventions. It is the case for most of these diseases that there is sufficient scientific and veterinary knowledge to enable successful control, or there is sufficient background understanding to enable the knowledge to be generated relatively quickly given the necessary resources. However, scientific and veterinary knowledge alone are not sufficient to result in disease control.

The detailed epidemiology of any particular disease is determined by the combination of biologically, socially and economically motivated processes operating at different levels. For an individual animal, the risk of infection is determined by the prevalence of infection in the herds and premises to which the animal belongs throughout its life. Animals in the UK (and elsewhere in the developed world) rarely spend their lives on one farm or premises – they are a tradable commodity and frequently move. This movement impacts on welfare, but also on infectious disease transmission since it greatly increases the numbers of animals that each animal contacts.[24] The range and frequency of animal movement has been explicitly linked to the spatial spread of bTB,[25] and was particularly important in the first stages of the FMD epidemic in 2001.[26]

For an individual herd, the pattern of infection is determined by contamination of the herd premises and transfer of infection between farms, especially through movement of animals. Essentially, every herd's exposure to disease is made up of the sum of exposures of each of its individual members. Diseases cluster within herds, so it is at the herd level that the effect of interventions has maximum effect since those interventions change the disease epidemiology within all the animals simultaneously; for example implementation of vaccination will be at a herd (or sub-group) level, and would have minimum impact if applied to animals individually.

Within the meta-herd, the patterns of movements of animals between herds as well as the state of the individual herds determine much of the epidemiology of disease. The national epidemiology is not simply the sum of the individual herds. Some diseases (e.g. BVD) probably have to move between herds to persist since their biological characteristics mean they will naturally fade out in all but the largest herds.[27] Other diseases (e.g. neosporosis, Johne's disease) can persist in the smallest of herds, and are transported to others through movement of

24 See, for example, Vernon, M.C. and Keeling, M.J., 'Representing the UK's cattle herd as static and dynamic networks' (2009) 276 *Proceedings of the Royal Society B* 469–476.

25 Gilbert, M., Mitchell, A., Bourn, D., Mawdsley, J., Clifton-Hadley, R. and Wint, W., 'Cattle movements and bovine tuberculosis in Great Britain' (2005) 435 *Nature* 491–496.

26 Anderson, I., *Foot and Mouth Disease 2001: Lessons to be Learned Inquiry Report*, London: The Stationery Office, July 2002.

27 Carslake, D., Grant, W., Green, L.E., Cave, J., Greaves, J., Keeling, M., McEldowney, J., Weldgebriel, J.H. and Medley, G.F., 'Endemic cattle diseases: comparative epidemiology and governance' (2011) 366 (1573) *Philosophical Transactions of the Royal Society B* 1933–1942.

infected animals. The ideal from an infectious disease perspective is a 'closed' herd in which animals are never moved into the herd, or if they are then they are subject to strict quarantine and health measures. A closed herd must rely on the productivity of its animals to create profit, and this we believe is the public perception of most dairy herds, in which the cattle have individual names and share their herd with their mother, aunts and daughters. However, closed herds are very rarely achieved in practice. The opposite extreme is herds that are essentially trading concerns, where animals (especially cattle in this context) are bought and sold, and the profit is made through exploiting differences in price rather than in animal production. Dairy farms rely on cows calving (and coming into milk), so the period between calves (the 'dry period') represents a period when cows require care and expenditure but are not generating income. A relatively recent phenomenon is the 'flying herd' where farmers buy cows that have just calved, milk them for a lactation and sell them on at the start of the dry period.

Disease influences the herd patterns of buying and selling. If animals are culled to control disease (e.g. in response to a diagnosis of bTB infection), then the farmer must find replacement stock to maintain profitability. Unless the farmer is prescient enough to have bred and kept sufficient replacements for this eventuality, the replacements must be purchased. Consequently, farmers can be drawn into a situation in which they are purchasing stock to replace animals culled for disease control, and as a result increasing the problem of disease within their herd.[28] Even if replacements can be found within the herd, the impact of culling is to change the demography of the herd (e.g. animals are kept for longer), which will have subsequent impact on the dynamics of all the diseases in the herd.

The reality, of course, is that farmers will use both types of activity to make profit. We do not propose a full categorisation of herd types, but it is clear that there are very different behaviours and these behaviours and their diversity are motivated by economic circumstances. It has clearly become profitable for some farms to act as 'rest herds' for cows between lactations before they calve and join a milking herd. The manner in which farmers behave, in terms of animal movement, is dependent on the economics of the industry. For example, were it to be the case that transport of livestock became more expensive, the amount of animal movement would decrease, and disease patterns would change.

Economic processes act on disease patterns in two ways. First, the extent of animal movement is determined by animals as commodities, and the decision to control disease on a farm is largely governed by costs and benefits. Second, farms are commercial enterprises, and disease-related reductions in production (growth, fertility, survival, etc.) or the perceived risk of such impairments determines

---

28 As one farmer we interviewed stated, 'We all aspire to have a closed herd, the benefits of that are huge – it's a long time since we were but we do try. But once you're into TB then you've no chance of keeping a closed herd because you're infected …'.

farmers' decisions about control of disease. Farmers are be able to mitigate loss, for example by breeding or purchasing animals on the basis that a certain percentage is likely to die. Whilst such an approach is a rational solution to livestock mortality, it does have the effect of making the mortality a requirement for the economic well being of the farm, because if the predicted deaths do not occur then the herd might be over-stocked with consequent loss of productivity. Farmers can also manage the risks associated with a disease or with disease generally. Maintaining a closed herd with proper regard to the possibility that animals will introduce new diseases or new types of disease is clearly a way of reducing risk of introduction. Similarly, vaccinating a herd against a disease which it does not have (but which is endemic in neighbouring herds and trading partners) will reduce the impact of the disease and reduce its chances of persisting should it be introduced.

Financial viability of the herd and farmers' actions are influenced by the farm's economic environment including market reactions and policies such as farm subsidies. A change in the price paid for milk or, as indicated above, the cost of transport will change the way in which farmers can make a profit from their animals. Compensation payments for culling diseased animals are paid by government when the benefit from culling is treated as a 'public good', i.e. when the principal beneficiaries are the whole industry or nation, but the individual farmer is losing money from the intervention. There is an important contrast here between exotic disease epidemics and endemic disease control. During an epidemic of an exotic disease, government is required to act to eliminate the infection by taking action and compensating farmers for their losses, which may be catastrophic. The expectation (and, to date, the practice) is that the intervention is relatively short-lived and, once the disease has been eliminated, the intervention stops and farmers can re-invest in their herd, as was the case for the elimination of brucellosis. However, compensation for endemic disease effectively changes the relationship between the farmer and the disease. Without compensation, the disease clearly has a negative impact on the economic performance of the farm, but with compensation the negative impact is mitigated or removed, and it might even create a situation in which farmers can make a profit from disease. During the BSE epidemic, it was argued that paying full compensation for BSE cases would encourage accurate disclosure and reporting, and that paying 50 per cent compensation would result in diseased cattle entering the food chain, i.e. farmers would make the decision on the fate of an animal based on the economic outcome.

Our argument is that the epidemiology of any particular disease is a consequence of the interaction between a plethora of natural science and social processes, and that the epidemiology acts on some of these processes. The consequence is that the epidemiology is a dynamic system in itself, in which economic factors both shape the epidemiology and are determined by the epidemiology. In order to be successful (in an ecological, evolutionary sense), an endemic disease must interact with the political and economic spheres to create a positive environment for itself. If a disease is zoonotic, then it is likely (but not always) to attract political attention and potential intervention against it. If a disease reduces growth rates of a few infectious individuals then they are more likely to be sold on by farmers as 'poor-doers', thereby facilitating transmission. So the economic/political/social system of livestock agriculture will effectively select the endemic diseases that are most suited to it. Simultaneously, the livestock agricultural system adapts *inter alia* to the endemic diseases within it. For example, the decline in livestock markets in the UK is largely due to the impact of disease and the measure to control disease, including the FMD epidemic, the over 30-months scheme to reduce BSE cases entering the food chain and pre-movement testing requirements for bTB.[29] The reduction in markets will change the epidemiology of other infections. If we accept that there will always be endemic disease in livestock, then the particular diseases and their epidemiology will be a product of the livestock industry, and the livestock industry will be influenced by the endemic disease it supports.

An alternative stance is that endemic disease is not to be accepted – just as we are unwilling to accept that measles causes death and disease in people, so we should not accept that BVD causes disease, death and reduced productivity in cattle. Endemic diseases in this case can be seen as exploiting the gaps, or disconnects, between the economic, political and veterinary/biological domains. In order for a disease to be eliminated, it must have met requirements in all domains. There must be a political will to eliminate, the right economic incentives and the appropriate veterinary/biological tools to accomplish the elimination. For a disease to remain endemic it need only fail on one of these requirements, or have too high a profile in one of these domains resulting in a skewed response with over-reliance on one aspect.

For example, there is a clear political will to eliminate bTB from the UK, but attempts to control disease are failing largely because of a lack of good diagnostic tools and unclear economic incentives. Previous successful elimination efforts (in the UK and Australia) have relied on market segmentation, as did brucellosis elimination. Creating an attested herd scheme with an economic advantage to being attested overcomes the deficiencies of the diagnostic test, resulting in a separation of cattle between those that are 'known' to be uninfected (through continued testing of herds over long periods of time) and those that are not known to be uninfected. However, such an attested herd scheme is very intrusive on market forces, and requires an economic incentive to make the investment to become attested. However, the dominance of the political profile (partly due to the involvement of badgers) skews discussion and debate, effectively excluding potentially rational economic and biologically motivated interventions.

29 *Livestock Markets in the 21st Century: A Review of the Livestock Markets in England – the Challenges and Opportunities*, Kenilworth: Meat and Livestock Commercial Services Ltd (MLCSL), 2010, www.eblex.org.uk/documents/content/publications/p_cp_livestockmarket20100 40111.pdf (accessed 27 March 2013).

A contrasting example is BVD, for which the diagnostic and invention tools are available, and there is some political interest (see Chapter 5), but there is little economic incentive. Consequently, control is reliant on the use of the vaccine, but without a concerted effort (i.e. political will and economic incentives) vaccination by individual farmers will not be sufficient for elimination. Similarly, for footrot in sheep, there are clear economic incentives and reasonable tools for intervention, but politically it has a very low profile.[30] It is quite clear that both BVD and bTB could be highly controlled or even eliminated from the UK if the other domains could be aligned, and we return to these examples in Chapter 5. The certainty for footrot control and elimination is less, but again it could be much better controlled if its political profile (and the consequent funding and incentives) were higher.

The state of a disease is defined not just by its epidemiology, but also by its economic impact and political profile. This state largely determines to what extent, and by whom, control is applied.

Determinants of disease control

In this section we consider the determinants of control programmes, and in particular at which level control is determined, i.e. the individual farmer or government or a mixture of the two.

Endemic disease

Endemic diseases are generally not subject to government-led interventions. At the lowest level, individual farmers are responsible for disease control. Farmers have a legal responsibility for the welfare of their livestock, and must make a profit from them to survive as farmers, so both are potential motivations for introducing control. However, individual farmers' actions lead to changes at the meta-herd level that might be beneficial or detrimental to other herds. Vaccination is beneficial to all the herds that an animal visits during its lifetime (presuming that the effect of the vaccine is long term). On the other hand, preferentially selling infected animals (e.g. 'poor-doers') will have the effect of disseminating infection to other farms. For infectious disease, at least, herds are not independent, so that the risk to any given farmer/herd is dependent not just on that farmer's actions, but on the actions of all the other farmers. A level of coordination and concerted action between farmers will result in a greater impact than farmers acting alone.

Farmers are also linked in terms of economics. Given that a disease has a negative effect on production, then farmers without the disease in their herd have a

---

30 See for example, Green, L.E., Kaler, J., Wassink, G.J., King, E.M. and Grogono Thomas, R., 'Impact of rapid treatment of sheep lame with footrot on welfare and economics and farmer attitudes to lameness in sheep' (2012) 21 (supplement 1) *Animal Welfare* 67–72.

competitive advantage over farmers who have it. Herds that harbour a disease pose a risk to other herds. Farmers who remove the disease from their herd/farm will enjoy an (economic) benefit of this removal, but it also benefits other farmers who have a reduced risk of moving infection into their herd. This linkage inevitably leads to the 'free-rider' problem, i.e. the farmer who does nothing benefits from the actions of all the others without bearing the costs of control. Clearly, if intervention against disease is to be effective and efficient then there must be sufficient coordination to overcome the economic incentives not to intervene if everybody else is intervening.

The lack of coordination between farmers in terms of infectious diseases can be explained in terms of the considerable differences between farmers in terms of experience and perception. As discussed previously, the clustering of disease within farms means that some farmers will be rightly sceptical of paying for an intervention against a disease that they do not regard as a problem. There is a suggestion that farmers who do not have a disease will explain their lack of disease as a difference in farming ability and expertise,[31] which reinforces the concept of competition between farmers. Alternatively, farmers who effectively eliminate a disease from their herd might experience a reintroduction from the meta-herd in the absence of concerted, successful effort. Indeed, a risk-adverse farmer might prefer to have a manageable level of disease permanently in the herd (against which he or she can mitigate) rather than face the risk of reintroduction. Uncertainty about other farmers' actions leads farmers to a situation in which their best option is not to take actions against disease, but to hedge the risk (e.g. buying from multiple sources) or transfer the risk to others (e.g. selling on 'poor doers' or suspect individuals). A more efficient allocation of resources would be for all farmers to address the infectious disease with appropriate intervention rather than to 'play' the risks.[32]

There are initiatives within the livestock industry to attempt to develop coordination between farmers to overcome the uncertainty and rationalise risk reduction. Dairy UK (sector trade association) initiated a Johne's Action Group in collaboration with DairyCo (levy-funded organisation) 'to identify current best practice measures for the control of Johne's disease',[33] and BPEX initiated Pig Health Improvement Projects with the 'aim [is] to assist producers in taking a more collaborative approach to pig health'.[34] However, it is not clear that any such initiative has developed to the extent to which any disease has been

---

31 Heffernan, C., Nielsen, L., Thomson, K. and Gunn, G. 'An exploration of the drivers to biosecurity collective action among a sample of UK cattle and sheep farmers' (2008) 87(3–4) *Preventive Veterinary Medicine* 358–372.
32 For an example of where profitability and disease control are not aligned, see Santarosa *et al.*, 'Optimal risk management versus willingness to pay for BVDV control options' (2005) 72 *Preventive Veterinary Medicine* 183–187.
33 DairyCo Research and Development, www.dairyco.org.uk (accessed 27 March 2013).
34 Pig Health Improvement Project, www.pighealth.org.uk/health/home.eb (accessed 27 March 2013).

significantly impacted. The examples of endemic diseases that were eliminated (brucellosis and warble fly) have been rehearsed, but both involved significant government involvement to the extent of legislation and mobilisation of considerable state veterinary resources.

Practically, then, it would appear that an endemic disease is set to remain endemic unless there is government intervention to enforce co-operation and concerted action amongst farmers.

Epidemic/exotic disease

In contrast to endemic disease, control of exotic disease is determined by government. For diseases that have been endemic in the UK in the past, this is situation is tautological, since in order to be eliminated there must have been some concerted, government-led action. For diseases that have never been endemic, it might be interpreted as tautological in that the reason the disease has never been endemic is because of government intervention and action.

Successful control of an epidemic is critically dependent on early recognition and intervention. Because epidemics grow exponentially, the impact of intervening two days earlier is much greater than intervening a day earlier.[35] Consequently, surveillance for disease and ensuring that there are plans in place for a prompt and appropriate response (i.e. restricting the movement of livestock) is the first line of response. Surveillance for diseases that are expected to be rare requires that a large number of animals be included in the sample increasing the cost. For budget managers, funding expensive surveillance programmes for a disease that is not expected to be there does not appear cost-effective, so there is always a pressure to reduce surveillance. Nonetheless, there is considerable effort and energy devoted to considering the response to future exotic disease outbreaks in the UK.[36]

Sources of information and risk perception

Currently, endemic diseases are controlled at the herd level by individual farmers, relying on the information available to them. The control a farmer chooses to apply is determined by the technical ability to diagnose, treat and vaccinate combined with the perceived potential commercial and welfare consequences of disease, expected costs and uncertainty of control, and social norms. Since infectious disease is heterogeneous (i.e. clustered so that not everybody experiences

35   Royal Society, *Infectious Diseases in Livestock*, London: The Stationery Office, 2002.
36   For example, see the Defra publications *Exotic Animal Disease Risk Pathways & Countermeasures:* Final Report, October 2009, www.defra.gov.uk/publications/files/pb13567-risk-pathways-countermeasures-100310.pdf (accessed 27 March 2013), and *A Review of the Implementation of the Veterinary Surveillance Strategy (VSS)*, February 2011, www.defra.gov.uk/publications/files/pb13568-vss-review-110204.pdf (accessed 27 March 2013).

the same prevalence) and dynamic (i.e. the clustering changes with time), infectious disease control is predominantly about assessing and managing risks. Where the presence of disease is more uniform and exists on virtually all farms (e.g. mastitis in dairy cattle, footrot in sheep and helminths in all livestock), the risk is that losses will be greater than normal, and intervention is required to contain the level of disease. In this case, an individual farmer has little information on which to base an estimate of the costs, either those due to lost production or those incurred by control.

In contrast, where the disease is characterised more by outbreaks, and 'jumps' from herd to herd (e.g. BVD), the risk is that the disease will be introduced so that intervention is required to reduce the risk of introduction and to mitigate its impact if it is introduced. In this case, the costs of an introduction to an individual farm can be assessed, as in the case of a diagnosis of bTB (a herd breakdown).[37] If a farmer has never experienced a disease, then it is likely to be treated as more of a threat than diseases that have always existed in the herd, regardless of their real impact.

This is a different process to that of government's assessment of the impact of disease to guide policy development, which normally takes a national perspective.[38] Consequently, government priorities will always be different from the majority of individual farmers. Frequently, cost and impact assessment are not confined to avoidable costs, i.e. those that the farmer can actually influence. A recent study of Johne's disease concluded that there was actually little incentive for farmers to control the disease,[39] even though there appears to be both government and industry interest in reducing it.

People involved in assessing and managing the risk can only react to the perceptions of risk and their effects.[40] The information on which the perception is based comes from personal experience, interaction with personal contacts (e.g. neighbours, veterinarians, trading partners), or through the media and information from organisations (e.g. Defra). Information, like disease, flows in networks which disseminate information about disease through the loose collective of those interested (the stakeholders), which includes consumers and retailers. The information spread by the networks is not accurate (e.g. it was a popular view outside the UK that FMD posed a threat to tourists in 2001), nor is it comprehensive. Nor is it 'valueless' in the sense that the receiver of the information will

---

37 Bennett, R.M. and Cooke, R.J., 'Costs to farmers of a TB breakdown' (2006) 158 *Veterinary Record* 429–432.

38 Bennett, R.M. and IJpelaar, J., 'Updated estimates of the costs associated with 34 endemic livestock diseases in Great Britain' (2005) 56 *Journal of Agricultural Economics* 135–144.

39 Stott, A.W., Jones, G.M., Humphry, R.W. and Gunn, G.J., 'Financial incentive to control paratuberculosis (Johne's disease) on dairy farms in the United Kingdom' (2005) 156 *Veterinary Record* 825–831.

40 Enticott, G., 'The ecological paradox: social and natural consequences of the geographies of animal health promotion' (2008) 33(4) *Transactions of the Institute of British Geographers* 433–446.

have some opinion about the motivation of the transmitter. Nonetheless, the information received via such networks is the basis for decisions.

Farmer survey

It is clear that farmers are the locus of control for endemic infectious disease. How farmers perceive the risks of disease and where their information comes from is therefore critical in determining endemic disease in the UK. Consequently, we undertook a series of semi-structured interviews to better understand the processes of information gathering, interpretation and consequent actions.[41]

Data collection

A purposive sample of 30 farmers was interviewed in the first half of 2010: 19 dairy farmers and 11 breeding/rearing beef cattle. Farmers were recruited via veterinarians and marketing groups. A semi-structured interview guide was followed. We specifically asked about the following diseases:[42] neosporosis, Johne's disease, leptospirosis, BVD, infectious rhino-tracheitis (IBR) and bTB, as well as more general questions about purchasing and selling cattle, sources of information and their attitude to disease. Interviews lasted between 45 and 90 minutes. With permission, interviews were recorded and transcribed and analysed using a thematic analysis approach.[43]

Knowledge of disease

Knowledge between diseases varied considerably. Most had an understanding of leptospirosis, BVD and IBR, but six interviewees had never heard of neosporosis and three were familiar with the name only. A number of farmers had experienced outbreaks of neosporosis and were actively involved in control programmes, and the fact that the main route of transmission is vertical[44] made farmers feel they could control the disease. Two farmers, who had experienced an outbreak, stated that neosporosis was the disease that caused them the greatest concern. Awareness of Johne's disease was high. Many farmers had experienced the disease in their herds and some were involved in active control programmes. Four farmers mentioned that leptospirosis is a zoonosis adding dimensions of

41   The interviews and analysis were undertaken by Dr Amy KilBride. Full details of the study are available at www2.warwick.ac.uk/fac/cross_fac/gld/results/survey.

42   Neoporosis is a unicellular parasite causing abortion; Johne's disease is a bacterial infection causing wasting and death in older cattle; leptospirosis is a bacterial disease that is also zoonotic, and for which there is a vaccine; IBR is a viral infection causing respiratory symptoms for which there is a vaccine. BVD and bTB are described in more detail in Chapter 5.

43   Braun, V. and Clarke, V., 'Using thematic analysis in psychology' (2006) 3(2) *Qualitative Research in Psychology* 77–101.

44   Cow to calf.

responsibility and ethical behaviour towards workers which played a part in their disease control decisions.

How much farmers had to say about bTB varied by geographical location; for farmers in bTB hot spots, it overshadowed all other disease concerns, while farmers in other areas ranged from nervously anticipating future trouble to being unconcerned. Twenty-two of the farmers interviewed rated bTB as the cattle disease they were most concerned about. Farmers perceived the comparative skin test as inaccurate, which undermined their confidence in the control programme. Occasions when cattle were identified as reactors by the skin test but this was not confirmed by laboratory examination or post mortem led farmers to perceive they had lost the animal unnecessarily.[45] Some attempts were made by farmers to explain the breakdown in one cow or farm rather than another, while some proclaimed the role of luck in the risk of contracting the disease. A small number of farmers interviewed stood out for their proactive attitude towards preventing their cattle contracting bTB. These farmers possessed a sense of self-belief that they could prevent the infection in their cattle. These farmers' herds were currently bTB free.

Attitudes to disease control

The farmers we interviewed appeared to be happy with the available cattle disease tests and vaccines, and perceived that these offered cost-effective control. Only a small number of farmers interviewed had herds that they knew were free from the diseases of interest and were actively trying to maintain this status. Two farmers mentioned concern about their herd becoming infected with IBR and one other farmer stated concern about his herd becoming infected with leptospirosis. For most farmers, infection in their herd with these diseases was seen as inevitable and not a cause for concern (as control methods are available).

For many farmers, vaccination was at the forefront of their disease management strategy,[46] and they appeared to be broadly satisfied with this approach; vaccination was generally thought to be relatively cheap and money well spent. Vaccination programmes once initiated tended to continue, although there was reticence over the management implications of administrating a number of different vaccines to their herd, as the logistics of administration was perceived to be more of a problem than the cost of the vaccine.

The majority of farmers were aware of the value of biosecurity, although there appeared to be general scepticism regarding biosecurity advice provided by those who are not farmers or veterinarians. Many farmers described their herd as closed (i.e. breeding all replacement cattle on farm) and referenced the disease status of bought in cattle as the motivation for this, as well as feeling their own

---

45 In fact, the specificity of the test is high (i.e. a positive result is likely to be accurate), but has a low sensitivity (i.e. infected animals return a negative test).

46 Ten, 15 and 20 farmers vaccinated their herds against IBR, leptospirosis and BVD respectively.

replacements were good cows. However, many 'closed' herds bought in cattle. It may be that farmers are using the term 'closed' to describe a general model of farming rather than specifying they never bring cattle into the farm. Or it may be that there is a considerable intention–behaviour gap. As a general rule, actions to control disease risk were under threat when farmers had to take action against factors that they perceived presented a bigger risk to their businesses (e.g. reducing fertility). Very few farmers who bought in cattle reported they had isolated them before introduction into the herd.

Farmers buying cattle put trust in social networks and buying from people they or their veterinarian knew. The flow of information appeared to be defined by social connections within the community. A minority stated the disease status of their cattle was no one else's business, but the majority took the view that, in theory at least, sharing information was the correct neighbourly thing to do, although they were generally unclear whether other farmers were sharing/ would share information with them. Information if offered was a gift, bestowed based on interpersonal relationship, not something farmers felt they had the right to expect or an obligation to provide. Not disclosing disease status to someone with whom you had no personal relationship was normal and accepted, and asking unsolicited questions about disease status would be difficult and generally unacceptable.

For some farmers general herd viability appeared to pass for information on herd health. That is, if a local farmer was perceived to have a healthy business, he must have healthy stock. While price and health risk matter when making decisions about where to buy and sell cattle, farmers are not simple profit maximisers. Many farmers are working for themselves, therefore their own time, effort and feelings have high value in making these decisions. In particular, ease of access (timing, transport and distance) impact on how cattle famers buy and sell.

Livestock markets functioned in different ways for different types of farmer. Farmers who produced pedigree breeding stock bought and sold high-quality stock at specialist markets. These transactions often involve information on the disease status of the animals. Non-pedigree farmers made a distinction between buying cattle to fatten and sell or slaughter – where disease risk was given minimal consideration and markets used – and cattle to keep and breed – where disease risk was given more consideration and markets were treated with suspicion. Two reasons were given for this suspicion: mistrust of the motive for sale as it was thought likely that farmers would be getting rid of their worst stock, and the perception that the mixing of stock would increase the risk of infection. While markets function on a clear 'buyer beware' presumption, when selling from home, farmers felt more responsibility for the quality of their product. Farmers perceived themselves as being able to distinguish a sick from a healthy animal.

Synthesis

Overall, farmers varied in their awareness of disease risk and their attitude towards controlling risk. Of the farmers interviewed, there were a small group whose knowledge of cattle disease was minimal and they tended to assume a low level of responsibility for disease in their cattle. Disease was not thought to be their responsibility; luck was part of how they understood the risk of their cattle contracting disease, and action to avoid disease risks was limited. A second group of farmers were characterised by their lack of awareness of disease problems. They were willing to call the veterinarian and address problems, but they were largely unaware of the disease status of their cattle. A third group – a large proportion of the interview sample – had good disease knowledge and were aware of the diseases in their herds through testing. Disease management was part of their farming process, although they saw disease burden in their herds as inevitable. The final group of farmers in our sample had a high level of knowledge about disease, which they saw as something to be tackled rather than something to be lived with. They initiated innovative approaches to reduce the disease risk in their herd, and were proactive and systematic in their approach.

Conclusions

The epidemiology and control of endemic disease emerges from the interactions between processes in the biological (physical) and social domains. The pattern of infection and disease cannot be understood adequately without recourse to both natural science (usually quantitative approach) and social science (usually qualitative). Transmission of infection in livestock is largely determined by the behaviour of farmers, and the risk of infection has at least some influence on the farmers' behaviour. Biologically, the interactions between pathogen and host start at the scale of the individual animal and build up to interactions between animals – the infection statuses of individual animals are determined by the state of the herd, and the state of the herd is determined by the collection of individual states. This process alone is sufficient to create heterogeneity between herds. The differences between herds are compounded by farmer behaviour, which is influenced by the state of their herd. The combination of dynamic interactions at different, interlinked scales creates a complex system from which the epidemiology of a disease 'emerges'. Government and other stakeholders operating at higher levels are able to influence the epidemiology, but without aligning the system at all levels, cannot control it.

One of the outcomes of this complexity is that endemic and exotic diseases become entrenched into almost separate compartments. Endemic disease survives below the political radar so that efforts to control it are variable and bound to fail because of the heterogeneity in response by farmers.[47] From an evolutionary

---

47 Although we are considering only livestock disease here, it is interesting that the same phenomenon is seen in relation to human disease. Diseases such as influenza, HIV and malaria attract the majority of political attention and research funding, whilst other 'neglected' diseases, especially helminths, get relatively little. This categorisation does not reflect the importance of diseases in terms of their impact on health, well being and economics.

perspective, brucellosis has been unsuccessful because it became a target for a concerted attempt to eliminate it, resulting in an alignment of objectives of different spheres (veterinary, political, legal, economic, etc.) and an alignment of the levels of organisation (farmers, government, etc.). Diseases that maintain non-alignment (or disorganisation) persist. Our view is that endemic disease is embedded as part of the livestock production system rather than being laid on top of it, and that the responses to the disease enhance its persistence. Disease is only one aspect of livestock production – it is easy for researchers to become bemused about farmers' apparently irrational behaviour, but farmers are not in business to control disease. Farmers' needs to maintain profitability, comply with legislation and exist within a social context create the environment in which endemic disease persists. Infectious disease is often viewed as an unnecessary burden, which if lifted would improve the experience of all. However, because endemic disease in enmeshed in the whole system, removal will change the system, with outcomes that might be perverse. For example, the current testing programme against bTB results in a considerable payment from government to veterinary services in rural areas, and were the disease to be suddenly eliminated, the impact on veterinary practice and coverage would be negative.

Farmers carry the responsibility for health and welfare of their livestock, motivated by legal requirements and profit. The role of government is to provide a framework which supports collective action where such action cannot be generated by farmers themselves because of the epidemiology of the disease, i.e. those diseases that are essentially outside the control of individual farmers. Although all infectious diseases exist within the meta-herd and are transmitted between herds, they differ in the importance of inter-herd transmission to their persistence. Some diseases (typically those in which animals are chronically infectious and there is environmental contamination, e.g. Johne's disease) are 'farm based'. Others (typically those that have a short infectious period and inspire long-term immunity, e.g. BVD) must move from herd to herd to persist and are 'industry based'. Carslake *et al.* suggested a four-way classification of endemic disease between these two epidemiological groups, and having a high or low political profile.[48] Diseases that are 'low-farm' (i.e. a low political profile and based in individual farms) are more vulnerable to individual farmer intervention, but very unlikely to attract government resources. Diseases that are high-industry (i.e. high political profile and disseminated in the meta-herd) are more likely to attract government-led intervention. Diseases that are low-industry or high-farm are starting from a position of non-alignment of organisational levels and create a tension between political and farmer/industry motivations. We believe that such classifications are useful in that they at least partially explain what might be required to achieve alignment in different spheres.

Overall, endemic diseases of livestock are challenging because understanding and control requires disciplines to be combined, and different organisational

48   Carslake *et al.*, op. cit., n. 27.

levels to be simultaneously considered. The best approach is to consider adapting and regulating a complex dynamic system; it is not a question of simply intervening directly to reduce prevalence and incidence. Neither the availability of a new vaccine nor a change in the law would solve a disease problem. Such measures alone change the endemic disease landscape, but successful, efficient control requires interventions along multiple avenues simultaneously.

5   Endemic diseases

Diseases (and the pathogens that cause them) are not per se endemic or exotic. The labelling of a disease as exotic or endemic is essentially a political decision to 'frame' or label a disease in a particular way. Once this labelling has occurred it creates a 'path dependency' which influences the future course of policy, particularly how involved government should be in tackling the disease and the level of resources that are devoted to its research and management.

Why should government concern itself at all with diseases of cattle? One powerful motive for intervention is if the disease is a zoonosis, capable of spreading to the human population. It then becomes a question of human health as much as animal health, creating a different set of priorities in the minds of decision makers.

If government sees itself as responsible for boosting the level of agricultural production, and in particular the efficiency of that production, then there is a case for some intervention in diseases of cattle. Government intervention in agriculture in Britain effectively began with the establishment of the Cattle Plague Department of the Home Office in 1865 to deal with a serious outbreak of the cattle plague known as rinderpest and was followed by the Cattle Disease Prevention Act 1866. One response could have been to restore the import ban that had previously existed on live imports. However, it was feared that this would force up the price of meat, increasing the risk of working-class revolt. Meat consumption was also seen as 'essential to muscle growth and energy levels. If workers failed to eat enough, their productivity levels – and capitalists' profits – would flounder.'[1]

Over time, government's involvement in agriculture became more extensive and systematic, exemplified by the Agriculture Act 1947. In addition to grants and subsidies, farmers were offered free advice through the Agricultural Development and Advisory Service (ADAS). Following a presidential address by Mr Sidney Jennings to the British Veterinary Congress in 1961, a debate started within government about whether there should be an equivalent of the National

1 Woods, A., *A Manufactured Plague: The History of Foot and Mouth Disease in Britain*, London: Earthscan, 2004, p. 13.

Health Service for farm animals and a nationalised veterinary service. One civil servant minuted, 'Since 1947 most farmers have been accustomed to free advice on technical matters. They do not get this in the veterinary field.'[2] Another civil servant noted, 'We believe that even with our present limited resources agricultural productivity could be largely improved by the provision of such a [free veterinary] service which would concentrate very largely on preventive measures'.[3] The subsequent debate that took place within the civil service emphasised the economic efficiency gains to be achieved from a reduction in the incidence of disease. It also proceeded on very statist assumptions with an anticipation that in time private practice would fade away when 'factors of a social, political or economic nature render its separate existence unnecessary or even anachronistic'.[4]

The debate about the possibility of a national animal health service, and even a Ministry of Animal Health, was the apogee of productionist interventionism in cattle disease. It did not lead to any outcome and, today, government would not intervene simply on the ground of improving productive efficiency. These problems are seen as for the farmer to resolve, even though collective action problems arise in any attempt to act in combination with other farmers. At most, there may be limited state intervention to 'nudge' farmers in a particular direction.

Three diseases considered

Each of these diseases has very different characteristics in terms of politics and policy, but before considering these the nature of the diseases themselves will be briefly explained.

BVD is a widespread viral disease of cattle which is not a zoonosis. The effects vary widely, are often mild and animals may display no clinical signs. It can be transmitted from bought in animals from nasal secretion and faeces, but also vertically from cow to calf. Infection in pregnant animals may cause abortion or the birth of calves which are persistently infected (PI) and invariably develop a fatal disease called mucosal disease which ulcerates mucosal surfaces such as the mouth, throat and intestines later in life. PI animals are highly infectious. Vaccines are available but are not fully effective, although the diagnostic tests are well developed and accurate.

bTB is caused by the bacterium *Mycobacterium bovis* and is a zoonosis, although the pasteurisation of milk and the removal of milk from diseased herds from the food chain means that a once prevalent source of human illness is no longer a significant problem. The most common means of transmission is through the respiratory system. The disease seldom becomes clinically apparent until a late stage of development. It has one of the broadest host ranges of all known

2 National Archives, MAF 287/101, J.N. Ritchie, 21 November 1961.
3 Ibid., A.G. Benyon to Mr Reid, 12 September 1961.
4 Ibid., 'Revised Draft (2): Report of the Working Party Set Up To Consider a Nationalised Veterinary Service'.

pathogens – it can exist in wildlife hosts and be transmitted from them to cattle, although the mechanism of transmission is uncertain. In Britain, the main wildlife reservoir host has been the badger, but wild deer can also be hosts and, in other countries, possum. It is currently dealt with by regularly testing animals and culling those infected, but work is being undertaken on vaccines. The diagnostic tests are relatively limited, and the lack of sensitivity of current tests is a concern.

Johne's disease is a chronic infectious intestinal disease caused by the bacterium MAP, shed in faeces in large numbers by infected cows and usually contracted by calves in the calving pen (susceptibility declines with age). Disease develops slowly and lies dormant in cattle for the first three to seven years of life. The main sign is chronic enteritis – rapid weight loss and diarrhoea. In clinical cases it leads to infertility, scouring, loss of condition and eventually death. It also has immunosuppressive effects, leading to a higher incidence of other diseases. Treatment is by testing and culling infected animals: there is no known cure. However, the diagnostics are very limited, so that most management is aimed at long-term control of infection in a herd rather than elimination. It is not known to be a zoonosis, although the bacteria can be found in milk and a link with Crohn's disease has been advanced as a hypothesis.[5]

In terms of public policy, elimination campaigns for BVD have been pursued outside the UK, and the state of knowledge in relation to the disease was reviewed by an EU thematic network. However, policy interventions have been largely absent until a recent attempt to contain the disease initiated by the Scottish Government.

Some government attention was given to Johne's disease during the period after the Second World War when 'maximum productivity [was] becoming more important every year'.[6] This was because it was seen as 'one of the most serious economic problems in cattle in this country for a long time'.[7] In Australia, there was a systematic approach to Johne's disease. Levels of the disease were substantially reduced and it is only in the twenty-first century that Johne's disease has been a clinical issue after 40 years with very low levels.

Neither Johne's disease nor BVD has attracted much in the way of public debate and attention. This is not the case with bTB, which has become highly politicised. Its containment has been the subject of successive reports by experts, the National Audit Office and House of Commons committees. Substantial demands have been made on government budgets to pay compensation to farmers, an increasing concern at a time of fiscal restraint. What have been particularly controversial, however, have been proposals for culling badgers as a means of containing the disease.

5 Greenstein, R.J., 'Is Crohn's disease caused by a mycobacterium? Comparisons with leprosy, tuberculosis and Johne's disease' (2003) 3(8) *The Lancet Infectious Diseases* 507–514.
6 Ministry of Agriculture, Fisheries and Food, *Animal Health: A Centenary 1865–1965*, London: HMSO, 1965, p. 249.
7 Ibid., p. 251.

Explanatory frameworks

Three explanatory frameworks are useful for considering both the differences between the political and policy treatment of these diseases and also how policy on each disease has developed:

(1) Policy communities and networks.
(2) Politics of expertise.
(3) Interpretive assessments of the framing of policy.

Policy communities and networks

Policy communities and networks have offered an influential analytical framework in political science for over 20 years, but one that has attracted increasing criticism of its limitations. Policy communities are relatively closed and a limited group of actors process policy. They are characterised by shared goals and agreement about procedures for reaching decisions and 'rules of the game'. Typically, a policy community might be made up of a government department and stakeholder organisations representing key interests.

An example is the annual price review process that set subsidies and guaranteed prices from the passage of the Agriculture Act 1947 until the UK joined the European Community. The membership in this case was very limited as it was effectively MAFF and the National Farmers' Union (NFU) as the organisation recognised by the ministry as representing farmers. Both the ministry and the NFU agreed that the principal objective of policy was to maximise domestic production in UK agriculture and to ensure that that production was as efficient as possible. The two parties then negotiated each year about the composition of the subsidies and other forms of assistance. There was always disagreement, but it was usually possible to reach a negotiated settlement broadly acceptable to both parties. Calls for militancy from NFU members had to be balanced by the leadership against 'the effect it would have on future negotiations with the Government'.[8]

Issue networks are much looser groupings of policy actors. Barriers to membership are much lower than in the case of policy communities. They may have a shared policy focus, but they do not agree on objectives or even sometimes on procedures. In the case of agriculture, the original emphasis on maximising production and productivity was challenged by new perspectives and organisations that were equally concerned with agendas of conservation and environmental protection. The policy community moved in the direction of being an issue network.

8 Plumb, H., *The Plumb Line: a Journey through Agriculture and Politics*, London: Greycoat Press, 2001, p. 64.

The principal objection to these approaches is that, while they offer a useful understanding of how policy is made and who the key participants in the policy process are, they are essentially descriptive. They tell us very little about policy outcomes. It has also been objected in the context of work on cattle diseases that 'very few examples can be found of cases which closely resemble either the policy community or issue network. The policy processes which occur in these numerous "intermediate cases" remain under-analysed, since they are too often seen to be anomalous or in transition from one type of policy network to another.'[9]

Nevertheless, we would argue that the policy communities/networks model can contribute to explanation, although by itself it is insufficient. First, pre-existing policy communities/networks can be used as a resource to tackle new items on the policy agenda, as in the case of BVD in Scotland. Second, the absence or fragility of a policy network may impede policy initiatives as resources must be devoted to creating a network within which policy options can be discussed and formulated, as in the case of Johne's disease. Third, if the subject matter becomes so contentious that pre-existing networks cannot handle them, normal techniques of stakeholder management break down and it becomes difficult to formulate and implement policy. In the absence of agreement on what constitutes legitimate policy, it may be necessary to turn to the coercive resources of the state, but these are deployed sparingly and reluctantly, and may bring new problems in their train. This is the case with bTB.

Politics of expertise

The treatment of cattle disease invariably involves the deployment of expertise. How can a disease be diagnosed? How is it transmitted? How can it be treated? The difficult question is who constitutes an expert for these purposes. Two groups of experts who are evidently relevant are veterinarians and epidemiologists. Veterinarians have had a role inside the civil service since the establishment of the State Veterinary Service (SVS) in 1937.

In the 2001 FMD outbreak

> many vets were angry that responsibility for FMD control policy had been transferred away from the [SVS] and the [Institute of Animal Health's] scientific experts, and handed to a group of epidemiologists who had no prior experience of the disease. Leading veterinarians were not alone in claiming that the epidemiologists had gained the ear of government as a result of undue political influence.[10]

---

9 Williamson, K., Lowe P. and Donaldson, A., 'Beyond policy networks: policy framing and the politics of expertise in the 2001 foot and mouth disease crisis' (2010) 88(2) *Public Administration* 331–345, 343.

10 Woods, op. cit., n. 1, p. 241.

'In the FMD outbreak, vets and epidemiologists clashed over their approaches to controlling the disease, with vets drawing on their local knowledge to challenge the legitimacy of the scientists' models.'[11] The epidemiologists represented veterinarians 'as being too close to the problem, and too much a part of the culture of those affected by the disease, to the extent that it impaired their scientific judgment, whereas by implication, epidemiologists' cultural distance and consequent "outsider" status afforded them greater objectivity'.[12] As a government veterinarian pointed out in an interview, diseases had been eradicated in the past without fully understanding epidemiological processes.

There have been a number of often recurrent issues about the roles, relationships and responsibilities of state veterinarians. What counted as a veterinary issue? Should veterinarians just deliver policy or could they also help to make it?

Reviewing the experience of coping with BSE, the former Permanent Secretary of the then MAFF noted that the BSE Inquiry found 'that the CVO and the Director of the [Central Veterinary Laboratory] unjustifiably operated a policy of restricting information flows within the [SVS], to others in the veterinary profession, to other research groups and more widely for a period of some six months at the beginning of 1987'. He records his surprise 'that the CVO did not inform Ministers or the Permanent Secretary about the new disease ... All this shows that vets, perhaps like other professionals, do not think like civil servants and are reluctant to involve others in decisions they regard as falling within their remit even when formally those others stand higher in the hierarchy.'[13] A somewhat similar view was taken by the head of the FMD inquiry who told the House of Commons Defra Committee that '"the SVS is, and in many ways rightly, very proud, but rather an isolated organisation" and that the silo culture he identified as a problem within the Government was also a problem within the then [MAFF]'.[14] The underlying concern here is that state veterinarians are part of a much larger profession, leading to a perception in some quarters that they may tend to be more concerned about their standing within the profession than adhering to the norms of the civil service. It may, however, be seen as primarily a question of allegiance: do they serve their profession first and the state second, or the other way round? At what point does their duty to the employer conflict with their legally underwritten professional responsibilities?

11   Wilkinson, K., 'Evidence based policy and the politics of expertise: a case study of bovine tuber-culosis', Centre for Rural Economy Discussion Paper Series No. 12, April 2007, Centre for Rural Economy, Newcastle, p. 11.

12   Bickerstaff, K. and Simmons, P., 'The right tool for the job? Modelling, spatial relationships and styles of scientific practice in the UK foot and mouth crisis' (2004) 22 *Environment and Planning (D)* 393–412, 405.

13   Packer, R., *The Politics of BSE*, Basingstoke: Palgrave Macmillan, 2006, p. 35.

14   House of Commons Environment, Food and Rural Affairs Committee, *Vets and Veterinary Services*, HC 703, Sixteenth Report of Session 2002–2003, London: The Stationery Office, 2003, p. 27.

These problems are also echoed in the Taig report on the development and use of scientific advice in Defra. Taig admits that 'The interface between policy people and veterinary advisers is complex', quoting a policy view as 'Vets are our greatest asset and greatest liability'.[15] As far as the field service is concerned:

'The SVS is very highly valued for its network of ears, eyes, hands and expertise. But it is also a large cadre of individually very highly qualified professionals who are used to doing their own diagnosis and prescription of solutions. They may in some cases undermine Defra policy by letting people know that their views are different.'

Taig was, however, writing at a time of transition. Defra was replacing the MAFF model of an independent science support function to one of having scientists located within policy divisions. Taig thought that there was 'a particular concentration of lower satisfaction policy customers in the Animal Health & Welfare area'. Wyn Grant's observations of this team in a variety of settings were that relations between policy staff and veterinary advisers (as they are designated) were effective and harmonious. Given the technical character of most of the material being dealt with, policy staff relied on the expertise of veterinary advisers. Given the emphasis on evidence-based policy-making, they needed to utilise the knowledge that the advisers had of the research literature.

It should be noted, however, that Wilkinson's account of the exotic diseases division portrays a much stricter separation of scientific and policy roles:

'In Defra's exotic disease division, there is a rigid split between "expert groups" which comprise scientific advisers, and "policy groups", which comprise officials. When expert groups meet, they are not supposed to discuss policy or political issues; their recommendations are taken to the policy groups where decisions will be made.'[16]

There is an internal politics of expertise within Defra in terms of the roles and status of veterinarians, but there are also broader tensions between State veterinarians, those in private practice and those in academic life. These make the mobilisation of expertise as a depoliticisation technique very difficult to use in practice. Indeed, rather than experts depoliticising the issue, what can be seen is a 'politicisation of expertise'.[17] This is discussed further in relation to bTB.

15 Taig, T., *The Development and Use of Scientific Advice in Defra*, London: TTAC Limited, 2004, p. 13.
16 Wilkinson, K., 'Organised chaos: an interpretive approach to evidence-based policy making in Defra' (2011) 59(4) *Political Studies*, 959–977, 964.
17 Wilkinson, op. cit., n. 11, p. 15.

Interpretive assessments of the framing of policy

Wilkinson argues that 'policy making in Defra is organised by socially constructed narratives that help officials and advisers to make sense of their roles in the policy-making process'.[18] She notes that 'Interpretivists focus on meaning because they see it as a component in the construction and understanding of social reality'. However, she also finds that interpretivism by itself is not enough because it 'has less to say about how ... beliefs inform action'.[19] She resorts to organisational sociology to explore the relationship between meaning and action.

The view taken here is that it is possible to enhance more traditional forms of policy network analysis by giving them a discursive turn. Policy communities are tied together by a definition of what the policy problem is and how it can be tackled. Policy networks may dispute the definition of the policy problem and the appropriate means of dealing with it. In either case, ideas are more than the expression of particular interests but become constitutive of the policy arena itself so that a particular discourse becomes prevalent (policy community) or alternative discourses are contested (policy network). As Schön and Rhein write, 'In order to reflect on the conflicting frames that underlie policy controversies, we must become aware of our frames, which is to say we must construct them'.[20] This task is undertaken in relation to bTB.

BVD: initiating policy

The National Archives contain no papers on BVD, and the official history of the first hundred years of animal health policy in the UK contains no reference to the disease (admittedly, it was not identified until 1946). Nevertheless, it has been argued that there are economic and welfare reasons to give BVD a higher profile than it currently receives. From the farmer's perspective, 'Diseases such as acute mastitis and lameness are more obvious and their link to impaired welfare and production is also obvious so such diseases grasp the farmer's attention'.[21] Coupled with this, because it has no known zoonotic implications, 'There is low public awareness of BVD and therefore of the public good associated with better control or eradication'.[22] Moreover, 'it is clear that there are differences in how stakeholders across Europe interpret BVD as a problem and

---

18 Wilkinson, op. cit., n. 16, p. 959.
19 Wilkinson, op. cit., n. 16, p. 962.
20 Schön, D.A. and Rhein, M., *Frame Reflection: Toward the Resolution of Intractable Policy Controversies*, New York, NY: Basic Books, 1994, p. 34.
21 Gunn, G.J., Saatkamp, H.W., Humphry, R.W. and Stott, A.W., 'Assessing economic and social pressure for the control of bovine viral diarrhoea virus' (2005) 72 *Preventive Veterinary Medicine* 149–162, 156.
22 Ibid., p. 155.

how they communicate about BVD control. These differences may in themselves constitute a constraint to reach any form of collective action regarding BVD.'[23]

The EU considered it worthwhile to fund a thematic network on the control of BVD. When the network reported in 2001 it found that:

> As a consequence of the ongoing national ... control programmes in Europe, differences in prevalence of ... infections are becoming increasingly pronounced. Politically, these differences are reflected in the acknowledgement of BVD as a notifiable disease in eight European countries: Austria, Belgium, Denmark, Finland, Germany, Norway, Sweden and Switzerland.

The thematic network took the view that 'the recent decision by OIE to list BVD as a priority disease in terms of animal trade is a strong signal to the Community to consider development of an EU wide strategy to control BVD'.[24]

The disease is eradicable and this has been achieved in Norway and, at least for a period, in the Orkney Islands in Scotland (where clear geographical boundaries and informal social networks helped overcome collective action problems). The Scottish Government has initiated an elimination programme which started with subsidised screening of herds completed in 2011, followed by mandatory annual screening from December 2011 and movement controls from December 2012 onwards.

The motivation for this policy stemmed in part of a broader 'quiet revolution' in animal health policy being pursued north of the border. This, in turn, can be seen as part of a broader narrative about Scottish political identity and the ability of the Scottish Government to deliver more cost-effective solutions to policy problems than the government in Westminster. It is believed that it would give the country's livestock a unique selling point in future globalised markets and would reinforce the quality image of Scottish meat as well as making a contribution to climate change objectives. Although the main objectives of the programme would be cost savings and efficiencies in the supply chain, 'Consumers want to know that animals are well looked after, bundle up [BVD] as part of health control programme'.[25]

The Scottish Government faced a situation in which there was no pre-existing policy network dealing with BVD. The commitment to a BVD programme had to be created. It was possible to do this by making use of an existing policy community concerned with quality meat production in Scotland, based around organisations such as NFU Scotland whose then vice-president played a key role

23 Lindberg, A., Brownlie, J., Gunn, G.J., Houe, H., Moenning, V., Saatkamp, H.W., Sandvik, T. and Valle, P.S., 'The control of bovine viral diarrhoea virus in Europe: today and in the future' (2006) 25 (3) *Rev. sci. tech. Off. Int. Epiz.* 961–979, 964.

24 EU Thematic Network on control of bovine viral diarrhoea virus (BVDV), BVDV Control, QLRT – 2001-01573, Position paper.

25 Quality Meat Scotland, interview by Wyn Grant, 14 July 2010.

alongside the chief veterinary officer for Scotland. The Institute of Auctioneers and Appraisers in Scotland (IAAS) was one grouping that played a key role. Its incentive for becoming involved was that it was 'always being held up as the route by which disease gets spread'.[26] Organisationally, the IAAS met Olson's criteria for a 'privileged' group where there are a small number of market participants and there is an incentive to provide a collective good even if the burden of doing so is not equally shared.[27] There were 'only seven or eight companies, 34 auction marts, pretty concentrated, ability to speak with one voice'. The IAAS was also seen within the Scottish Government as being 'experts on market forces'. The Scottish Beef Association was also interested, more so than dairy farmers, while the BVD group within the Scottish Agricultural College was seen as important and provided a local source of expertise.[28]

The process of formulating and building support for the policy was facilitated by the relatively informal and close links between decision makers in Scotland. One interview respondent commented, 'In Scotland tend to be forced together. [There] does seem to be more contact because smaller.'[29] 'You can get everyone in one room and get the official answer at one time. You don't get backsliding or Chinese whispers.'[30] What also helped was that the Scottish National Party Government was 'very sympathetic to farmers and livestock farmers in particular'.[31]

It may be, however, that EU or government-led solutions are not the best approach to dealing with a production disease like BVD. The theoretical work of Elinor Ostrom is relevant here. She notes that 'Analysts who find an empirical solution with a structure presumed to be a commons dilemma often call for the imposition of a solution by an external actor'.[32] An alternative solution would be for 'herders themselves [to] make a binding contract to commit themselves to a cooperative solution that they themselves will work out'.[33]

At least some of the conditions Ostrom[34] specifies for the creation of institutions that supply joint welfare apply in the case of BVD:

(1) 'Most appropriators share a common judgment that they will be harmed if they do not adopt an alternative rule.' (Getting all farmers to recognise BVD as a problem is a hurdle.)

---

26 Quality Meat Scotland, interview.
27 Olson, M., *The Logic of Collective Action*, Cambridge, MA: Harvard University Press, 1965, p. 50.
28 Scottish Government, interview by Wyn Grant, 13 July 2010.
29 Interview by Wyn Grant, Inverness, 15 July 2008.
30 Quality Meat Scotland, interview.
31 Scottish Government, interview.
32 Ostrom, E., *Governing the Commons: The Evolution of Institutions for Collective Action*, Cambridge: Cambridge University Press, 1990, p. 13.
33 Ibid., p. 15.
34 Ostrom, op. cit., n. 32, p. 211.

(2) 'Most appropriators will be affected in a similar way by the proposed rule changes.' (The epidemiology of a beef herd is likely to differ from that of a dairy herd because of variations in contact and calving patterns.)[35]

(3) 'Most appropriators highly value the continuation activities from the [common pool regime].' (Having eliminated BVD, one would want to maintain that status.)

(4) 'Appropriators face relatively low information, transformation and enforcement costs.'

(5) 'Most appropriators share generalized norms of reciprocity and trust that can be used as initial social capital.'

(6) 'The group appropriating from the [common pool regime] is relatively small and stable.'

Two practical examples of such arrangements can be found in the UK. The Orkney Islands are located to the north of the Scottish mainland. They have 'the highest density of cattle in Europe with approximately 30,000 suckler and dairy cows'.[36] There was a significant problem with BVD. 'In the late 1990s, post mortems of abortions and neonatal deaths in Orkney calves showed 45 per cent of them were caused by BVD.'[37] In order to run a BVD eradication scheme, the Orkney Livestock Association was established, making use of local social capital. An employee of the auction mart acted as secretary and a local veterinarian played a prominent role. There were very few free riders, as 550 cattle farmers joined the eradication scheme with only 13 not joining. In the first two years of the scheme, 378 PI cattle were identified and removed. The experience of largely eradicating BVD (there are occasional breakdowns) has led the Association to start a campaign to eradicate Johne's disease, with the Orkney Islands Council meeting 80 per cent of the cost of laboratory testing over a three-year period.

A more ambitious scheme has been launched in the East of England in an attempt to make the region BVD free. This is predominantly an arable area. The project was started by members of the Norfolk and Suffolk Holstein Club because of their concern regarding the severe economic impact of this disease. East Anglia has traditionally had a lower number of infected farms (about 75 per cent) than the national average (about 95 per cent). Funding was provided by a company for the laboratory costs of initial testing for 100 farmers. A prominent veterinary academic was also involved in the scheme. A similar scheme has been initiated in Somerset. It would seem that BVD is likely to be tackled through co-operative schemes of this kind for the foreseeable future. Although they always raise free rider problems, this could be offset by requiring farmers to give more information about the disease status of an animal at the point of sale.

---

35 Gunn, G.F., Stott, A.W. and Humphry, R.W., 'Modelling and costing BVD outbreaks in beef herds' (2004) 167 *The Veterinary Journal* 143–149, 143.

36 www.orkneylivestock.co.uk (accessed 13 April 2010).

37 www.farmersguardian.com/story.asp?storycode=8589 (accessed 14 March 2008).

The more general question that arises is whether self-regulation offers a neo-liberal alternative to centralised regulation? Or might it be seen, as is apparent in the two examples discussed, as an example of a local democratic initiative which might forestall imposed forms of regulation? There is a third interpretation in which, in accordance with the prescriptions of behavioural economics about 'nudging' behaviour,[38] a limited and inexpensive state intervention in collaboration with an industry body facilitates effective action by producers which is of direct benefit to them. An example of this kind of enabling role is the BVD scheme initiated in Wales in 2011 through the red-meat promotion body Hybu Cig Cymru. £40,000 was made available from the Rural Development Plan for Wales which enabled farmers to claim up to £400 towards the cost of testing up to 100 cattle, the objective being to raise awareness and allow farmers to remove PI animals from the herd. The beneficiaries are the producers in terms of reducing losses of cattle and also the animals themselves. Consumers do not benefit directly, although it is thought that BVD-free status might help marketing.

The BVD case shows the importance of pre-existing policy networks as a means of facilitating policy innovations to control cattle disease. In particular, it has been possible for the state to perform an enabling role in the devolved administrations. Although there is some disagreement among BVD experts, for example about vaccines, there is a sufficient pool of expertise, including work in economics, to provide a basis for decision making. Discursively, an attempt was made in Scotland to portray BVD elimination as a contribution to greenhouse gas reduction, as well as a means of reinforcing the wholesome image of Scottish cattle.

Johne's disease: prioritising responses

The case of Johne's disease offers insights into the way in which priorities are decided in relation to combating cattle diseases, both at different times and in different countries. The causative agent was identified at the end of the nineteenth century and it was first discussed in official reports in 1909, but after that 'very few references to Johne's disease were made officially until 1934'.[39] It was one of four diseases, along with mastitis, BVD and infertility, included in the wartime Panel Scheme in 1942. This was a joint venture of MAFF, NFU and the National Veterinary Medical Association which sought to encourage preventive management on a herd basis. 'It never played a very prominent part in the scheme',[40] but it raised the profile of the disease.

38   Thaler, R.H. and Sunstein, C.R., *Nudge: Improving Decisions about Health, Welfare and Happiness*, New Haven, CT: Yale University Press, 2008.
39   Ministry of Agriculture, Fisheries and Food, *Animal Health: A Centenary 1865–1965*, London: HMSO, 1965, p. 250.
40   Ibid., p. 251.

Accordingly, the ministry initiated some surveys of the incidence of the disease after the war. This was followed by a study, 'Disease, Wastage and Husbandry in the British Dairy Herd', carried out in 1957–1958. The report published in 1960 showed that 'Johne's disease and acute mastitis were the two diseases causing the greatest total loss through depreciation in market value'. Mastitis was more common but did not necessarily lower the carcase value, while 'the productive life of a cow affected by Johne's disease is nearly halved and its commercial value is practically nil'.[41]

Given that it recognised that Johne's disease was one of the more serious economic problems in cattle, and that this was still a period when production losses were seen as giving grounds for government intervention, why was the ministry less active on Johne's disease than other cattle diseases, as is reflected in the extent of the files in the National Archives? Apart from the very real problems of diagnosis, it was feared that action on Johne's disease would undermine the greater policy priority of tackling bTB and that in particular the use of an available oil-pumice vaccine would interfere with the reading of the tuberculin test (there were also doubts about the efficacy of the vaccine). The Secretary of the Animal Health Division wrote to the British Veterinary Association stating:

> We are aware that Johne's Disease is a serious problem in many herds and that many people think its incidence may be on the increase. On the other hand it is surely obvious that nothing should be done which would prejudice the biggest single task the profession has undertaken at least during the twentieth-century and one moreover which has a public-health as well as an agricultural significance.[42]

Returning to the issue in 1963, it was admitted in internal discussions in the ministry that 'The loss from the disease is … considerable. This may suggest that the disease ought to have been tackled earlier. The fact is, however, that it has no public health significance.'[43] This confirms the extent to which policy was driven by concern about zoonoses. However, it also suggests a time lag in adjusting to changing circumstances which may itself suggest the existence of a path dependency. Given that all except the small percentage of 'green top' milk was pasteurised and that bTB had been brought under control in many parts of the country by the end of the 1950s, it is interesting that the zoonosis issue was still influencing the selection of policy priorities. 'A decision was made in 1964 that, despite the recognised complications to the tuberculin test that might result from its use, vaccine would be made available for herds with a Johne's

---

41 Ministry of Agriculture, Fisheries and Food, op. cit., n. 39, p. 251.
42 National Archives, MAF 35/625, 'Vaccination against Johne's disease', letter from W.E. Crump to F. Knight, 2 March 1959, p. 4.
43 National Archives, MAF 287/194, minute by J.N. Ritchie, 13 December 1963.

disease problem, providing that the tuberculin testing of the herd over the past two years had been satisfactory.'[44]

The vaccine was quite effective, together with recommended management to decrease the incidence of disease, and Johne's disease was brought under control in Britain, but levels have been increasing again in the recent past. It has never occupied as large a political space as bTb as it has not had the same public expenditure implications, nor has it involved attempts to control a wildlife reservoir.

The diagnosis issue remained a real practical constraint. The Scottish Government gave some consideration to prioritising Johne's disease rather than BVD. 'When BVD came in [to the policy discussion] my team were saying we should be looking at Johne's, potential link to Crohn's, but going on BVD, tools are all there, don't have a test that works in a practical time scale. Not able to detect animal early enough. Johne's a hidden one.'[45] For the Scottish Government it was a case of 'pick[ing] off the most achievable'.[46] Moreover, the prevalence of Johne's disease in Scotland was lower than that of BVD.

'Australia is in the fortunate position of having relatively little JD [Johne's disease] compared with most developed agricultural countries.'[47] To prevent the further spread of Johne's disease, Australia has invested considerable resources in the reduction of its incidence. It is 'essentially a disease of four states, really three who would dictate policy for other states'.[48] It is limited to the states of South Australia, Victoria, New South Wales and Tasmania (just 16 herds). In New South Wales it is largely found along the border with Victoria, but there are outliers related to the former dairy industry. Western Australia was declared Johne's disease free in 1999. Queensland and Northern Territory have been traditionally free of the disease. It should be noted that each state has legislative responsibility for endemic diseases.

There has been a National Johne's Disease Control Program covering a variety of species in Australia since 1996. It provides a set of standard definitions and rules to facilitate trade between jurisdictions. In 1999, Animal Health Australia (AHA) commissioned a discussion paper on the future of Johne's disease control in the Australian cattle industries. Following extensive discussions with stakeholders, a meeting in 2003 endorsed a national strategic plan. The Market Assurance Programme (MAP) is an audited voluntary quality assurance programme incorporating animal health risk assessment, testing and movement controls. MAPs are intended to give increased assurance that herds are not infected with Johne's disease. It is a 'relatively expensive programme ... that is

44   Ibid., p. 255
45   Quality Meat Scotland, interview.
46   Scottish Government, interview.
47   Animal Health Australia, 'What is Johne's disease?', www.animalhealthaustralia.com.au/programs/johnes-disease/what-is-johnes-disease (accessed 3 April 2013).
48   Animal Health Australia, interview by Wyn Grant, 24 February 2009.

not for everyone'.[49] A CattleMAP costs about $A10 per head tested. The main target is livestock producers who sell replacement stock to breeders who want low-risk stock.

Johne's disease zones based on a region's level of disease risk and control were introduced in 1999 to prevent the disease from spreading further, and involve movement controls. Higher-status zones protect their favourable status by placing controls on animals moving from lower-status zones and by dealing with incursions or existing infections Western Australia is designated as a Johne's disease free zone. Queensland, the Northern Territory, the northern pastoral areas of Southern Australia, most of New South Wales and Flinders Island plus the Furneaux Group are protected zones which have traditionally been free of the disease. Tasmania is a residual zone. Victoria, southern South Australia and parts of New South Wales are treated as control zones.

In New South Wales and Southern Australia it is mandatory to declare the National Dairy BJD Assurance Score for all dairy cattle offered for sale. The higher the score, the lower the risk. By making more information available to potential purchasers of cattle this then affects the price the farmer receives for cattle that are sold, providing incentives to control Johne's disease through the market place. A score of zero is allocated to non-assessed herds and a score of one if the herd is infected or suspect. Scores of two to six are allocated to herds in a control programme, with a score of two being allocated to herds with more than 4 per cent reactors. A score of seven or eight is given for the first clean test depending on the zone. A score of eight to ten is awarded if the herd is in the CattleMap, and a score of ten if it is in a Johne's disease-free zone.

An industry-funded assistance package developed by AHA is not a compensation package, but is intended to help owners of infected and suspected herds to identify and remove for slaughter high-risk animals from within the herd and recover from the effects of Johne's disease. A counsellor is provided to assist the producer to consider management and trading options and develop a business plan. Limited funds may be made available for the development of the business plan.

The main driver for the adoption of the Johne's disease policy in Australia appears to have been concern about the purported link with Crohn's disease. This is also known about in the UK, but the greater displacement of the cattle industry in the Australian economy would also appear to be a major consideration. As one respondent put it, 'Most of the benefits we get from Johne's control relate to the ability to market cattle anywhere both overseas and in Australia'.[50] A Johne's disease specialist at AHA noted that it was 'management of human perception risk rather than science based risk. Many of our markets are public health sensitive, risk averse markets, useful to demonstrate that we have a management and control programme in place. That's certainly the driver.' Overcoming production

49 Animal Health Australia, interview.
50 Agriculture, Food and Wine, South Australia, interview, 20 February 2009.

problems would of itself not stimulate intervention, 'Programmes are either emergency response or zoonosis type conditions, unlikely to have a national programme if just a production disease'.[51]

Given the varying priorities and perspectives of different jurisdictions, AHA provides a forum in which common ground can be sought at the federal level. AHA emerged out of the bTB and brucellosis eradication campaign and was established by government and the livestock industries in 1996. It brings together a whole range of stakeholders, the Australian federal government and state and territory governments, as well as meat processors, stockyards and animal welfare organisations. From the perspective of government:

> Strength is industry buy in, consultation, active involvement, other companies do not have control on how funds spent, creating problems for us in government, industry leaders often disparate and have disparate views, but are within fold. There is joint ownership, responsible to members for success. Driver of all this is beneficiary pays principle. AHA enables endemic diseases which do not have trade implications to be discussed around table.[52]

For example, Western Australia does not have Johne's disease and can question why levies should be used to help farmers in the east, while South Australia favours regulatory control.

AHA sees itself as an 'honest broker in terms of negotiations'. Should the debate get 'politically intense, AHA seen as neutral ground, can identify areas of commonality in divergent views, use that as a basis to build. It can be a fragile arrangement, but if you can find a little area of commonality, you can build on that, a place to put a stop to the bitterness that can go with the political debate.' The underlying philosophy is 'everyone taking responsibility for mitigating risk, not just cost sharing, but responsibility sharing'.[53]

Similar processes were evident at State level. In New South Wales there was an extensive consultation process with industry through a Johne's disease summit that included abattoirs, milk processors, veterinarians and saleyard managers. A Summit Executive Committee included stock and station agents who were seen as having a critical function in getting the message across, an independent chair and a Department of Primary Industries (DPI) representative. The fact that the DPI has an extension branch, something that is absent in the UK, facilitated an extension campaign that directly targeted every farmer.[54]

What was evident throughout the interviews at federal level and in four different States was the emphasis and real commitment to active stakeholder

51   Animal Health Australia, interview.
52   Department of Agriculture, Food and Fisheries, interview, 25 February 2009
53   Animal Health Australia, interview.
54   DPI, New South Wales, interview, 6 March 2009.

involvement in decision making and policy implementation. In principle, the right structures properly operated should permit this to be achieved in the UK, although there may be some cultural differences, such as greater frankness without giving offence being easier for Australians. It was noted in an interview, 'In the agricultural sector got a long history of involvement by industry bodies. Co-operatives involved in marketing. [There is a] history of working together, part of national ethos, mateship.'[55] The federal government also has a structural incentive to find ways of working effectively with the states and the industry as it lacks direct controls other than in the area of international trade.

In England and Wales a Johne's disease initiative has been undertaken by Dairy Crest Direct Limited (DCD), which represents 1,350 farmers who are direct suppliers to the processing firm Dairy Crest. The incidence of the disease appears to have increased in part because of increased cattle movements due to FMD, bTB and herd expansion. The original motivation came from the fact that 'Johne's disease had almost gone off the agenda'. In particular, 'Vets were not pushing Johne's', possibly because it is a disease which brings few financial returns. As in Australia, the possibility of a link with Crohn's disease was a concern, 'Started to have relationships with retailers, don't want a *Daily Mail* exposé'.[56] There was some initial nervousness that doing anything would arouse consumer interest in Johne's disease.

It was evident that there was a considerable range in the knowledge base of farmers about the disease. In an effort to raise awareness, DCD developed a strategy with partners National Milk Records (NMR), Cattle Information Service (CIS) and DairyCo. Cows infected with Johne's disease produce antibodies to fight off the disease and it is therefore possible to test for it using milk samples. Funding was provided for an initial 30-cow screening test free of charge, which would normally cost £75, and 679 farms enrolled – about 65 per cent of the membership. The results were that 75 per cent of the tests showed at least one infected animal on each farm compared with a supposed national average of around 35 per cent. This suggests that the disease is more widespread than had been assumed.

There has been a long-term reluctance to develop programmes to deal with Johne's disease, which is seen as more difficult to tackle than other cattle diseases given the long incubation period and the absence of any cure. 'With BVD, IBR, you can reach for a bottle and vaccinate.'[57] Nevertheless, the existence of concerns about a possible link between Johne's disease and Crohn's disease has stimulated government action in Australia and an industry initiative in England and Wales. This shows once again how a zoonosis status can be a powerful driver for action on a cattle disease.

55   DAFF, interview.
56   DCD, interview, 11 October 2010.
57   DCD, interview.

Bovine tuberculosis

The original driver for government involvement in the eradication of bTB was a public health concern, although high levels of infection of cattle were also a factor with as many as 30 per cent of cattle in Britain dying from the disease in the early twentieth century. In the 1930s, some 2,000 human deaths a year were attributed to bTB derived from cows' milk. This particular route of infection was overcome by pasteurisation (except where raw milk was consumed), although transmission could occur through an aerosol effect to someone in contact with infected animals. bTB is therefore no longer a major zoonosis, but this has not diminished political interest in the subject.

The Gowland Hopkins Report in 1934 found that 'at least 40 per cent of cows in dairy herds were infected with tuberculosis to some extent'.[58] The way in which government sought to reduce this level of incidence was through an attested herds scheme, which paid a bonus on milk sold by owners of herds free of bTB. When the scheme was reviewed at the end of the Second World War there was some disagreement within government in both England and Scotland about whether its principal objective was protecting public health, improving the quality and saleability of milk or increasing milk production.

In any event, more and more herds entered the scheme as there was a clear financial incentive to do so. The Treasury was always concerned about the cost implications of the scheme, but by 1963 these concerns were shared within MAFF. The Milk and Milk Products Division wrote a paper pointing out that since all herds were now attested, the only feature that distinguished tuberculin tested (which was 97 per cent of the total) from other milk was that it had been tested by ministry officials. This was placing an increasing strain on resources and to some extent duplicated testing by buyers. Too much time was spent on tuberculin licensing procedures and the Ministry of Health had agreed that they could be dropped.[59]

By 1960 it was accepted that bTb had been brought under control in the British cattle herd. Complete eradication may not be achievable but 'between 1960 when the whole country became an attested area and the end of 1964, the incidence of reactors had fallen from 19 in 10,000 to 6 in 10,000'.[60] Subsequently, the Attested Herds Scheme was brought to an end in October 1964 and testing was relaxed, and the constraint on the movement of cattle from infected herds to uninfected herds was removed. The chief veterinarian said at the time that if there was a relaxation in accreditation and testing, bTB would increase again, which it did. bTB was discovered in a badger for the first time in 1971 and badger culling began in 1975. It is arguable that initial and subsequent policy responses

58   Ministry of Agriculture, Fisheries and Food, op. cit., n. 39, p. 221.
59   National Archives, MAF 251/297, 'Arrangements for the control of the hygienic quality of milk in England and Wales', 2 July 1963.
60   Ministry of Agriculture, Fisheries and Food, op. cit., n. 39, p. 227.

relied too heavily on a perception of the badger as the problem and hence the focus of any solution. It is only since the mid-2000s that faced 'with scientific evidence which confirms the importance of cattle-to-cattle transmission, the NFU, the British Veterinary Association (BVA) and other farming organisations have been forced to accept the necessity of cattle based control measures'.[61]

In 1979, the incoming Minister of Agriculture, Peter Walker, established a review of policy chaired by Lord Zuckerman which endorsed existing policy.[62] There was always provision for a follow-up review to Zuckerman, generally referred to by civil servants as 'son of Zuckerman', and this appeared as the Dunnet Report in 1986.[63] This recommended a scaling down of badger culling, the so-called 'interim strategy'. This remained in place for ten years, despite criticism from both farmers and conservationists, in part because attention switched to the problem of BSE, which constrained the resources available for dealing with bTB. In practice, badger control was

> influenced by practical and political expediency, field experience, research, public relations considerations, the perplexities and imponderable nature of TB badger/cattle relationships and much discussion among interested parties, especially the views of veterinarians whose primary concern, rightly, is the health and welfare of cattle.[64]

In 1996, the government commissioned a new independent review of policy chaired by Professor Sir John Krebs. This report recommended a programme of experimentation to determine whether badgers were responsible for the spread of bTB in cattle and whether culling strategies would reduce its incidence. The Independent Scientific Group on Cattle TB was set up by the government in 1998 to conduct the Randomised Badger Culling Trial (RBCT) in order to establish the effects of badger culling on the incidence in herds of bTB. This led to complex results and contradictory reports in the media, and the Defra secretary, Hilary Benn, decided not to proceed with a cull. Whilst a cull might work, 'it might also not work' and would be too risky. One factor he took into account was that public opposition would render a cull more difficult.[65]

A continuing problem in the development of bTB policy has been the existence of gaps in the scientific evidence and disputes about the interpretation of that evidence. This gives ammunition to those on both sides of the debate and makes

---

61 Wilkinson, op. cit., n. 11, p. 13.
62 Zuckerman, Lord, *Badgers, Cattle and Tuberculosis*, London: HMSO, 1980.
63 Dunnet, G., *Badgers and Bovine Tuberculosis*, London: HMSO, 1986.
64 National Archives, MAF 459/19, 'Wildlife and Storage Biology Discipline: Badger Management Group. Report of the Wildlife and Storage Biology Discipline Management Group to the Tuberculosis in Badgers and Cattle Coordinating Group. An Alternative Course of Action for Controlling Badgers', 1986, p. 12.
65 Stocks, C., 'Too risky: Hilary Benn decides against a badger cull', *Farmers Weekly*, 11 July 2008, p. 6.

it difficult to follow recommended processes of evidence-based policy-making. 'Critical gaps in the knowledge about cattle TB and the way it spreads remain.'[66] There is substantial evidence that badgers contribute significantly to the disease in cattle, but 'The evidence is ... mainly of a circumstantial nature, proving that infected badgers *can* cause infection of cattle, that infected badgers *can* shed significant amounts of infectious material, that cattle *may* interact with badgers in real situations'.[67] However, 'what is still not known is the precise method of transmission from badger to cattle, i.e. it is still not known whether direct contact is necessary for the transmission of the disease'.[68] In addition, 'The role and extent that cattle-to-cattle transmission plays in the maintenance and spread of TB is unknown'. Moreover, 'Current tests for bovine TB in cattle are not completely reliable. Tests for TB in badgers and other wildlife are less reliable.'[69]

Could badgers be catching TB from the cattle? This issue is certainly raised in the scientific literature. There is discussion about whether badgers are acting as 'spill over' hosts (i.e. that badgers become infected from cattle but do not disseminate it) or 'reservoir' hosts (i.e. badgers become infected and maintain the infection and can pass it back to cattle at some point in the future). What is still unclear is whether badgers are 'maintenance' hosts, i.e. whether TB can remain in the badger population indefinitely without continual exposure to infection from cattle.

It is the perturbation effect that makes culling badgers not cost-effective on anything but the largest scale. Essentially, it means that we kill all badgers or none. Put at its simplest, perturbation means that disrupted social groups disperse and relocate. Moreover, 'perturbation increases incidence of bTB in badgers' and 'can cause the spatial distribution of bTB in badgers to change from one in which it is contained within spatially discrete patterns of high prevalence to one where it is more widely, or thinly spread'.[70] Thus, 'to have any prospect of contributing significantly to controlling bTB in cattle, a badger cull would have to be undertaken over a very large area'.[71] Given the level of emotional attachment to the badger, such a large-scale cull would be highly politically unpopular. The lack of any consensus among scientific experts is shown by two

---

66   House of Commons Environment, Food and Rural Affairs Committee, *Badgers and Cattle TB: The Final Report of the Independent Scientific Group on Cattle TB*, Fourth Report of Session 2007–08, HC 130-1, London: The Stationery Office, 2008, p. 4.

67   House of Commons Research Paper 98/63, *Bovine Tuberculosis*, London: House of Commons, 1998, p. 14.

68   House of Commons, op. cit., n. 66, p. 10.

69   Welsh Assembly, *Final Report of the Rural Development Sub-Committee Inquiry into Bovine Tuberculosis*, Cardiff: Welsh Assembly, 2008, p. 2.

70   Macdonald, D.W., Riordan, P. and Matthews, F., 'Biological hurdles to the control of TB in cattle: a test of two hypotheses concerning wildlife to explain the failure of control' (2006) 131 *Biological Conservation* 268–286, 286.

71   Ibid., p. 268.

contrasting reports, both commissioned by Defra, although the second after a change of secretary of state.[72] The final report of the Independent Scientific Group (ISG)[73] stated, 'we conclude that badger culling cannot meaningfully contribute to the future control of cattle TB in Britain'. The government then commissioned a review of the ISG's report by the then Government Chief Scientific Adviser Sir David King, assisted by a group of five experts. The King Group concluded that, 'In our view a programme for the removal of badgers could make a significant contribution to the control of cattle TB in those areas of England where there is a high and persistent incidence of TB in cattle, provided removal takes place alongside an effective programme of cattle controls'.[74] Apart from this contradictory advice, a further complication for policy makers is that there is evidence of a perturbation effect when badgers are culled.

Discursive constructions of the badger have been important in the debate and have little connection with the available scientific evidence. The badger is an omnivorous mammal which is the largest surviving land carnivore in the British Isles, following the elimination of the wolf and the bear. It has lived in the islands for at least a quarter of a million years. Around a quarter of the population is estimated to be concentrated in the south-west of England and only 10 per cent in Scotland. It is a largely nocturnal animal with poor eyesight. It is estimated that there are some 300,000 badgers in Britain and it is not an endangered species, although it receives strong legal protection. Cultural constructions of the badger in literature and elsewhere treat it as a cherished species endowed with elements of magic and mystery.

Perhaps it was the very mysteriousness of the badger, and the lack of real (as distinct from self-proclaimed) experts on the badger that led to the development of the myth of 'the old rogue badger' which had a significant and continuing influence on public policy. The concept of the rogue badger is still present in frames of reference as it was referred to in a discussion between the author and the Defra bTB team in May 2009. The myth of the rogue badger permitted the construction of an image of a bad, deviant or anti-social badger, a 'senile and virtually toothless'[75] creature, whose actions could be presented as a basis for intervention against a cherished animal. This was only possible by asserting that there were very few rogue badgers. The categorisation could not be extended to the much larger number of badgers afflicted with TB.

Prior to the discovery of bTB in a badger carcase in 1971, MAFF had generally taken a benevolent view of the badger: 'On the whole, the badger is generally

---

72 Spencer, A., 'One body of evidence, three different policies: bovine tuberculosis policy in Britain' (2011) 31(2) *Politics* 91–99.
73 Independent Scientific Group on Cattle TB, *Bovine TB: The Scientific Evidence*, Final Report of the Independent Scientific Group on Cattle TB, Defra: London, June 2007, p. 14.
74 King, Sir D., *Tuberculosis in Cattle and Badgers: A Report by the Chief Scientific Adviser*, London: London, 2007, para. 5.
75 National Archives, MAF 285/39, Badgers: consultation with Ministry of Agriculture, Fisheries and Food on control and protection, 'Badgers in Forestry Commission areas', 1965.

regarded as a friend of the farmer since it has some beneficial effect in its destruction of many harmful insects and other pests.' However, no quarter was to be shown to an old rogue badger that was believed to have been responsible for the depredations that such deviant badgers were believed to undertake: 'we recommend that it should be shot by an expert marksman when emerging from its sett at dusk'.[76] Such a drastic measure was necessary because it was believed that it could not be easily trapped. 'The so-called "rogue" badger is less afraid of such things [traps] than other members of his species and, if his accusers are to be believed, will push through the small pop-hole entrance to a hen-house.'[77] This was somewhat at odds with the characterisation quoted earlier of the rogue badger as a senile animal, but it was the orthodoxy rather than its internal consistency that seemed to be important. Anyone deviating from the departmental line was likely to draw a sharp rebuke from Animal Health Division. Commenting on a draft ministerial reply, a civil servant in the division stated, 'because of the activities of "rogue" badgers, we could not say that badgers are not harmful'.[78]

One of the difficulties was that these issues were being dealt with by generalist civil servants and even when they sought the advice of specialists, such as the Infestation Control Laboratory at Worplesdon, they were advised that 'Very few scientific investigations have been made of the life and habits of the badger and all but one or two of these have been uncritical and superficial. The literature abounds with conflicting theories'.[79] Nevertheless, within the Nature Conservancy, which was then the official advisory body on flora and fauna, officials shared among themselves their doubts that the 'rogue badger' really existed: 'Between ourselves, I find the reference to "rogue" badgers puzzling. Do we *know* that such a creature exists or is it merely that badgers (along with other species) are likely to become opportunists when the occasion arises?' (original emphasis).[80] However, the Nature Conservancy Council was more of an external advocate than an internal adviser in the policy process and did not see fit to challenge the established orthodoxy. Indeed, the Council was characterised as 'unhelpful' in one policy review document.[81]

76 National Archives, MAF 131/170a, 'Badgers: proposals for control', letter from E.A. Ricot to H.J. Montgomery, 5 November 1965.
77 National Archives, HO 285/40a, 'Badgers: proposed private member's bill presented by Donald Chapman MP. Note on letter from Mrs R Murray to Chairman of League Against Cruel Sports', 1966.
78 National Archives, HO 285/40b, 'Badgers: proposed private member's bill presented by Donald Chapman MP'. Letter from V.H. Bath to P.E. Baker, Home Office, 5 December 1966.
79 National Archives, MAF 131/170b, 'Badgers: proposals for control', letter to G.R. Hill, 27 July 1960.
80 National Archives, FT 1/59 (1965), Badgers: Mammalian Predator Working Party minutes, letter from Michael Blackmore to G. Christian, 5 February 1965.
81 National Archives, MAF 459/37, 'Badger control policy: Consideration of the recommendations of the Dunnet Report on Badgers and Bovine Tuberculosis', K. Wilkes, 9 October 1985 revision.

Resolution of the issues through a policy community or network was difficult because of uncertainty about who was a legitimate and credible participant in the process. Relations with stakeholder groups in the area were very difficult in spite of the prevalent British policy style of seeking to consult and work with a range of interests. In some quarters of MAFF, particularly among those with scientific backgrounds, there was deep suspicion of conservationist groups because of their lack of scientific understanding and their perceived lack of openness to argument: 'I would suggest that very few local naturalists and conservationists will have much to contribute on badger social groups.'[82] There was a concern that badger organisations might be 'wholly comprised of "cranks"'.[83]

Creating spaces where the views of opposing stakeholders can be exposed to expert evidence, mediated and hopefully reconciled is one technique available to government for dealing with an intractable policy problem. The Badger Panel was set up in 1976 'for the express purpose of providing a forum for the views and advice of leading experts and interested organisations on the problems posed by bovine tuberculosis in badgers. The membership ... includes a wide range of scientific, veterinary and conservation interests and individuals.'[84] As an advisory body, it is evident that their effect on policy was limited, in part because 'Given the wide spectrum of opinion represented on the Badger Panel it has frequently not been easy to achieve a unified view'.[85]

The Badger Panel ceased to meet after the establishment of the Krebs review in 1996 and was disbanded in 2003. The ostensible reason given was that it was no longer necessary as an expert group would supervise culling.[86] However, it also reflected an attempt by Defra to construct a more evidence-based approach to policy on bTB. The strategy of creating encompassing groups which attempted to reconcile differences between highly divergent positions was seen not to have worked and reliance was placed on much smaller, more exclusive groups. In 2006, Defra created a small Bovine TB Advisory Group which was set up to 'consist of those with experience of working with the disease rather than a representative selection of interested organisations. The group is not intended to provide another forum for the usual debates over badger culling to be rehearsed

---

82 National Archives, MAF 459/14, 'Bovine tuberculosis: methods of badger control: discussion on need to research other methods following suspension of gassing, June 1982'. Views of interested organisations on methods of badger control, 1985.

83 National Archives, MAF 459/26, 'Consultative Panel on Badgers and Tuberculosis: Agenda, briefs and minutes', R.J. Jeffery, Consultative Panel on Badgers and Tuberculosis. Further Briefing for 28th meeting, 29 February 1984.

84 National Archives, MAF 458/26, 'Quangos review 1979: Consultative Panel on badgers and tuberculosis. Reappointment of Consultative Panel on Badgers and Tuberculosis, submission to the Management Board', 1984.

85 National Archives, MAF 459/37, 'Badger control policy: consideration of the recommendations of the Dunnet Report on Badgers and Bovine Tuberculosis. Submission to the minister. Badger Panel's views on the Dunnet recommendations', 1986.

86 Defra, *Animal Health and Welfare: The Government's Response to the Krebs Report*, London: Defra: London, 1998.

by farming and wildlife organisations.'[87] The in-built preference for veterinary expertise in this new arrangement was not necessarily a way of generating a workable solution, as large animal veterinarians tended to be sympathetic to their farmer clients and were inclined to see the problem in terms of the badger rather than cattle-to-cattle transmission. 'The use of veterinary advice is likely to cause further controversy ... as their approach to disease control is frequently at odds with other forms of scientific expertise.'[88] In November 2008, Defra created a small Bovine TB Eradication Advisory Group for England which, apart from Defra officials, was composed just of farmers and veterinarians and was charged with developing a strategy to reduce the incidence of bTB.

It appeared for a while that the first cull of badgers might be undertaken in Wales after the Welsh Assembly Government approved a culling programme, but the way in which it was drawn up was challenged in court and found to be legally flawed. Before a revised programme could be implemented, the political composition of the Welsh Assembly Government changed and the programme was withdrawn.

Attention switched to England following the formation of the Coalition Government in 2010. With their substantial bases in rural areas, both the Conservatives and Liberal Democrats were sympathetic to the arguments in favour of a cull put forward by the NFU, which emphasised that any policy to tackle the problem had always included any wildlife reservoir. Moreover, the Conservatives held all the ministerial posts in Defra until the ministerial changes in 2012. Although a Liberal Democrat minister was then included, he was not an opponent of culling, while the new Secretary of State, Owen Patterson, had a track record as an enthusiastic advocate. Apart from bringing bTB under control, a further consideration at a time of fiscal consolidation was that the cost of compensation and disease management was estimated at £1 billion over the next decade.

Following a consultation, two areas in parts of the country severely affected by bTB, Gloucestershire and West Somerset, were selected for pilot culls in January 2012. The culling would be carried out by cage trapping followed by controlled shooting undertaken by marksmen who had completed a special training course. It was thought that perturbation could be avoided by choosing culling areas with hard boundaries such as motorways, rivers and coastlines. Vaccination would be used around the edges of the cull areas to mitigate against any negative perturbation effects and £250,000 was made available to encourage vaccination. The culls would be monitored and evaluated by an independent panel of experts to assess the welfare implications and effectiveness of farmers killing badgers before ministers took a decision about whether to roll the cull out more widely after 2013. If that went ahead 50,000 to 90,000 badgers could be killed over four years in 40 designated zones. A legal challenge by the Badger Trust was rejected

87   Wilkinson, op. cit., n. 11, p. 11.
88   Wilkinson, op. cit., n. 11, p. 11.

in July 2012, and a second legal challenge was rejected in September. It was then discovered that the badger population was much larger than had been thought and culling on the scale required would not be possible in 2012. In February 2013 it was announced that it was intended to proceed with the culls in the summer of 2013 with a reserve pilot area in North Dorset. However, substantial resistance to the cull led to doubts about whether it could be carried out effectively.

Needless to say, the decisions only intensified controversy about the justification of such measures, their likely effectiveness and the efficacy of alternative measures such as badger vaccination. The level of police protection necessary and its cost became an issue. Adrian Tudway, the police officer in charge of domestic political extremism 'warned a cull could spark clashes between farmers and animal rights protesters which stretched police forces would struggle to control ... police forces could be overwhelmed by protesters'.[89] The combination of incomplete and contested evidence; alternative framings of the policy problem, including emotions surrounding the badger, that were polarised and difficult to reconcile; and the inapplicability of normal techniques of stakeholder management through co-option and mediation created a situation in which it was difficult both to formulate an agreed policy and to implement it in a way that dealt effectively with the underlying problem. Even the containment of bTB poses challenges and the policy dilemmas are likely to continue to challenge government for some time into the future.

Conclusions

Of the three analytical frameworks advanced, the policy communities and networks framework assisted the understanding of the relative difficulty of the formulation and implementation of policy. The development of BVD policy in Scotland made use of the resources of the existing policy community, while AHA provided a focus for a functioning policy network on Johne's disease in Australia. The Johne's disease policy network in Britain was weak, reflecting the absence of government policy, while the conflicts surrounding bTB made it difficult for policy networks to function effectively. Defra resorted to a 'core insider' strategy which emphasised the role of farmers and veterinarians. The RSPCA was effectively shut out of this network, particularly after the formation of the Coalition Government, while the Badger Trust resorted to challenging policy through the courts.

Evidence-based policy making favours a resort to expertise as dealing with policy problems, but leaves open the question of which expertise is seen as relevant. Veterinarians understandably have had a central role in the policy-making process, but there have been some concerns about how far those in government service are influenced by their wider professional responsibilities. In the case of bTB there was contestation between different experts, which made it more

---

89 Case, P., 'Police warn badger cull could spark clashes', *Farmers Weekly*, 24 November 2011, 7.

difficult to arrive at a settled policy. Expertise became politicised and hence lost its neutral, adjudicating function.

The framing of policy was especially important in the case of bTB, although it also helped to explain differences of perception of the importance of Johne's disease between Britain and Australia, while the emergence of BVD policy required the construction of a justifying narrative. Emotional symbolism surrounding the badger became significant in the policy debate, while constructions of the 'rogue badger' affected how the policy problem was perceived.

The difficulties associated with such policies, the public expenditure and reputation costs associated with them and the move away from a production-based view of agriculture mean that governments are motivated to shift the cost of, and responsibility for, policy elsewhere. In the long run, the role of the government in England in relation to endemic cattle diseases is likely to be confined to a facilitating or enabling one, placing a responsibility on the industry to make its own collective arrangements.

6 Regulating animal health and welfare

Law and economics in an era of fiscal uncertainty

Introduction

Responsibility and cost sharing offers a useful economic instrument on which to build a partnership relationship between private and public sectors[1]. The aim is to deliver effective value for money where it is intended to transfer costs from the public sector to the private sector. Animal keepers and various stakeholders are being asked to share cost and responsibility for animal health and welfare. The Final Report of the England Advisory Group on Responsibility and Cost Sharing in December 2010 (Advisory Group Final Report)[2] recommended adopting cost sharing for animal health and welfare. After considerable discussion, the Coalition Government created a new regulatory body, the AHWB, within Defra. The Government Chief Veterinary Officer was appointed as an adviser and is employed by the AHWB. The first meetings were held in November and December 2011. Decision making is intended to be based on the best evidence and a proportionate response to risk, balanced by costs and benefits. There is, however, an expectation, on the part of the government, that there should be accompanying funding for the AHWB to support 50 per cent of the costs of tackling exotic disease outbreaks. The government's agenda by creating a regulatory body is to take forward cost-sharing policies for animal health and welfare, within a scientific context of advice. The 2001 FMD outbreak cost the UK Government in terms of compensation and related public spending £6 billion to £9 billion.[3] In 2010/11, the government spent £91 million in compensation for farmers with bTB.[4] This is a sizeable proportion of Defra's budget and is unsustainable given the current cuts in public spending. This chapter offers a legal and economic analysis of how the cost-sharing principle may amount to a distinctive form of

---

1 This chapter relies on the collaboration with Jonathan Cave, a member of the Gold Team.
2 England Advisory Group on Responsibility and Cost Sharing, *Responsibility and Cost Sharing for Animal Health and Welfare: Final Report*, London: Defra, December 2010.
3 Ibid.
4 Department for Environment, Food and Rural Affairs, *Bovine TB Eradication Programme for England*, London: Defra, July 2011.

economic regulation that may have lessons for other sectors of the economy. It concludes that the claims made in support of cost sharing assume that risks are being adequately quantified and that stakeholders will agree. These assumptions are problematic as understanding market forces requires a deeper understanding of the legal responsibilities and economic costs of regulation than may be initially assumed. The complexity of any cost assumptions should not be underestimated. This raises serious questions about how future regulation should proceed in a period of fiscal uncertainty.

Responsibility and cost sharing in the context of animal health and welfare

Responsibility and cost sharing offers a useful economic instrument on which to build a partnership among private and public sectors. The aim is to deliver effective value for money and transfer costs from the public sector to the private sector. There are claimed for benefits which may or may not be legitimate. These include lowered regulatory and cost burdens, regulation based on better understanding (closer to the action), avoidance of perverse subsidies and the opportunity to minimise capture and opportunism given to stakeholders. Responsibility and cost sharing is expected to solve a number of regulatory problems, such as institutional capture, creep, institutionalisation, inefficiency, ineffectiveness and loss of transparency. This gives raise to issues about how to develop transparency strategies as against systems of accountability.

There are also some criticisms that need to be weighed against the desirability of responsibility and cost-sharing. These are that in many cases the private-sector parties are effectively delivering what should be public governance services; this is particularly true when they bear the burden because they are best-placed to ameliorate the harms, rather than because they benefit from breaking the rules. It is clear that this is neither a cost-free nor a risk-free transfer; it may wind up costing more in aggregate, even when the presumably enhanced benefits are taken into account. Also, to the extent that the transferred costs are affected by shocks and/or changes in government action, the transfer of risk imposes additional costs on the private parties (maybe no bad thing) and may induce them to adopt hedging strategies (possibly a very bad thing). Lastly, the transfer of costs raises the issue of subsidies; if the government is policing the industry, it is in effect subsidising the private parties who benefit from the regulation; but this in turn creates incentives for the industry to invest in capture. The current attempt by the financial services industry to delay regulation is a good case in point.

Responsibility and cost sharing provides the potential for co-operation between the private and public sectors in their different roles and functions[5] fostering a

---

5 See Gunn, G.J., Saatkamp, H.W., Humphry, R.W. and Stott, A.W., 'Assessing economic and social pressure for the control of bovine viral diarrhoea virus' (2005) 72 *Preventive Veterinary Medicine* 149–162. Grant, W., 'Policy Failure: the Case of the Old Rogue Badger', presentation

sustainable approach to regulating risk. As a regulatory device, responsibility and cost sharing is likely to gain increasing favour with the Coalition Government precisely because cost sharing may reduce regulatory burdens on the public purse. Certainly, sharing costs has the potential to incite the exchange of good practice between both sectors. In this chapter we develop this theme based on analysis of the regulation of animal health and welfare, which has been the subject of an intensive research project over five years funded by RELU and supported by Defra. The first part of the chapter considers how the regulatory debate in the current economic climate might be informed by the introduction of responsibility and cost sharing. The key point here is the prisoner's dilemma that is emphasised by the tension between reducing government budgets (which is the same as maximising the shifting of costs to the other side) versus pursuing budget reductions as part of an overall growth strategy (thus reducing the aggregate cost of running the economy or maximising the surplus, or even the difference between expenditures and tax revenues). Also, note the pressure for deregulation/regulatory withdrawal. If each side simply attempts to minimise its costs (or even to maximise the excess of benefits over costs as it experiences them), the result will generally *not* be minimisation of overall cost or maximisation of overall welfare, or even an efficient allocation of responsibility. That is true under conditions of certainty; it is true in spades for uncertain conditions when the two parties are asymmetrically informed, because the cost-shifting tussle interferes with the communication of information.

The chapter moves on to consider how responsibility and cost sharing might work in the context of animal health and welfare. Specifically, in animal health and welfare there is considerable potential to adopt the insurance principle to provide a cost effective way to ensure accurate, consistent and widely accepted risk assessment and the attribution of responsibilities where required. We might sensibly differentiate idiosyncratic risk (the kind that can be diversified away by co-insurance or reassigned to follow the power to monitor or reduce risk) from systemic risk (undiversifiable and difficult to transfer) – the reason is that regulatory arrangements can have the (unintended) consequence of converting idiosyncratic to systemic risk; that is why it is necessary to differentiate prudential from macro-prudential regulation.

Lastly, the chapter considers the future direction of regulatory reform including the role of cost sharing and responsibility in terms of the Advisory Group

to the Department of Politics and International Studies, Warwick University, 2008. House of Commons Environment, Food and Rural Affairs Committee, *Badgers and cattle TB: the final report of the Independent Scientific Group on Cattle TB*, Fourth Report of Session 2007–08, HC 130–1, London: The Stationery Office, 2008. Jordan, L., *The Eradication of Bovine Tuberculosis*, London: HMSO, 1933. Stott, A.W., Jones, G.M., Humphry, R.W. and Gunn, G.J., 'Financial incentive to control paratuberculosis (Johne's disease) on dairy farms in the United Kingdom' (2005) 156 *Veterinary Record* 825–831. Woods, A., *A Manufactured Plague: The History of Foot and Mouth Disease in Britain*, London: Earthscan, 2004.

Final Report, published in December 2010[6] and the National Audit Office Report, *Delivering Regulatory Reform* (February 2011),[7] which considers the future of regulatory reform in the context of the financial cuts.

Responsibility and cost sharing has the advantage of developing risk analysis and potentially making risk more transparent and encouraging stakeholder accountability. However, there are doubts as to how effective any partnership among the various stakeholders might prove in terms of reducing overall costs, let alone maximising the excess of total benefit over total cost. Risk assessment must be appropriately calibrated within any regulatory system to be effective, and sharing costs and responsibility must be affordable and competitive. In the case of animal health, this applies to the farming industry as a whole. In the case of health and safety, it leaves unclear how enforcement will work.

Regulating in the context of regulating animal health and welfare in a period of fiscal responsibility

The starting point is fiscal 'responsibility' – or fiscal pressure that has two interesting applications: one is (of course) as a motivation for increasing the cost-effectiveness of regulation by decreasing the cost, regardless of anything else. This point is the key issue which is a recurrent theme in assessing any analysis of costs. The other is the adoption of fiscal responsibility as a central 'principle' in principles-based regulation. There are several 'varieties' of regulation and several 'architectural' principles. The former include:

- rule-based regulation;
- principles-based regulation;
- risk-based regulation.

The latter include:

- citizen-centric regulation;
- 'smart' (incentive-aware) regulation;
- better regulation, such as light touch.

Cost sharing should be placed in the context of the role of the state in the regulation of business and society.[8] Many principles found in cost sharing have a

---

6 Advisory Group Final Report, op. cit., n. 1.
7 National Audit Office and Comptroller and Auditor General, *Department for Business, Innovation and Skills: Delivering Regulatory Reform*, HC 758, Session 2010–2011, 17 February 2011, London: NAO, 2011, pp. 4–5.
8 Ayres, I. and Braithwaite, J., *Responsive Regulation: Transcending the Deregulation Debate*, Oxford: Oxford University Press, 1992. Baldwin, R. and Cave, M., *Understanding Regulation*, Oxford: Oxford University Press, 1999. Black, J., 'The Emergence of Risk-based Regulation and the New Public Risk Management in the UK' [2005] PL 512. Grant, W., *Pressure Groups and*

common history within the development of regulation. Inspections and inspectorates formed a coherent basis approach to regulation in use in the nineteenth century. There was a government obligation to provide assurance that the system was 'regulated' in the nineteenth-century sense – this is entirely consistent with regulation by markets, self-regulation, co-regulation, etc. provided the government meets a duty to establish a basis for intervention (e.g. market failure) and to conduct a rigorous impact assessment/monitoring type of exercise to ensure that the system is 'working' and that interference meets at least a second-best test of efficiency and effectiveness, proportionality and transparency.

That legacy remained with a command and control methodology employed for a wide range of different functions.[9] In the 1970s, the command form of regulation came under criticism coinciding with an examination of the role of government in the economy. Costs, rigidity and strains on the systems of regulation emerged as a consequence of the privatisation of the major utilities and concerns about over-reliance on juridical rules that might serve to inhibit the growth of the market economy.[10] The 1980s and 1990s saw an examination of the need for regulation and the precise form such regulation[11] should take. Regulatory reform encompassed a good governance agenda for developing countries.[12] In such cases of regulation the strong underlying political risk formed part of the challenge for developing countries, but also for developed countries, as regulators are given a measure of responsibility that also carries forward political policy matters that may be unpopular or have less of a political mandate.

By the 1990s the future of regulation became caught up in the regulatory reform agenda linked to the ideology of the government of the day.[13] A general desire to shrink the size of government and reduce burdens as well as contribute to controls on costs led to a recalibration of the need for regulatory agencies. These proliferated with ever more detailed codes, regulatory instruments and

---

British Politics, Basingstoke: Palgrave Macmillan, 2000. Moran, M., *The British Regulatory State*, Oxford: Oxford University Press, 2004. Nielsen, V.L., 'Are regulators responsive?' (2006) 28 *Law and Policy* 295. Parker, C., *The Open Corporation: Effective Self-Regulation and Democracy*, Cambridge: Cambridge University Press, 2002. Scott, C., 'Accountability in the regulatory state' (2000) 27(1) *Journal of Law and Society* 38–60.

9   In environmental law, for example, the work of Rachel Carson (*Silent Spring*, New York, NY: Fawcett Crest, 1962) was influential. In the USA, see Udall, S.L., *The Quiet Crisis*, New York, NY: Holt, Rinehart & Winston, 1963.

10 See DTI, *Lifting the Burden*, Cmnd 9571, White Paper, London: HMSO, 1985. DTI, *Building Businesses Not Barriers*, Cmnd 9794, London: HMSO, 1986. DTI, *Releasing Enterprise*, Cm 512, London: HMSO, 1988.

11 In the financial sector, see Gower, L.C.B., *Review of Investor Protection: Report Part 1 (Cmnd. 9125)*, London: The Stationery Office, 1984. DTI, *Financial Services in the United Kingdom: A New Framework for Investor Protection (Cmnd. 9432)*, London: The Stationery Office, 1985.

12 Richardson, B.J. and Wood, S., *Environmental Law for Sustainability*, Oxford: Hart Publishing, 2006.

13 Black, J., 'Tensions in the regulatory state' (2007) *Public Law* 58, and also Ogus, A., 'Regulation revisited' (2009) *Public Law* 332.

complexity in the role of the state through the proxy of 'better regulation'. The privatisation strategy merely postponed many hard decisions. The key message was that privatisation would bring a better mix of *ex post* and *ex ante* regulation and allow costs and demand to become key riders. However, this did not prove as easy as first thought. Public ownership was relinquished to private-sector bodies regulated through an arm's length relationship with regulatory agencies. Sophisticated economic price caps and performance measurements became an important part of the regulatory tool box. A greater dependence on public audit to regulate regulation and provide the necessary assurance that the sectors and activities in question were efficient, etc. gave rise to targets, performance indicators and value for money examinations.

In the context of regulatory approaches, the impact of privatisation should not be underestimated. The privatisation of sectors of industry such as the public utilities should be distinguished from the privatisation of market governance that was delivered by deregulation and self-regulation, as well as indirectly by 'smart regulation' with its decentralisation of choice of objectives and the activities of regulated stakeholders. It introduced enormous changes in the nature of the state and in the relationship between the citizen as 'consumer' and 'customer' and the public sector as service provider. In so doing, privatisation has changed the system of public management and administration[14] in Britain. In many cases, the purchaser of services is distinct from the consumer (or recipient) of services, for example the healthcare system. Two points are relevant: the first is that in many instances the traditional bundling of roles (suppliers of services receive payment; recipients of services make payments) is replaced with more complex and contingent arrangements; and that, in addition, the relationships may be extended to the point where the supplier and recipient no longer have privity of contract (or direct contact). The most obvious example is healthcare, where providers and patients interact about platforms (the National Health Service itself, insurance companies, hospitals) that prevent them from agreeing directly on who gets which treatment.

However, there is an animal health and welfare example in the form of supermarkets and insurance companies, which provide platforms that constrain the interactions between farmers and food consumers. This matters because in this indirect or networked arrangement it is not appropriate to assume that what people are observed to do represents what they should optimally (or efficiently, etc.) be doing. The reform agenda known as new public management effectively shaped and re-shaped the contours of public life and the private sector. This has had long-term effects on the way public and private services operate and, as a consequence, many of the values of public service have changed. The tradition of stewardship and public duty has been replaced by a market-orientated approach to the delivery of public goods and services. The blurring of the distinction

---

14 Oliver, D. and Drewry, G., *Public Service Reforms*, Oxford: Oxford University Press, 1996, pp. 1–15.

between public and private has brought the admission of the values of economy, efficiency and effectiveness into the public sector. The distinction is two-fold: the recognition that the government's responsibility to ensure that certain public services are delivered in the right way (which is not the same as the obligation to deliver them itself or even directly to commission their delivery), and the recognition of a well-regulated environment as a vital public good. Beyond this, we can note the extreme reductionism of market discipline; all sorts of objectives are valorised using the same metric (money), and market outcomes (prices) are presumed to encapsulate a full, fair and accurate accounting of all stakeholders' information, preferences and potential to contribute to the collective enterprise. We might also observe that the tautology at the heart of formal regulation (these things are in the public interest because a public servant says they are) is thus replaced with the collective tautology of the market (these things are societally optimal because anything better would be more profitable). What is gained is the economy and inherent democracy of a marketplace in which anyone can trade and in which each party can decide for itself how to trade off one objective against another and how much to do on their own (instead of paying others to do it for them). What is lost is the ability to incorporate non-tradeable and unquantifiable interests, to give voice to those without opportunities to trade and to direct society towards specific outcomes that have more than Pareto optimality (which is blind to transfers between people and to intensity of preference) to recommend them. Standards and terms recognisable in the vocabulary of auditors are given new fluency in the language of inputs and outputs. The scale is vast and the application spans education, the police and the courts, health and the environment. The principle is that the purchaser or consumer of services is distinguished from the provider. The latter may be part of the pre-existing public service or form a new competitive element whereby private and voluntary sectors bid to supply goods and services. The provider is then engaged in the award of the contract, including the negotiation of various conditions for the performance of the contract. This changes the nature of government and the relationship between the citizen and the state. The Private Finance Initiative (PFI) formally introduced in 1992 has proved controversial and politically sensitive. Currently, there are over 800 PFI projects worth in excess of £56.9 billion in capital value terms. PFI provides that private companies undertake capital spending on behalf of the public sector.[15] This is important in addition because it creates a long-term relationship that results in institutionalised capture and the creation (as we have seen) of secondary markets. This is particularly difficult when only the cost (and

---

15 Chote, R., Emmerson, C., Miles, D. and Shaw, J. (eds), *The IFS Green Budget: January 2008*, London: Institute for Fiscal Studies and London: Morgan Stanley, 2008, p. 54 estimated that: 'In total, PFI deals signed up to November 2007 that are still current are set to finance a total of £56.9 billion (4.1% of national income in 2007–08) of capital spending. Of this, 43% (£24.4 billion) is cored on the public sector balance sheet, with the remaining 57% (£32.5 billion) not on the public sector balance sheet.'

commercial risk) can be transferred, but the political or public service responsibility (e.g. for a school or hospital) cannot. Another example of indirect contact is public procurement, with the potential separation of customer 1 and customer 2, and the need to account for agency costs that are not wholly visible.

Significantly, Gavin Drewry has pointed out, 'Public administration has been displaced – at least in part – by a "new public management" (NPM) which rejects bureaucratic methods and structures in favour of market-based and business-like regimes of public service'.[16] This may be regarded as a global phenomenon or, as Hughes[17] refers to it, 'a new global paradigm'. It also raises serious questions about the adequacy of accountability systems. There is a tension between transparency, accountability and responsibility.

Smart regulation or responsive regulation[18] was in vogue in the 1990s. The role of regulation was designed to set only general directions rather than having a more intrusive interventionist role. Light touch[19] was seen as characteristic of setting overall directions while leaving day-to-day operational control vested within the organisation itself. Gumingham explains how smart regulation means involving government capabilities in 'harnessing the capacities of markets, civil society and other institutions to accomplish its policy goals more effectively with greater social acceptance and at less cost to the state'.[20] It is arguable that the government is there to help the stakeholders identify and attain their goals, which is why empowering them works. There is a need to preserve innovation incentives.

Gunningham noted, '… the principles of smart regulation suggest the use of a broad range of policy instruments, which might include information or education, voluntarism, self- and co-regulation, market based instruments and direct regulation'.[21] There is a difference between the co-optation view of smart regulation which is how to get private parties to do what the government sees as its job and the more defensible objective of reframing the regulatory relationship as a partnership.

16 Drewry, G., 'The new public management' in Oliver, D. and Jowell, J. (eds), *The Changing Constitution*, 4th edn, Oxford: Oxford University Press, 2001, pp. 168–189.
17 Hughes, O., *Public Management and Administration*, 2nd edn, Harlow: Longman Pearson, 1998, quoted in Drewry, ibid.
18 Baldwin, R., 'Is better regulation smarter regulation?' (2005) *Public Law* 485.
19 Black, J., 'Constitutionalising self-regulation' (1996) 59 *Modern Law Review* 24–56. Moran, M., 'Not steering but drowning: policy catastrophes and the regulatory state' (2001) 72 *Political Quarterly* 414–427. See Gunningham, N., 'Regulating biotechnology: lessons from environmental policy' in Somsen, H. (ed.), *The Regulatory Challenge of Biotechnology*, Cheltenham: Edward Elgar, 2007, p. 5. See also House of Lords Select Committee on Regulators, *UK Economic Regulators, Volume I: Report*, 1st Report of Session 2006–07, HL Paper 189-I, London: The Stationery Office, 2007.
20 Ibid., p. 6.
21 Ibid. See Gunningham, N.A. and Grabosky, P., *Smart Regulation: Designing Environmental Policy*, Oxford: Oxford University Press, 1998.

Smart regulation therefore seeks to adapt regulation appropriately through a problem-based learning appraisal. A broad and inclusive range of actors are brought inside the regulatory system and this public participation is fostered through a transparent decision-making process. This raises the question of how are tensions between transparency and effectiveness mediated?

Smart regulation has been blamed for the recent financial crisis. In this context, the regulatory approach of the Financial Services Authority[22] was heavily criticised[23] for failing to act. The Turner Review into the banking crisis, concluded in March 2009 that, for the future, the Financial Services Authority must be able to spot emerging issues: 'This failure to spot emerging issues was rooted in the paucity of macro-prudential, systemic and system wide analysis.'[24]

A key point here is that smart regulation is meant to engage the regulated parties as the eyes and ears as well as the hands of society. The Financial Services Authority example is one where prudential aspect of regulating individual institutions may have functioned more or less but the detection and managements of emergent risks did not. It is appropriate to consider the effectiveness of one kind of regulation over another and, in specific circumstances, the form of regulation that is best able to detect and respond appropriately to regulatory problems. Responsibility and cost sharing is a constructively incomplete compact between private and public systems that needs to address many of the questions about the most appropriate form of regulation.

It is accepted that there is no single ideal system of regulation. What is required is a balanced discussion of principles-based versus rule-based approaches. The following discussion is an attempt to draw out some of the main issues. Responsibility and cost sharing is a way of introducing a subset of the relevant principles and the rules that follow from them with a delegated or shared responsibility to agree their modification and application as the circumstances demand. It is hard to be certain. It would appear that principles may be too sweeping, ambiguous or even subjective and difficult to apply to real events; rules are limited in their applicability and invite all kinds of ingenious forms of exploitation that may bypass them and also favour corruption. A regulatory system that uses a partnership to manage a combination of rules and principles can benefit from self-organisation of its complex constituents; it can even manage crisis,

22 Black, B., 'Managing the financial crisis – the constitutional dimension', LSE law, society and economy working papers, 12-2010, London: Department of Law, London School of Economics and Political Science, 2010. McEldowney, J.F., 'Managing financial risk: the precautionary principle and protecting the public interest in the UK' in Labrosse, J.R., Olivares-Caminal, R. and Singh, D. (eds), *Risk and the Banking Crisis*, Cheltenham: Edward Elgar, 2011. McEldowney, J.F., 'Defining the public interest: public law perspectives on regulating the financial crisis' in Labrosse, J.R., Olivares-Caminal, R. and Singh, D. (eds), *Financial Crisis Management and Bank Resolution*, Abingdon: Informa, 2009, pp. 103–132.
23 Financial Services Authority, *The Turner Review: A Regulatory Response to the Global Banking Crisis*, London: FSA, March 2009, p. 87.
24 Ibid.

even when of its own making, and in that lively way it minimises the risks of capture. Some brief consideration follows of the debate about regulation currently in play.

Warning of the dangers of adopting a principles-based approach for financial regulation, Julia Black identified a number of concerns: the generality with which the principles are drafted; the call for qualitative assessment rather than quantitative analysis; the diversity and breadth of their application; that the principles assume behavioural standards; that breaches of the principles are largely based on fault; and the assumption that, through enforcement, sanctions will be applied.

There are clear risks associated with the principles-based approach and, not least, considerable ambiguity over the form such approach might take. Within the overall umbrella of principles-based regulation there is variation in its application and the rigour with which it is applied. There are complex legal obstacles when seeking to enforce the rules because of technical and divergent interpretations of EU rules. Vagueness and ambiguity may arise about the delegation of so much discretion to the markets as interpretations may vary. There may be a lack of certainty in the standards that are being applied and if and when they are to be enforced; there may be a proliferation of rules to the point that they may be ignored or simply contested; minimum standards and best practice may become blurred and impossible to apply; unpredictability in enforcement and inadequate training, knowledge and skills of the regulators or those being regulated may make the rules impossible to apply; lastly, accountability issues may arise. This may occur through inadequate consultation or a degree of institutional capture of the regulators by the industry they regulate.[25] There is also an increasing need to identify and reinforce the public interest in the future of regulation.[26]

It is important that the experience of regulation generally and the lessons from the banking crisis caused, in part, by regulatory failures are understood in terms of the participation and incentive effects of regulatory relationships, in order that cost sharing or responsibility sharing is properly understood. In particular, it is necessary to distinguish two benchmarks: the first is the efficient joint sharing and allocation of costs and, second, there is responsibility among the public and private sector stakeholders. This 'optimal contract' will ensure that all relevant costs and benefits are taken into full account by those whose actions influence them, and thus that the overall benefits (considering opportunity costs, externalities, monitoring and enforcement costs and likely levels of compliance) are as large and as fairly distributed as possible. However, this requires a vast amount of information, much of which will not be known, will not be truthfully disclosed and may not be understood at the point where it is needed; more worryingly, these

---

25 Black, J., Hopper, M. and Band, C., 'Making a success of principles-based regulation' (2007) *Law and Financial Markets* 191–206.
26 Treasury Committee, Memorandum from the Financial Services Authority, evidence 461.

arrangements may not adjust to a changing world, because they foreclose learning or crowd out innovation. Lastly, the sharing may not reach far enough to engage those whose information or powers of action are necessary to identify and implement socially optimal arrangements. Therefore, cost and responsibility sharing have a second-best or pragmatic instantiation; parties who bear costs will seek to understand them better and to minimise them as best they can – and to seek to change the arrangements when the world changes; those whose interests are affected are most likely to seek to participate in order to gain an efficacious voice.

There are some difficulties in ensuring that smart regulation is appropriate for the regulation of animal health and safety. In that context, there are some important considerations. Risk assessment and its various progenies have a long history in this area. This is partly understandable because of the specialist and technical nature of the subject matter. Insights and benefits need to be shared and there are many lessons to be gained from adopting cost-sharing agendas. There may not be sufficient consensus between government, industry and stakeholders about what is desirable and whether policy making is the appropriate choice for the problem defined by regulating animal health and welfare. The extent of consensus is variable across the various animal diseases. There may be contradictory versions of the same analysis and there may be public distrust over the entire regulatory framework as a result of its ineffectiveness and vice versa.

There are three points to be made about regulatory arrangements in general. First, there is a need for an understanding of how participation and action respond to the 'rules of the game' and the various economic incentives that this give rise to.[27] Second, there is the issue of mechanism design. This involves writing new rules in order to bring the rational behaviour of the parties as close as possible to the societal optimum. Third, there is the issue of complexity. This is recognition of the self-organising and emergent behaviour of regulation practice. There is a considerable challenge. The most important changes may not be manageable by old-style individually orientated prudential regulation. Changes may lead to systemic risk that may not always be perceived by individual stakeholders or be informative of their behaviour. There may be a tendency towards regulating a big crisis with a system designed to deal with a single major shock.

The experience of complex regulation and regulatory systems provides useful lessons. It is clear that when selecting the most appropriate type of regulation, rigid rule setting may not provide the most suitable strategies for animal health and welfare because of the lack of consensus about what may be achieved and the costs involved. Specifically, there are questions about how to address the contagious aspects of disease, the conflation of welfare, medical and economic objectives, and the impact of specific outbreaks, as well as policy objectives having to be tailored to meet risky outcomes

---

27 The Nash equilibrium – understanding response to the effects of participation and action.

This is an area where setting standards and appropriate means to ensure compliance are required. Compliance and standard setting require a variety of solutions that will best meet the requirements of the industry and strike the most appropriate balance between the market and costs.[28] Gunningham makes some useful conclusions when considering the best way forward in selecting the most suitable regulatory structure: 'In terms of meta-regulation, the perceived solution is to establish regulatory structures that strengthen the capability of individual institutions or enterprises for internal reflection and self-control.'[29]

Indeed, the regulators themselves should strive to put themselves out of business. Increasing reliance on regulators and their services can weaken the industry and become, in effect, a perverse subsidy. How should the selection of the most appropriate regulatory system take place? Baldwin and Black argue that particular attention should be given to the problems of regulatory enforcement and compliance, and regulatory regimes that adopt with different compliance strategies are in need of continual adjustments. They admit that while smart regulation 'is more holistic than responsive regulation', it suffers from the difficulties of addressing various escalating problems and a myriad of detail that may not always ensure consistency, fairness and accountability.[30] The power of commitment is important here, as one of the key problems with smart regulation is its credibility in terms of ensuring stakeholder information and the promise of what is needed to be undertaken. Baldwin and Black argue that risk-based regulation has become the norm in the UK and suggest that really responsive regulation should have a framework that is both flexible and sufficiently robust to address the needs of enforcement and compliance.

It is clear that an emphasis on enforcement and compliance gives really responsive regulation the potential of providing an appropriate framework that facilitates evaluation. This allows the selection of the most appropriate regulatory framework when addressing different problems. It is essential that choosing the appropriate regulatory strategy should take account of the means for assessing and monitoring as well as re-assessing the needs of society. Reflexive decision making is a crucial part of the regulatory system, with various regulatory strategies dependent on the nature of the problems that are being addressed. Julia Black has recently drawn regulatory lessons from the financial crisis.[31] She concludes:

> If the financial crisis has a broader lesson for regulators elsewhere it is this it is not enough to ask regulators or others to engage in self-critical learning, to

---

28 See Baldwin, R. and Cave, M., *Understanding Regulation*, Oxford: Oxford University Press, 1999.
29 Ibid., p. 15. See also Baldwin, R., 'The new punitive regulation' (2004) 67(3) *Modern Law Review* 351–383.
30 Baldwin, R. and Black, J., 'Really responsive regulation' (2008) 71 *Modern Law Review* 59–64.
31 Julia Black, 'Paradoxes and failures: "new governance" techniques and the financial crisis' (2012) 75(6) *Modern Law Review* 1037–1063.

assess whether they are performing their tasks well. It has to be asked whether they are performing the right tasks at all.[32]

Black's analysis is worth serious consideration in taking forward lessons of past regulatory failures.

Animal health and welfare in the context of cost sharing

The Coalition Government has adopted a strong policy preference in favour of reducing regulatory costs, simplifying regulatory systems and cutting regulatory burdens. Animal health and safety provides a clear policy example by promoting cost sharing and responsibility amongst animal keepers and various stakeholders. The Advisory Group Final Report[33] recommended adopting cost sharing for animal health and welfare. In 2009/10, Defra spent over £365.5 million on animal health and welfare, with almost 50 per cent of costs related to bTB. This is a sizeable proportion of Defra's budget and is unsustainable given the current cuts in public spending – unsustainable because it has become an inefficient form of subsidy and there is a desire to share costs with the private sector to minimise public expenditure. The pre-eminent aim should be the rebalancing of public and private expenditure in order to enhance the growth and competitiveness of the industry. Aggregating public and private requires the transfer of the right *amount* of costs that are proportional to the benefits of the industry and the right *kind* of costs that are driven by the needs of the industry in terms of precaution. Transfer of costs may need be contingent upon the transfer of certain kinds of responsibility. Insuring against a potential outbreak of disease may be a good example of how insurance may enrich cost sharing.

The proposals made by the Advisory Group were significant as they provide general lessons for the UK in terms of how the cost-sharing principle may amount to a distinctive form of economic regulation that may have lessons for other sectors of the economy. The main findings of the Advisory Group Final Report were that the arguments in support of cost sharing are well supported with risks being adequately quantified and that stakeholders are more likely to agree during the current economic climate. Some of the assumptions underlying the Final Report are problematic as they assume that there is a well-understood expectation on how market forces may be brought together when the aim is to reduce public spending and transfer costs onto the main stakeholders. Will farmers vaccinate if the upfront cost is to be borne by the farmer? It is also possible to see that farmers may take the opportunity to implement effective alternatives to vaccination that are more efficient provided their cost shares and market rewards are in place. Transferring costs will inevitably lead to higher food prices and this is at a time of high inflation. Not all the legal responsibilities and economic costs

---

32 Ibid., p. 1062.
33 Advisory Group Final Report, op. cit., n. 1.

of regulation are known and fully transparent. Price and cost transparency will require a vigilance on the part of regulators.

The cost-sharing principle comes with governance arrangements. Here the two need to be distinguished but the link between cost sharing and certain kinds of actions engages with policy making and is part of the regulatory structures. The Advisory Group Final Report envisaged that the main governance system with oversight over cost sharing should be carried out by a Partnership Board located within Defra, with the assumption that it would be effective through the prudent choice of its membership with a 'high-profile' Chief Executive. There are echoes of the early post-privatisation regulatory structure when gas, electricity and water were privatised and it will take some time for the new regulatory system to take shape.

The Advisory Group recommended a very wide remit for the Partnership Board. Its purpose was broadly defined to include '... within its remit strategic oversight of the whole of animal health and welfare policy and delivery undertaken by Defra in relation to England'.[34] The inclusion of policy making within the strategic oversight role raises the question of how this would fit with the role of ministers and accountability. Reassuringly, the Advisory Group recognised that this would not undermine the role of ministers in terms of Parliamentary Questions and the Treasury's role of oversight through Defra's Accounting Officer. However, this leaves a large question unanswered – how would the Partnership Board be accountable? Would it simply be a conduit of advice or a decision making body? Given that the Partnership Board would be expected to meet only six to ten times a year[35] the relationship between its formal roles and responsibilities is far from clear. The Advisory Group proposed that ' ... the Board should be the sole source of Departmental advice to the responsible Minister on all strategic health and welfare matters relating to all kept animals in England. There should be no "parallel track" of advice to the Minister from officials within the Department on these matters.'[36]

Why is this desirable? How would the proposal work in practice? Replacing the current civil service advisory role by moving some key senior Defra civil servants to work with an external Partnership Board and external members raises questions about how the mix would work and whether it would achieve legitimacy as an independent body. Again, the arguments for doing so are not supported by substantial evidence that this is desirable, possible or needed. The Advisory Group claimed that the Partnership Board would act independently as having 'an external Chair; the other external members, whilst acting collectively would individually be independent of Government',[37] but later on the Advisory Group claimed:

34   Advisory Group Final Report, op. cit., n. 1, para. 4.10, p. 51.
35   Advisory Group Final Report, op. cit., n. 1, para. 4.32, p. 56.
36   Advisory Group Final Report, op. cit., n. 1, para 4.11, p. 52.
37   Advisory Group Final Report, op. cit., n. 1, para 4.8, p. 51.

The Board's agenda should be aligned to the Defra and wider Government business cycle, such as the financial and business planning cycles, so that it can make decisions effectively and at the appropriate time. The Board's deliberation should be consistent with better regulation principles.[38]

Mixing up various roles and responsibilities is not desirable. The Partnership Board would be too susceptible to government changes in direction and would not be easily able to identify its own direction, priorities or ways of working. The mix of external and internal members appears to offer a model drawn from a Company Act company but lacking its own resources and ability to manage. Would senior Defra officials, once members of the Partnership Board, act as civil servants under the various rules and procedures or as a new species of hybrid status with not always compatible roles and functions? Also included on the Partnership Board would be the Chief Veterinary Office as an *ex officio* member.

The Advisory Group placed enormous reliance on the ability to attract the most suitable person to serve as external Chair. This is familiar territory in the history of regulatory bodies. If given a public profile through a charismatic chair, the regulatory body becomes closely connected with the personality, opinions and predilections of the individual. This is a high-risk strategy, however, as stakeholders in the area of animal health and welfare face formidable, well-organised lobbyists, with this being one of the most politically contested area of regulation.

There are further concerns. The role and responsibilities of the proposed Partnership Board require clarification and focus. The key issue of independence is also linked to proper accountability and as the Advisory Group assumed that this could be achieved through ministerial responsibility, this adds to the lack of clarity about the Partnership Board. It would not have its own forms of accountability outside the political control of ministers and its remit would be 'strategic oversight of the whole of animal health and welfare policy and delivery undertaken by Defra in relation to England'.[39] The boundaries between operational or day-to-day decisions would be blurred with strategic policy making, making it difficult to know who would take responsibility for the Partnership Board as distinct from the policy itself. The fact that:

Routine advice to the Minister from officials within the strategic policy framework already considered and approved by the Board and determined by the Minister would not normally go to the Board (e.g. day-to-day policy development, routine correspondence, Parliamentary Questions (PQs), Parliamentary debates, speeches).[40]

38 Advisory Group Final Report, op. cit., n. 1, para 4.12, p. 52.
39 Advisory Group Final Report, op. cit., n. 1, para. 4.10, p. 51.
40 Advisory Group Final Report, op. cit., n. 1, para 4.13, p. 52.

underlines the need for clarification of role, responsibility and functions of the Partnership Board from the relevant minister.

A good regulatory system must set high standards but must also be designed to secure the particular objectives to be achieved. In particular, the regulatory structure ought to be able to detect undesirable behaviour, encourage good practice and develop adequate responses, including enforcement tools and strategies that engage with the various stakeholders. The interests of the public, including the interests of animals, must be addressed in terms of animal health and welfare policy that protects human health and sets standards for animal health and welfare. It may be necessary for an animal perspective to be part of the regulator's role. The robustness of the design must take account of differing tensions and at the same time engage in a need for flexibility.

There is also the need for the creation of incentive mechanisms and an enforcement capability. In the case of animal health and welfare, public and private groups must be accommodated. In order to engage with the public interest, priority must be given to achievable aims that provide legitimacy and respect for the regulatory system. The regulatory structure should endeavour to achieve adequate enforcement strategies that fall within existing resources. This may be achieved through the following approaches involving:

- setting regulatory objectives that are clear and realisable;
- providing adequate enforcement functions that are well coordinated;
- providing a means for testing and evaluating the effectiveness of regulation and reviewing strategies for improvement;
- monitoring compliance and enforcement and adjudicating success or failure;
- providing a coherent and responsive system of regulation that commands the support of the public and stakeholders;
- providing an adequate reporting system and transparency in decision making.

Despite some doubts about how future regulation will work, especially in a period of fiscal uncertainty, it is clear that cost sharing and responsibility may set the trend for the future. Responsibility and cost sharing offers an innovative regulatory structure for animal health and welfare[41] and the potential for both private and public sectors to co-operate through their different roles and functions[42] in a sustainable approach to regulating risk. In animal health and welfare currently, the public-sector finances many of the compensation schemes, provides

---

41 See Black, J. 'Paradoxes and Failures: "New Governance" Techniques and the Financial Crisis' (2012) 75(6) *Modern Law Review* 1037–1063.

42 See Gunn *et al.*, op. cit., n. 4. Grant, op. cit., n. 4. House of Commons, op. cit., n. 4. Jordan, op. cit., n. 4. Stott, A.W., Jones, G.M., Humphry, R.W. and Gunn, G.J., 'Financial incentive to control paratuberculosis (Johne's disease) on dairy farms in the United Kingdom' (2005) 156 *Veterinary Record* 825–831. A. Woods, A., *A Manufactured Plague: The History of Foot and Mouth Disease in Britain*, London: Earthscan, 2004.

welfare standards and their enforcement, and assesses and protects the public from health risks associated with animal diseases, including the operation of border controls.[43]

The sharing of responsibility and costs has a long history. The current discussion comes from the experience of the BSE crisis in the 1980s, followed by the Swine Fever outbreak in 2000 and the FMD epidemic in 2001. The latter cost the UK £8 billion and gave rise to a Policy Commission on the Future of Farming and Food under Sir Don Curry. His analysis attributed to a sustainable farming industry the need to allocate risk and ensure that the degrees of responsibility between animal keepers and the government needed attention. Endemic diseases such as bTB cost Defra annually around £80 million. Since the 1980s there has been a considerable amount of discussion including various consultation papers as to how to allocate appropriate cost sharing and responsibility objectives. Since 2004, the Animal Health and Welfare Strategy has been focused on achieving improvements in animal health and welfare. The approach to reform and systematic analysis has been *ad hoc* rather than strategic. The legislation has reflected this in a piecemeal way – regulation in the form of legal duties and responsibilities under the consolidation found in the Animal Welfare Act 2006, most of which dated back several centuries. The EU has been active in setting the pace of future strategy, including a new framework for animal health and welfare with a systemic approach to identifying risk consistent with cost sharing and responsibility. The previous government proposed an independent regulatory body (Non-Departmental Public Body) with associated regulatory powers, but the details of cost sharing were not included in a published Animal Health Bill 2009. The proposed Bill did not address animal health and welfare collectively, preferring to look at animal health alone. It also omitted cost sharing and responsibility, which had been held over pending the preparation of a separate Treasury Bill. The Coalition Government decided not to reinstate the Animal Health Bill, but supported the continuation of the work of the England Advisory Group on Responsibility and Cost Sharing, established in late 2009. The work of the Advisory Group has had to take account of the Coalition Government's cuts agreed soon after the General Election (June 2010). The Advisory Group also made a number of operational assumptions, namely that both animal health and welfare were best considered together and that public consultation should be actively part of the working methodology of the Group.

Current regulatory reform strategies

The National Audit Office Report, *Delivering Regulatory Reform* (February 2011) sets the future direction of regulatory reform. The Report makes clear that regulation is a 'key tool' used by departments to achieve policy objectives:

---

43 Defra Consultation Paper (2007). The Consultation Paper is part of a strategy set out by Defra in *The Animal Health and Welfare Strategy for Great Britain*, London: Defra, 2004.

Complying with regulation can create costs, for example, for businesses. The cost of compliance can be a direct cost, such as licences or buying equipment to comply with regulation, often known as the policy cost. Regulated entities also face indirect costs for example the time spent understanding legislative requirements, which are usually referred to as administrative burdens.[44]

The premise on which regulatory reform is currently based includes the following:

- regulatory reform seeks to achieve the right balance between the benefits of regulation and its costs;
- improvements are ongoing to the 'better regulation' agenda, and place emphasis on improving the regulatory and policy making framework;
- the Coalition Government operates under the assumption that 'current levels of regulation are excessive and reducing regulation for business is one of its key commitments'.

There are a number of key strategies that have been adopted, including the setting up of the Reducing Regulation Committee in May 2010 as a new Cabinet Committee to ensure that there is a robust case for any new regulations. In choosing how and when to regulate, there are a number of additional strategies, including:

- the system of 'one in, one out' applies where the cost of new regulation must be compensated for by a corresponding cut;
- a policy for departments to challenge the costs and the need for regulation;
- the use of 'sunset clauses' to end tick the box systems[45] and require that regulations should automatically expire after a certain time period;
- rolling review programmes to review current approaches to regulation and ensure that additional costs and burdens are being controlled.

What are the implications of the approach analysed by the National Audit Office? There are clear signs that the cost and responsibility sharing agenda is beginning to take shape, not only within Defra, the department responsible for animal health and welfare, but also in other departments. The adoption of cost and responsibility sharing is evident in the health and safety area. In March 2011, the Department for Work and Pensions published *Good Health and Safety, Good for Everyone*, which provides an example of current approaches to regulation. Costs have had to be reduced because of a 30 per cent cut in the Health and Safety Executive's

---

44   National Audit Office, op. cit., n. 6.
45   The term refers to time limits on the life of the legislation – one year, for example. After the time elapses the legislation ceases to apply.

(HSE's) current budget. The aim is to reduce inspections by one-third, and this is to be achieved through various risk strategies:

> HSE will achieve this reduction in proactive inspections through the better use of intelligence to target inspections towards higher risk industries and duty holders where there is information indicating that they may be operating in material breach of health and safety law or that there are higher risks arising from the work being carried out.[46]

The underlying assumptions are that the system of regulation will be self-reporting and enforcing. Responsible management is expected to behave prudently and the worst offenders will be readily exposed. There is also an assumption that vigilance will be rewarded by a robust deterrence coupled with effective detection systems. Confidence in self-regulation and vigilance as well as the competence of managers were some of the weak aspects of the Financial Services Authority's adoption of principles-based regulation found to be at fault in the Authority's own review of its failings in the regulation of Northern Rock.

Taken together, the trajectory of government thinking is in the direction of cost sharing and responsibility. Section 5 of the Advisory Group Final Report[47] contains an itemised list of options including fees, charges and levies as a way of attempting to share costs and reduce the burden of regulation on the public purse. Current Defra policy is to deliver 'significant rationalisation across the fragmented, overlapping, inconsistent and complex framework' of regulation.[48]

There are some concerns about the absence of a statutory framework and linked systems of accountability for the AHWB. Lessons may be learned in this context from the following two examples. The first is of the Forensic Science Regulator (FSR) when faced with the challenges of regulating forensic science providers, which have increasingly been private-sector businesses. The second example is the adoption of a regulatory body within Defra, the AHWB, to regulate animal health and welfare through the principle of co-regulation engaging with private and public sectors.

Forensic Science Regulator

The government-run Forensic Science Service (FSS), which was mainly publicly financed, closed in 2012. Since then, private-sector providers have helped to fill the niche left by the closure, resulting in a mixture of privately funded and publicly funded providers. This is a good example of cost sharing between the sectors. Private providers as well as the police are free to develop their own

---

46 Health and Safety Executive, CD 235 – *HSE proposal for extending cost recovery*, consultation document, London: HSE, 2011, p. 8
47 Advisory Group Final Report, op. cit., n. 1.
48 'DEFRA pushes ahead with red-tape reforms', *ENDS Report 452*, 25 September 2012, p. 6.

services, which will create new challenges during a period of intensive change. Regulating forensic scientists will require addressing both public and private entities. The importance of uniform and fully accredited forensic services includes the need for proper resources, training and appropriate processes and integrity in setting benchmarks and accreditation schemes. For example, International Standard ISO/IEC 17025 sets the competence levels for testing and accreditation of laboratories. The current arrangements for regulation are in the hands of the FSR alone, who was appointed in February 2008.[49] The FSR is sponsored by the Home Office and is a public appointee operating independently of the Home Office. His main function is to ensure the provision of forensic sciences services to the criminal justice system and that there is an appropriate regime of scientific quality standards. The FSR currently has no statutory powers. There is a separate and independent Forensic Science Society, which is the professional body for forensic practitioners. It is largely supportive of the work of the FSR and operates a full range of related services. There is a Membership and Ethics Committee of the Forensic Science Society, which applies a strict criteria for membership, engages in supervising continuing professional development activities and ensures that there is supervision of the Chartered Forensic Practitioner status. It holds workshops and conferences, and seeks to enhance the education of forensic scientists.

In the future, there is also considerable EU regulation planned for forensic science with an EU Framework Decision requiring DNA and fingerprint laboratories to conform to ISO/IEC 17025. Changes due to the abolition of the FSS will require the FSR to be vigilant especially as many of the newly created police laboratories will be non-accredited. Addressing these matters has resulted in various drafts and guidance to be issued by the FSR, including the draft Codes of Practice and Conduct for forensic science providers and practitioners in the criminal justice system (2010), and various attempts to build into the regulatory structure the main components of ISO/IEC 17025 (2011).

A major complaint against the FSR is that the appointment lacks statutory powers. Having established a regulatory framework, the FSR is planning to issue enforceable standards for the UK. This, however, was postponed in April 2011 and is now planned for December 2013. The FSR has admitted that enforcing such standards is difficult when there is no statutory leverage for enforcement or compliance with the standard.

The crucial question of whether or not to adopt statutory powers has proved difficult to resolve. It is instructive to consider this point in some detail. In oral evidence to the House of Commons Science and Technology Committee, the FSR stated:

> During the research phase leading up to the development of my role, Home Office Officials spoke to many regulators and said, 'What sort of regulatory

---

49 Mr Andrew Rennison.

model should we have?' The overwhelming recommendation from them was: 'Avoid some sort of statutory model, if you can, because it tends to restrain you' The recommendation at the time was to go for light-touch regulation but with the regulator having the freedom to move into areas that he or she saw fit. I enjoy that freedom at the moment ... However, I am now reaching the conclusion that we have to seriously consider some sort of statutory underpinning of my role and some powers to mandate standards. Now that we have developed and consulted widely on the standards, it is entirely appropriate to consider whether we should be mandating those – bolstering the European regulations and translating that into domestic law with some sort of domestic powers to mandate standards.[50]

The government is currently considering whether or not to grant the FSR statutory powers, and the arguments for doing so are familiar ones. The FSR must take into account many organisations within the justice system, including the courts and the police, that have wide statutory powers. The House of Commons Select Committee has accepted that the FSR should have statutory powers to regulate the provision of forensic services. Statutory powers in this context are very much seen as an evolutionary phase in the development of effective regulation. As discussed in Chapter 8, the government's attitudes to policy making and statutory regulation are influential. As Julia Black has noted:

> Designers and regulators do need to build in structures for cognitive challenge and experimentation.[51]

Animal health and welfare board

The decision to set up a non-statutory regulatory body within Defra came after the Coalition Government took office. Previously, Defra had been actively engaged in a number of consultations and deliberations. Beginning with the inquiry into the FMD outbreak in 2001 under Sir Iain Anderson,[52] there have been a number of working parties and public consultations.[53] Consultation on a new independent body for animal health concluded in June 2009, with the government's response at the end of 2010. Prior to the election of May 2010 it was proposed to have a statutory framework for an independent regulatory body. An Animal Health Bill was drafted and lost in the period before the election.

50 House of Commons Science and Technology Committee, *The Forensic Science Service*, Seventh Report of Session 2010–12, HC 855, London: The Stationery Office, 20 June 2011, para. 127.
51 J. Black, *op. cit.*, p. 1063.
52 *Foot and Mouth Disease 2001: Lessons to be Learned Inquiry Report*, HC 888, London: The Stationery Office, 22 July 2002.
53 Public consultations were in 2006 and 2007 and there was a UK Responsibility and Cost Sharing Consultative Forum.

Selecting the most appropriate regulatory regime for animal health and welfare requires careful consideration to ensure the 'right fit' between the design of the best regulation and the requirements for animal health and welfare.[54] It is clear from the previous Labour Government's consultation process that there are a number of goals in the regulation and governance of animal health. These goals are:

- to reduce the overall levels and total costs of animal diseases;
- to ensure that investment in disease prevention and management is effective, efficient and economical;
- to share costs between main beneficiaries and risk managers;
- to improve confidence of the livestock industry and that of other stakeholders in the way disease risks are managed.

It is clear that many of these principles are to be found in the AHWB. Cost sharing is one of the key issues to be addressed and is likely to mean that livestock owners gain financial responsibilities that were hitherto largely held by government through subsidy and support. This will empower livestock owners' awareness but also require a much more open debate and informed decision making; a substantial departure from the lobbying stance taken by stakeholders in the past. The new regulatory structure has high expectations, as follows:[55]

- to ensure more independent and better informed decision making;
- to increase the involvement of livestock awareness amongst farmers and other key stakeholders;
- to provide incentives to reduce the cost of managing disease;
- to provide incentives for better risk management; and
- to ensure greater financial transparency and accountability in the livestock industry.

The success or failure of the AHWB is likely to depend on the effectiveness of consultation and the transparency in decision making. Engaging with accountability systems is important especially with parliamentary select committees and MPs. Setting priorities is also challenging when there are conflicting pressures. Will the AHWB have sufficient status and authority to take forward its policies? How effective will it be in identifying its independence when working closely within Defra? How will it be able to respond rapidly to short-term decision making when under considerable public pressure? It is too soon to tell whether the AHWB will meet its design expectations. The success of its

54 See May, P.J., 'Regulatory regimes and accountability' (2007) *Regulation and Governance* 8–26. Scott, C., 'Accountability in the regulatory state' (2000) 27(1) *Journal of Law and Society* 38–60.

55 Defra, *Consultation on a new independent body for animal health*, London: Defra, 2009.

endeavours will be tested in the coming years and the implementation of budget costs at a time when cost sharing is likely to become highly contested in a period of austerity amongst the main stakeholders.

Conclusions

Cost sharing and responsibility is likely to become an important means of developing future regulatory strategies. Our interest in cost and responsibility sharing is that it fits a strategy to develop a regulatory system suited to addressing animal health and welfare issues as well as taking account of the current economic climate. Good governance regulation based on needs and effectiveness derives from the allocation of responsibilities and costs. This offers economic and legal mechanisms to encourage dialogue between stakeholders linked to animal health and welfare strategies, with the potential for private and public sectors to co-operate in a sustainable approach to regulating risk. Our research considers the principles of more effective regulation including taking decisions closely related to fact finding; transparency and fairness; minimisation of costs and market distortions; and proportionality in decision making.[56] As outlined above, cost and responsibility sharing offers a useful economic instrument on which to build a partnership relationship between private and public sectors. The aim is to deliver effective value for money in regulation and to transfer costs from the public sector to the private sector. Animal keepers and various stakeholders are asked to share cost and responsibility for animal health and welfare. It is a form of co-regulation consistent with the strategy of moving costs from the public onto the private sector. There is an additional dimension. Defra's long experience as broadly a publicly supported insurance provider for animal health and welfare has been formulated with stakeholders, including the private and public sectors working together through informal working groups, strategy groups and individual consultation arrangements. Essentially, Defra combined its role as a government department developing and implementing policy with its role as a 'broker' between business and government. The fact that this has proved difficult to achieve in terms of clear goals and objectives makes regulation and a regulatory body a critical issue, especially when cost sharing is expected to deliver less public subsidy than in the past.

Lastly, there are some doubts and uncertainties in terms of the architectural arrangements for cost sharing and responsibility. For example, the value of the AHWB without primary legislation requires details in terms of the clarity of its role, responsibility, powers and duties. Animal health and welfare has, in the past, not been well considered or adequately addressed. To reiterate – the economic dimension has made animal health a high priority, but this is generally not as clearly evident when it comes to welfare. Stakeholders must feel confident

---

56 See n. 42.

in the role of the proposed Partnership Board and public confidence including parliamentary scrutiny and accountability should be addressed.

Cost and responsibility sharing offers a co-regulation strategy that connects private and public sectors. Lessons from the PFI and existing forms of co-regulation need to be taken into account. Sharing costs also means shifting levels of responsibility including information competences, objectives and responses. More explanation is required of how this form of co-regulation will address both animal health and welfare considerations. The regulatory style and design of the various regulatory instruments to be undertaken by the proposed Partnership Board need to be mapped out in full, taking account of the general historical context of the role of the state in the regulation of business and society. Addressing the history of past attempts to regulate animal health and welfare is the primary challenge facing the Partnership Board. The Partnership Board's regulatory strategy needs to take account of risk-based regulation and the precautionary principle discussed in Chapter 7. Really responsive regulation should engage with regulatory problems within a framework that is both flexible and sufficiently robust to address the needs of enforcement and compliance. Placing emphasis on enforcement and compliance gives really responsive regulation the appropriate framework for evaluation to take forward and improve animal health and welfare strategies.[57] Finally, the lessons of past regulatory failures provide precautionary lessons for the future. Underestimating complexities and tensions within regulatory systems holds warnings of future regulatory effectiveness.

---

57 Carslake, D., 'Endemic cattle diseases: comparative epidemiology and governance' (2011) 366 (1573) *Philosophical Transactions of the Royal Society B* 1975–1986.

7 Policy making and future regulatory strategy

Introduction

This chapter explores contemporary policy making and regulatory strategy in the context of animal health and welfare and the governance of animal diseases. The analysis is intended to contribute to the current debate in the UK on the future of regulating animal health and welfare. It is hoped that it will be particularly relevant to the AHWB in relation to its responsibility for policy making and risk assessment. Contemporary policy making and regulation must be considered in the context of reductions in public spending, which is in sharp contrast to the past experience of government involvement in agriculture since the Agriculture Act 1947,[1] and which comes at a time of increasing threats from animal diseases.

As outlined in previous chapters, in the aftermath of the Second World War, subsidies, grants and a paternal approach to farmers extended well into the 1960s, and serious consideration was given to a national animal health service. Today, the focus has moved considerably towards recognising animal welfare and health. It is difficult to optimise the welfare of a diseased animal, and there are significant economic consequences arising from animal diseases. Consequently animal health is much to the fore, especially given the volatility of the economics of agriculture, and this represents a major policy challenge. Several years of low farm incomes[2] have raised concerns about the future viability of the agricultural industry, especially in livestock farming and dairy farming. However, farm income is cyclical and, recently, some farm prices have improved. Food security has recently become a matter of serious concern for the first time in peace time in the UK, with a particular focus on the vulnerability of food production. The EU, for example, is implementing a scheme for all sheep over 12 months to be electronically tagged as a means of tracking animals and ensuring that appropriate health checks and surveillance are carried out.[3]

---

1 See Chapter 2.
2 See House of Commons Library, 'Farm incomes: statistics, SN/SG/2246', London: House of Commons Library, 4 February 2011.
3 Burrell, A., '"Good agricultural practices" in the agri-food supply chain' (2011) *Environmental Law Review* 251.

Policy makers, in the area of animal health and welfare, have had to consider environmental objectives as part of the justification for continued public financial support for farming. The effects of climate change and globalisation of food markets make it more difficult to prevent and control disease.[4] Environmental challenges arising from climate change are difficult to predict, making responses difficult to plan. The drought in 2010 that led to the Russian ban on wheat exports has highlighted the vulnerability of agriculture and possible impacts on supply. Similarly, in China, the past six years of increasing crop production could come to an end. Floods in Australia and Pakistan underpin the vulnerability of countries to major weather events and climate change. Increases in food prices are also seasonal and difficult to predict, and vary in relation to climate impacts and animal disease. Consequently, the UK Government has undertaken a risk assessment of the agricultural sector in terms of the potential impact of climate change. The study[5] is required under the Climate Change Act 2008. This is an important risk assessment of the likely impact in each sector of the economy including agriculture. Specific concerns for future policy making are the increase in flood risk at certain times in the season coupled with drought affected regions. Crop yields may be affected, leading to food shortages including animal feedstuffs. Pigs and poultry may be particularly vulnerable to heat stress. Poultry may produce fewer eggs and heat waves may damage their health. This may also impact on milk production and insufficient forage for grazing animals.

One of the most challenging aspects of policy making is in respect of bTB and how best to address the disease in cattle. The question of adopting control measures that include badger culling is controversial. The Coalition Government has favoured introducing proactive culls in England in designated areas as a test of the efficacy of its strategy. Public opinion is sharply divided and there are also diverse scientific opinions about the effectiveness of the badger-cull arrangements and the long-term strategy to be adopted. Due to administrative difficulties in assessing the number of badgers within the designated area for the cull, at the end of October 2012 it was decided to suspend the cull until the summer of 2013. Arrangements are currently in place to begin the cull as soon as practicable.

Livestock disease and policy making

Challenges and perceptions

Policy making in the agricultural sector must also be considered in the context of recent EU changes that may affect the UK's farm economy where there are lower farm incomes across many sectors of the industry. The Common Agricultural

4 Defra, *Agriculture in the UK 2009*, London: Defra, 2009. Macleod, M. *et al.*, *Review and Update of UK Marginal Abatement Cost Curves for Agriculture: Final report*, Prepared for the Committee on Climate Change, 2010.
5 Defra, *UK Climate Change Risk Assessment*, London: Defra, 2012.

Policy (CAP) must also be viewed within the current difficult economic cycle and fiscal downturn. Global growth prospects are sensitive to the financial crisis in the eurozone, and the UK is sensitive to changes in trade and finance.[6] Brent Crude oil prices have doubled since January 2007 and are likely to maintain at a steady high for some years to come. Recent food price increases might result in government pressure to keep food prices low and consequently adversely affect standards of animal health and welfare.

Intensive farming methods and changes in the economics of farmed animals links disease prevention the welfare of animals, the environment and public health with the economy. Agricultural expansion is driven by population changes. Globally, there is an increased reliance on livestock at a time when the UK is also facing an increased risk of livestock disease. Globalisation has also contributed to the risk of diseases. Increases in animal movements and trade, climate change and economic recession all have the potential to reduce the capacity of preventing and controlling disease. The emergence of new diseases in new locations is also a sign of climate change. Variable amounts of rainfall and rising temperatures may facilitate an increase in vector-borne diseases and parasites. Increasing pressure falls on biosecurity measures and surveillance techniques to ensure the prevention and early identification of disease.

Indelibly associated with the Coalition Government is an agenda of public sector cuts and a focus on cutting 'red tape' thereby reducing regulatory burdens. In this context, various animal diseases are influenced by shifting policy, for example, in the attempts to tackle bTB. Policy making must also take account of past and present governments' attempts to refresh regulation of animal health and welfare. The political dimension of policy making is always an ongoing debate. It finds expression in many polemical accounts of what policy making may mean and how it may engage with stakeholders. Party political splits are also much in evidence, and lessons of previous mistakes rarely admitted or accepted. Currently, this has relevance through the Coalition Government's approach to the CAP and the strategy to reduce regulatory burdens and red tape. The AHWB within Defra is the most recent institutional manifestation intended to promote self-regulation and a light touch regulation, with no express statutory powers and serious questions about its transparency and oversight. Sub-optimal control has serious dangers that have been raised in the past.[7]

The AHWB must work within Defra in discharging its primary responsibility for animal health in England,[8] but the question is how might this be achieved? These include the following: the methodology used, the approach adopted to

---

6   Emmerson, C., Johnson, P. and Miller, H. (eds), *The IFS Green Budget: February 2012*, London: Institute for Fiscal Studies and Oxford: Oxford Economics, 2012, pp. 1–2.

7   Ogus, A., *Regulation, Legal Form and Economic Theory*, Oxford: Clarendon Press, 1993.

8   In Scotland, there is the Scottish Government Rural Directorate for Animal Health and Welfare; in Wales, the Department for Environment, Planning and the Countryside; in Northern Ireland, the main department is the Department for Rural Affairs Northern Ireland.

shared learning and support as a means of achieving common understanding and meeting the challenges of taking forward a future regulatory strategy. The cross-disciplinary nature of the collaborative experience is intended to support better understanding. Stakeholder engagement and gaining public trust are also important aspects. The role of public trust creating a link to responsibility and cost sharing carries an underlying lesson, namely that loss of public confidence through lack of transparency or accountability creates a crisis of legitimacy in future policy making that takes a long time to be restored. Examples include the FMD outbreak in 2001, the BSE crisis and current concerns about bTB with a proposed badger cull, which are all hallmarks of reactive policy making with science heavily contested.

Understanding disease and identifying its epidemiological pathway is only one part of the policy analysis. Presenting findings to the public and engaging with stakeholders is a separate skill set involving economic, legal and political perspectives. The challenges can bring advances only through combining and interpreting different disciplines to a limited degree. The outcome is largely dependent on formulating and building support for policy making, which must take a holistic approach for the agricultural industry as a whole. In many sectors the underlying economy of farming is fragile. However, recent changes in farm prices because of the weakened euro may have a significant impact in the short term. It is also inherently complicated in many cases by the CAP and the future of European policy making for animal health and welfare. Assessing the underlying trends within each agricultural sector is highly revealing, and illustrates the way in which government policy making interacts with complex markets. It also reveals another underlying systemic problem with policy making – the contested values of the regulatory state beyond agriculture, but with a profound effect upon the future of regulating agriculture. This point is often difficult to appreciate within the agriculture sector.[9]

The UK's recent regulatory experience has been likened to a 'regulatory laboratory',[10] but also has strong lessons about 'political' tinkering with specialist and expert systems. The previous New Labour Government's desire for the regulation of financial institutions in a 'light touch' way is only one aspect of a complex subject.[11] The various arm's length agencies bequeathed from the years of Conservative Governments (1979–1997) have given way to consolidations

9 *Foot and Mouth Disease 2001: Lessons to be Learned Inquiry Report*, HC 888, London: The Stationery Office, 22 July 2002.

10 Moran, M., *The British Regulatory State: High Modernism and Hyper-innovation*, Oxford: Oxford University Press, 2004.

11 DTI, *Deregulation: Cutting Red Tape*, London: DTI, 1994; DTI, *Thinking About Regulation: A Guide to Good Regulation*, London: DTI, 1994; DTI, *Getting a Good Deal in Europe*, London: DTI, 1994. Baldwin, R., 'Is better regulation smarter regulation?' (2005) *Public Law* 485. Hampton, P., *Reducing Administrative Burdens: Effective Inspection and Enforcement Final Report*, London: HM Treasury, 2005.

and realignment. The regulatory state gained from increasing demands for detailed evidence of impacts to accompany every regulatory episode. More data collection and greater attention to risk assessment suggested a greater regulatory grip over the day-to-day running of the state. Juridical in nature, technical and complex in detail, the regulatory domestic state was also working in parallel with an increasingly expanding EU preference for regulation. Paradoxically, just as the Labour Government was coming to the end of its term in May 2010, the Animal Health and Welfare Bill was in a forward trajectory into law – bringing the subject of animal health and welfare into alignment with the regulation of the major utilities. However, the Bill did not survive the election of the Coalition Government.

As discussed in Chapter 6, the Coalition Government decided to create a regulatory body within Defra, the main sponsoring department for animal diseases. The decision to do so without primary legislation is consistent with the Coalition Government's policy known as the 'one in, one out' system, which is intended to reduce unnecessary regulation. By cutting red tape, the Coalition Government hopes to deliver economic growth. Poorly designed, disproportionate or uncoordinated regulation is seen as an impediment to innovation and productivity.[12] The policy to increase deregulatory measures and refrain from additional legislative burdens is tightly policed and is monitored by a Regulatory Policy Committee. Any proposed regulatory responsibilities including statutory powers must be assessed and subject to Impact Assessment. The one in, one out system requires that the cost of new regulations must be compensated for by a corresponding cut.

We have already seen how the analysis of the prevention and cure of animal diseases is interlinked with the question of how best to regulate animal health. Defra has been actively engaged in a number of consultations and deliberations. Beginning with the inquiry into the FMD outbreak in 2001 under Sir Iain Anderson,[13] there have been a number of working parties and public consultations, some of which are ongoing.[14] The consultation on a new independent body for animal health had taken place over many years and through a change of government. Designing the most appropriate regulatory regime for animal health and welfare has required careful consideration to ensure the 'right fit' between the design of the best regulation and the requirements for animal health and welfare.[15] It was clear from the Coalition Government's consultation process

12 HM Government, *One-in, One-out: Second Statement of New Regulation* Department for Business, Innovation and Skills, 2011.
13 Foot and Mouth Disease 2001, op. cit., n. 9, p. 8.
14 Public consultations were in 2006 and 2007 and there was a UK Responsibility and Cost Sharing Consultative Forum.
15 See May, P.J., 'Regulatory regimes and accountability' (2007) *Regulation and Governance* 8–26.
    Scott, C., 'Accountability in the regulatory state' (2000) 27(1) *Journal of Law and Society* 38–60.

that there are a number of goals in the regulation and governance of animal health. These are:

- to reduce the overall levels and total costs of animal diseases;
- to ensure that investment in disease prevention and management is effective, efficient and economical;
- to share costs between main beneficiaries and risk managers;
- to improve confidence of the livestock industry and that of other stakeholders in the way disease risks are managed.

It is clear that sharing costs and introducing any form of independent regulator will substantially alter the largely self-regulatory nature of current arrangements. Cost sharing is likely to mean that livestock owners will gain financial responsibilities that were hitherto largely held by government through subsidy and support. This will empower greater awareness of livestock needs but also require a much more open debate and informed decision-making. This will mark a substantial departure from the lobbying stance taken by stakeholders currently. The Government has an expectation that any new regulatory structure should achieve a number of benefits and ensure more independent and better-informed decision making amongst ministers:

- increasing the involvement of livestock awareness amongst farmers and other key stakeholders;
- providing incentives to reduce the cost of managing disease;
- providing incentives for better risk management; and
- facilitating greater financial transparency and accountability in the livestock industry.

Under the new Coalition Government, and after much discussion, Defra transferred its existing animal health policy responsibilities to the AHWB, with the Government Chief Veterinary Officer as an adviser and employed by the AHWB. The AHWB has not been created by statute and operates within Defra.

The first meetings of the AHWB were held in November and December 2011. Decision making is intended to be based on the best evidence and a proportionate response to risk, balanced by costs and benefits. In Chapter 6 the importance of cost sharing and responsibility is discussed in some detail. The government's animal health and welfare strategy has proposed that responsibilities and costs of livestock health and welfare should be balanced between the industry and taxpayers. This is intended to reduce substantially the main burden of the costs of compensating farmers for the compulsory destruction of animals during notifiable disease outbreaks. The AHWB is charged with the main responsibility for achieving this strategy. It is not an easy task and likely to become very contentious amongst farming groups, the public and also within government itself. There is, however, an expectation, on the part of the government, that there should be accompanying funding for the AHWB to support 50 per cent of the costs of tackling exotic disease outbreaks. By creating a regulatory agency, the government's agenda is to take forward cost-sharing policies for animal health and welfare, informed by sound scientific advice.

Livestock disease and animal welfare set considerable policy challenges. The strategy to share responsibility for decisions on disease prevention and control with stakeholders leaves an important role for government – to retain overall responsibility for funding research, to undertake disease surveillance and also to maintain a competent veterinary service for the prevention and control of exotic disease. The responsibility for livestock health is retained by livestock keepers and the livestock industry. The surveillance and early detection of animal disease remains a prime responsibility of the livestock keeper, who will pay for veterinarian advice. As this is a cost burden on the livestock keeper, it may lead to shifting costs onto the consumer. In the case of animal loss, the main compensation arrangements could be shifted from the government to the livestock keeper through a system of insurance. The details of these arrangements need to be worked out in full. This leaves uncertainty over the effectiveness of the new arrangements and public trust in their reliability.

Defra's role in managing its relations with arm's length bodies is a cause for concern. The National Audit Office has expressed doubts about Defra's role in measuring full cost of front-line activities including animal health. It has found that a projected reduction of 30 per cent of Defra's budget to be given effect by 2014–2015 will require 'a good understanding' of its arm's length bodies' costs 'in order to exercise scrutiny and challenge'.[16] The National Audit Office also doubts the capacity of Defra to meet the challenges of monitoring and ensuring that value of money is achieved.

The vulnerability of animals to disease and the dependency on the vigilance of livestock owners remains. In the current economic downturn there is a key additional question, that of the profitability of each agricultural sector. There are also serious questions about the adequacy of biosecurity measures and the need to give incentives to encourage farmer compliance. The variability of farmer compliance is an unknown factor that raises doubts and uncertainties over the adequacy of surveillance. Recently, the Environment, Food and Rural Affairs Committee expressed concern about changes to the Animal Health and Veterinary Laboratories Agency (AHVLA) as part of the rationalisation of laboratory services and the introduction of competitive tendering for Official Veterinarians. The effectiveness and public trust in the AHVLA is interlinked to adequate funding and the competence of specialist skills within the Agency. The Committee is undertaking a review of the AHVLA, which was due to be published in the

---

16 National Audit Office and Comptroller and Auditor General, *Department for Environment, Food and Rural Affairs: Managing front line delivery costs*, HC 1279, Session 2010–2012, 22 July 2011, London: NAO, 2011.

summer of 2012, but is still ongoing.[17] Animal-disease patterns are difficult to predict and come under the influence of climate change. Concerns are that if the focus is too much on cost saving, this may have longer-term economic impacts of serious animal disease outbreaks in the UK in the future.

Sound science and policy making

Defra's policy on animal health makes a distinction between three classes of animal diseases which threaten the UK: diseases usually not present in the UK but which may affect animals and humans, such as Avian influenza; diseases that may or may not show clinical signs in animals but cause diseases in people, for example salmonella and *Escherichia. coli*; and diseases that do not present a significant public-health risk but affect animal welfare, its productivity and profitability. There are a number of key considerations in setting priorities and the allocation of resources. The highest priority must be given to zoonoses, which are diseases that are transmissible between animals and humans. Sporadic outbreaks of such diseases may also give rise to major public-health scares that may affect consumer choices and confidence in food safety, with adverse consequences to the market. The obvious example is salmonella, which is transmissible from poultry or pigs to humans.

Consideration should be given to protecting and promoting the welfare of animals. The UK animal health and welfare legislation makes it explicit that animals are protected as they are cable of experiencing pain and distress. The five freedoms are: freedom from hunger and thirst with a requirement for access to fresh water and diet to maintain full health and vigour; freedom from discomfort that requires an appropriate environment including shelter and a comfortable resting areas; freedom from pain, injury or disease, which requires prevention or rapid diagnosis and treatment; freedom to express normal behaviour with provision of sufficient space, proper facilities and company of the animal's own kind; and freedom from fear and distress that requires conditions and treatment which avoid mental suffering.[18] Defra has established a Farm Animal Welfare Committee comprising a group of experts with terms of reference that include providing independent, authoritative and impartial advice to Defra and the Devolved Administrations in Scotland and Wales. This is evidence-based scientific advice that contributes to Defra's policy making and provides technical support. Currently, a number of animal health and welfare working groups, such

---

17 See House of Commons Environment, Food and Rural Affairs Committee, *The Rationalisation of The Animal Health and Veterinary Laboratories Agency (AHVLA), written evidence*, December 2011, HC 1805-i-ii, London: The Stationery Office, 28 February 2012.

18 See Brambell, F.W.R., *Report of the Technical Committee to Enquire into the Welfare of Animals kept under Intensive Livestock Husbandry Systems*, December 1965, London: HMSO, 1965. See also the Farm Animal Welfare Council (FAWC) set up on 1 April 2011, which succeeded the Farm Welfare Council which closed on 31 March 2011. See FAWC, *Farm Welfare in Great Britain: Past, Present and Future*, London: FAWC, October 2009.

as the Farm Animal Welfare Committee, are working on distinct welfare reports. For example, there is a working group on disease and farm welfare, whose aim is to undertake research that seeks to understand the past, present and emerging trends by species. This includes the five freedoms and aims at reducing the current disease challenge at national, sectoral and farm levels. There is also a working group on evidence base for farm and animal welfare policy making. Particular attention is given to the EU, CAP reform and the potential for welfare incentives in the context of World Organization for Animal Health (OIE initiatives). These are good examples of the value of informed evidence-based policy making.

There is the added dimension in animal health and welfare policy of EU expansion and harmonisation that must be taken into consideration. The existing EU *Animal Health Strategy 2007–2013* is under active review. Plans are well advanced to create a simplified EU framework that is convergent to international standards. The UK may find this the most challenging part of its policy-making strategy. There are concerns that maintaining higher standards of health and welfare in the UK may result in the UK being at a commercial disadvantage to other trading states. This is especially the case within the EU where trade is fundamental. Given the economic fragility of the euro zone, there may well be downward pressures on animal health and welfare standards to meet rising costs, lower farm incomes and increasing competition from outside the EU.

Lastly, the interests of the wider economy and the environment must be protected. This has already been mentioned above. Increasingly, disease outbreaks must be seen in the context of wider considerations, including the impact on international trade, particularly if there is a ban on exports of live animals and animal products under EU controls for notifiable disease outbreaks.

There are many overarching considerations, including policies on disease prevention and disease control. Disease prevention is seen as the most effective way to tackle animal health and welfare problems. The EU's *Animal Health Strategy 2007–2013* insists that 'prevention is better than cure'. Disease prevention involves surveillance, a prime responsibility that falls on livestock keepers and veterinarians, which is overseen by Defra. There is also a keen need to ensure that there is appropriate liaison between stakeholders, Defra and the laboratories used to test for diseases. Monitoring diseases at national, EU and international levels is very important. This includes monthly and quarterly reports on exotic diseases published and available on the Defra website. There is a great deal of work being undertaken to ensure that the control of diseases by Defra at source to reduce the risk of global diseases threat that puts the UK at risk is effective. There are various strands to this strategy[19] – good biosecurity is essential,

---

19 Endemic diseases are those that are found in the UK, and are distinguished from exotic diseases, which are usually found outside the UK. The latter are kept under close scrutiny and a monthly list is published setting out the main exotic disease threat prevalent in the UK.

Table 7.1 UK farming industry

UK farming	2006	2010
Full-time farmers	146,000	134,000
Commercial holdings	248,000	222,000
Average (ha) of holdings	69.3	76.7

as is addressing future disease threats in a way that is consistent with future EU policy making. Sound science must inform the debate and the policy matters that arise.[20]

Policy making: a sectoral analysis

The UK has witnessed many changes in the farming industry in the recent past. As seen in Table 7.1, since 2006 there has been a marked decline in the number of farmers and in farming units.

The key question is how to form policy making in each agricultural sector and what are the main social, economic and legal drivers at work?

Sheep

The sheep sector has suffered decline throughout Europe. It is estimated that sheep meat production has fallen in the last 15 years by at least 20 per cent. This is partly attributable to low wool prices and a marked decline in sheep meat consumption. This general trend may be subject to change in different economic circumstances. In the UK, tough movement restrictions, including criminal sanctions, were imposed in Autumn 2007 in response to the FMD outbreak, and similar restrictions were introduced to meet the threat from bluetongue. These restrictions adversely affected sheep farmers, and specifically hill farmers. In the summer months, sheep graze on pastures and are normally transferred to safer areas for pasture to meet winter weather conditions. The movement restrictions left many farmers with too many sheep on green pastures. The government's response was to make a special aid package available to farmers affected by FMD in England.

Disease may have long-term effects on the industry. Bluetongue is a good example as it may have serious long-term implications. The use of immunisation is possible but the costs are increasingly being transferred onto animal keepers. Many Defra restrictions can also have implications for selling at major animal

---

20 See Doremus, H. and Tarlock, D., 'Science, judgment and controversy in natural resource regulation' (2005) 26 *Public Land and Resources Law Review* 1.

markets and fairs. Electronic tagging under EU Regulation 21/2004, which is mandatory for sheep born after 2009, has improved the tracking and surveillance of sheep. Some UK concessions have allowed sheep in England not to be tagged before they are 12 months old and are intended for slaughter. There are further concessions in terms of recording individual sheep movements and reducing some of the costs and administrative burdens. Estimated costs are £31 million across the UK, with a cost of £8.37 million in Wales. Such costs must be considered in the context of the sheep market. As consumption of sheep meat has fallen, it is clear that the sheep sector generates income levels that are the lowest in the agricultural industry. The sheep sector may be found in marginal geographical areas and is often crucial to the survival of that region. Sheep production is also related to an important environmental role for the regions where sheep are to be found.[21] The unprofitability of sheep farmers is a serious challenge amidst declining sheep numbers and reductions in consumer demand. Currently, wool prices are low because of competition from synthetic materials.

Poultry

Poultry farming has become a highly competitive market. Under the CAP, poultry farmers can receive Single Farm Payment, which has important economic consequences for them. Welfare issues in the poultry sector have significant potential to affect the industry, and before 2007 there were no specific animal welfare rules that related to broiler chickens. Since EU Directive 2007/43/EC came into force on 30 June 2010, there are now regulations that apply to broiler chickens as part of the egg industry. They cover stocking density, the inspection of premises and the control of production. Free-range birds are also included in terms of welfare standards and registration purposes.

The EU Directive was implemented in England under the Welfare of Farmed Animals (England) (Amendment) Regulations 2010, SI 2010/3033, implemented in December 2010. These are important regulations intended to improve the conditions for meat chickens across the EU. It is part of the general approach to all farmed animals under general regulations (see Council Directive 98/58/EC and the Welfare of Farmed Animals (England) Regulations 2007, SI 2007/2078) and the introduction of specific regulations for each animal sector. Good chicken welfare is seen as desirable in terms of public interest and addresses media attention. The regulations provide regulatory supervision for the use of chicken for meat chicken, those who have more than 500 chickens, breeding hatcheries and conditions for free-range chickens. The regulations set conditions for the welfare of chickens including drinking, feed, litter, ventilation and heating, noise and light, inspection and cleaning, and record keeping. For example, since 2012, egg producers must no longer use battery cages. There are also regulations on poultry

---

21 See House of Commons Library, 'Sheep, SN/SC/116', London: House of Commons Library, 14 May 2012.

producers who produce meat. One of the great challenges for Defra is how might avian disease, a notifiable disease, be controlled.[22]

Pig producers

Pig-meat production in the UK has operated in a highly competitive market without any direct support payment from the EU, which is common to other agricultural sectors. The UK has always prided itself in having stricter welfare laws than in the rest of the EU, which has resulted in an increase in imports from outside the UK. Stricter EU animal welfare laws for pigs are likely to have a major impact on this sector, with the regulations due to come into force from 2013. Many British farmers believe that consumers are not fully aware of the higher welfare standards in the UK when compared to elsewhere. Strictly speaking, the definition of 'British bacon' is pigs reared only on British farms. In fact this may not always be the case, which causes a problem in relation to labels of origin within the EU. Strictly speaking, food labelling falls under EU competency rules, and the EU offers only limited protection that covers only traditional products from particular regions. The rules do not cover meat in general and do not apply to all the Member States.

Some British farmers have been attempting to persuade the large supermarkets to favour only British pork. This strategy has only had a limited success.

The pig industry in the UK has suffered a severe economic decline over the last ten years. The average number of pigs in the UK was 7.9 million in 2000, with a steady decline to 4.5 million in 2010.

Animal health and welfare considerations have had an impact on the economy of the pig industry. Since 1999, UK regulations have banned the use of stalls and tethers, which led to an increase in costs making the export of UK pork or bacon more difficult. The labelling of produce as British bacon covers bacon from pigs reared abroad. As a response the UK government, has co-operated with supermarkets to label pork and bacon products in a way that will assist UK consumers to purchase British produce. This has not been entirely successful, as higher costs have been a key determination in market choices. The EU regulatory arrangements that will come fully into force in 2013 may provide a solution – stricter standards and welfare requirements will arise from Council Directive 2001/88 EC, and Commission Directive 2001/193/EC amending Directive 91/630/EEC will lay down minimum standards for the protection of pigs including the ban on close-confinement stalls.

In assessing this sector, it is clear that it is a cyclical industry, highly susceptible to competitive pressures and external competition. The prices received by UK farmers seem to be inadequate and, although there has been some limited relief due to changes in the exchange rate with the euro, this has not stopped the general

---

22 See House of Commons Library, 'Broiler chickens and poultry meat, SN/SC/1386', London: House of Commons Library, 14 May 2012.

decline in pig-farming profitability by 40 per cent in the 2010/11 financial year. Higher cereal prices and feedstuffs have not been passed on to consumers.

Dairy

The UK is the third largest milk producer in the EU after Germany and France, making the UK the ninth largest producer in the world. Milk production amounts to 16.1 per cent of total UK agricultural production. This sector is worth £3.3 billion at market prices in 2011.[23] Despite market share, UK milk production has come under economic pressures. Since 1980, the UK dairy herd has declined at a steady rate of 43 per cent from 1980 to 2010. In 1980, there were 3.2 million cows, which fell to 1.8 million in 2010. Similarly, the number of registered dairy producers has fallen from 35,741 in 1995 to 15,716 in 2010. How has milk production managed to increase, especially from 2008?

The answer appears to be through an increase in the yield per cow. Statistical data from 1995 to 2005 shows that milk production has been increasing at a steady rate up until 2005. However, the average yield per cow has increased every year. Reductions in milk outputs during the same period have also been experienced in other European countries, but not in China, Pakistan, India, Brazil and New Zealand, where production has been increasing steadily.

There is little overseas trade in liquid milk but there is a vibrant trade in processed products. The UK imports remarkably small amounts of milk – in 2010, less than 1 per cent of the milk used in UK dairies was from overseas.

Increased milk yields per cow have significance in the priority that has to be given to disease control and the necessity to address animal health and welfare issues. The price of milk is an important part of the overall strategy. The decline of door-step deliveries (delivery to homes and residences) to only 5 per cent of sales has seen a significant rise with retail sales making up the remainder. The price marginal costs are a factor. Door-step delivery prices are an average of 57.7 pence per pint while retail sales are 36 pence. In terms of milk producers, the key issue is the farm-gate price for milk. Up until 2007 there had been a sharp decline in prices from around 25 pence per litre to 18 pence in 2007. Since then, the price has increased to an average price of around 25 pence per litre. It is arguable that pricing has had a marked impact on milk producers, with many farmers finding prices an incentive to return to dairy farming.

Bovine TB, badgers and policy making

bTB is discussed in Chapter 5. In the UK, the compulsory culling of infected cattle began in the 1930s. In the past, because milk was often unpasteurised,

---

23 On latest statistics in 2011, 51 per cent of milk processed in the UK was used for liquid milk; cheese amounted to 26 per cent and the remainder was used for milk powder and condensed milk; cream was 2 per cent, yoghurt 2 per cent; and other dairy produce amounted to 3 per cent.

milk-borne human *M. bovis* was a major public-health risk in humans and an important TB source. There were on average an annual 50,000 cases of human TB and an annual human death toll of 2,500 attributed to the disease. Various measures have been adopted to respond to the problem, including developing an effective vaccine, reducing cattle movements and reducing the badger population amongst badgers, regarded by many as being responsible for the spread of bTB.

The incidents of bTB are recorded by Defra on the basis of two systems. The first is the number of herds affected with at least one case of bTB, and the second is the number of animals slaughtered after a positive test. All cattle herds are regularly tested and the frequency of testing is based on the profile of the local disease. In 2010, there was a marked increase in new cases of bTB – 4,703 herds recorded with new cases of the disease – the second largest number of new herd incidents in a single year in the last decade. The regional distribution of the disease is highest in terms of the highest number of cases in Western England followed by Wales and Northern England. To date, Scotland has the lowest incidence of bTB among the five major regions.[24] The annual number of cattle slaughtered due to the disease is set out in Table 7.2.

Policy making in the context of legal challenges to badger culling

One of the most controversial areas is badger control[25] through badger culls. The previous government decided not to introduce a badger cull. The government conducted a UK Randomised Badger Culling Trial. The results were widely interpreted. The trial concluded that a reactive cull of badgers might cause a significant increase in bTB and a proactive cull might have only limited success in reducing bTB within the specific area but cause an increase in an adjoining area. In the case of the Welsh Assembly, the Randomised Badger Culling Trial was conducted in full. A proposed randomised Badger cull was stopped because of a successful challenge undertaken by the Badger Trust.[26] The Court of Appeal's decision arising out of the Welsh badger cull, in *Badger Trust v The Welsh Ministers*,[27] set an important precedent after finding that the proposed badger cull in Wales was illegal. The implications of the case included legal

---

24 The five regions are Wales, Scotland, Western England, Eastern England and Northern England. See House of Commons Library, 'Bovine TB statistics: Great Britain, SN 06081', London: House of Commons Library, 14 October 2011.

25 Jenkins, H., Woodroffe, R. and Donnely, C., 'The duration and effects of repeated widespread badger culling on cattle turberculosis following the cessation of culling' (2010) 5 *Plos One* 1. Wagner, W., 'The "bad science" fiction: reclaiming the debate over the role of science in public health and environmental regulation' (2003) 66 *Law and Contemporary Problems* 63.

26 See Bishop, P., 'Badgers and bovine tuberculosis: the relationship between law, policy and science' (2012) 24(1) *Journal of Environmental Law* 145–154.

27 *Badger Trust v The Welsh Ministers* [2010] EWCA Civ 807.

Table 7.2 Number of animals slaughtered as reactors to bTB

Date	England	Scotland	Wales	Great Britain
1998	4,102	73	774	4,949
1999	4,958	51	920	5,929
2000	6,029	58	986	7,073
2001	3,804	24	1,578	5,406
2002	15,482	178	4,305	19,965
2003	15,120	199	4,809	20,128
2004	15,093	200	4,682	19,975
2005	20,145	112	5,520	25,777
2006	14,585	169	5,241	19,995
2007	18,543	357	7,171	26,071
2008	26,038	432	10,542	37,012
2009	24,500	314	9,951	34,765
2010	24,213	145	7,321	31,679

observations on the mechanisms used for public consultation and policy making. Badgers are a protected species under section 1(1) of the Protection of Badgers Act 1992. The unauthorised killing of badgers is a criminal offence. However, the Tuberculosis Eradication (Wales) Order 2009, SI 2009/2614, provides the legal basis for any proposed badger cull. The Order is made under section 21 of the Animal Health Act 1981, which is the primary legislation. Section 1 of the 1981 Act gives ministers order-making powers where the ministers:

... think fit—
(a) generally for the better execution of this Act or for the purpose if in any manner preventing the spreading of disease ...

Section 21 of the Animal Health Act 1981 provides the criteria for the law-making powers exercised under section 1 of the Act. This is the critical section in terms of the decision made by the Court of Appeal. In particular, section 21(2) (b) requires that the minister, if satisfied in the case of any area:

(b) that destruction of wild members of that or those species in that area is necessary in order to eliminate, or *substantially reduce the incidence of, that disease in animals of any kind in the area* ... [emphasis added]

The Animal Health Act 1981 is compliant with Council Directive 77/391 EEC (May 1977), which provides that Member States may draw up schemes for the eradication of TB within their regions. Two issues arose in the Court of Appeal. First, under the 1981 Act, the minister designated that the badger cull would take place throughout Wales. The point was conceded by the minister in the appeal that this was without legal foundation and that the appropriate course of action would have been to designate specific regions within Wales where the badger cull was appropriate. This leaves open the question of whether within a small area of Wales the badger cull was legal and appropriate. The second issue is whether the Order made by the minister was justified in law. The test (set out in italics), is whether the evidence before the Court of Appeal amounted to showing that the badger cull would *substantially reduce the incidence of, that disease in animals of any kind in the area*. The main question was whether or not the Welsh Government had satisfied the test of *substantially reduce the incidence of* TB under section 21 of the Animal Health Act 1981.

The interpretation of whether the minister could satisfy the Court of Appeal that the badger cull would meet the criteria set out in the legislation is at the centre of the case. What does *substantially reduce the incidence of* TB mean? The factual and scientific evidence in favour of the badger cull had to convince the Court of Appeal that there was a sufficient potential to reduce bTB in cattle. The evidence had to be more than insignificant or trivial. In applying the scientific evidence, the Court of Appeal took the view that the scientific evidence had to justify the cull in terms of balancing the harm to badgers set against the benefit to cattle. Justification of the cull required both the application of a balancing test as well as the evidence showing that the a substantial reduction in bTB might be achieved. The Court of Appeal took very seriously that the harm to badgers might ultimately lead to the eradication of badgers and the species becoming extinct. Underpinning this approach is section 1(1) of the Protection of Badgers Act 1992, which provides a legal protection for badgers that cannot be lightly diminished as the unauthorised killing of badgers is a criminal offence. The Court of Appeal concluded that the minister had acted unlawfully in misinterpreting the meaning of section 21 of the Act.

A major influence in the Court of Appeal was a scientific finding accepted by both parties to the case, that the number of herds likely to protected by the badger cull is probably in the order of 9 per cent of the Welsh herd. That figure is a critical one in terms of assessing the likely outcome of a badger cull, which was not considered sufficient in terms of the 'substantial' reduction of disease.

The case has significant implications for the law on badger culls and policy making. First, unless the Animal Health Act 1981 is amended, the 'substantial merits test' will have to be applied. Unless there is stronger scientific evidence in favour of badger culls, then the judiciary will be reluctant to be persuaded that badger culls will meet the criteria set in the legislation. The strategy of badger culls over wide areas is also problematic. Small areas where the incidence of bTB is very high might be more easily brought within the terms of the legal requirements and be regarded as offering a substantial impact on bTB in cattle. There is also a broader question, not dealt with directly by the Court of Appeal, as to the current state of scientific evidence relating to badgers and the use of the mechanism of the cull as opposed to vaccination or other strategies. The need to balance the interests of the badger and the benefits of eradication of bTB is also an interesting part of the decision and one that might be addressed by risk assessment or proper pilot studies.

In Wales following the Court of Appeal decision, the Welsh Assembly undertook a badger vaccination policy.[28] This is in sharp contrast to England where, in December 2011, the Coalition Government decided to go ahead with a badger cull trial to be carried out in West Gloucestershire and Somerset. This has led to a number of challenges in the courts. The Badger Trust sought a judicial review. In the Administrative Court Mr Justice Ouseley considered a challenge by the Badger Trust arguing that the policy of a badger cull was not a rational operation of policy making, that the Secretary of State was acting outside her powers under section 10(2) of the Protection of Badger Acts 1992. The Badger Trust's main arguments were that the cull might risk spreading the disease beyond the cull zones and that this risk did not meet the strict legal test of 'preventing the spread of disease' under the Protection of Badgers Act 1992. The Trust also claimed that the costs of the cull had not been properly considered in the impact assessment and that the assessment was flawed. Interpreting the law required careful consideration of the available scientific evidence. Mr Justice Ouseley heard evidence from both Defra and the Badger Trust. The RSPCA was also permitted to provide evidence as an interlocutor. There are two striking features of the decision. The first is the way in which scientific evidence and debate informed the decision in the case, but did not determine the outcome. The outcome rested in the interpretation of the legislation including the main distinction between a cull as a trial mechanism to eradicate bTB rather than as a decided policy to be applied without the cull being considered a success or not. The second feature is the extent to which the judge reviewed the details of the main evidence relating to the impact assessment and the issue of costs. Attention was given to the continued threat of bTB, its high costs and also the failure of the current control programme involving the slaughter of 250,000 cattle in 2010/11 and the cost to tax payers of over £91 million.

Mr Justice Ouseley was clear in the way in which the law needed to be interpreted. Citing earlier decisions[29] involving the role of the courts when confronted with policy-making issues that are challenged on the basis of their legality, Mr Justice Ouseley followed the interpretation offered by Lord Diplock that the main question rested on the Secretary of State asking the 'right question' and ensuring that 'reasonable steps' were taken to ensure that the relevant information had been carefully considered. The conclusion reached was that the cull was legal and might be taken forward, Natural England had been given appropriate guidance under the terms of section 1(2) of the Natural Environment

---

28 House of Commons Library Standard Note: *TB vaccination of Badgers* SNSC6647 (28th November, 2012).

29 See *Secretary of State for Education and Science v Tameside MBC* [1977] AC 1014.

and Rural Communities Act 2006 and this resulted in the dismissal of the Badger Trust case.

On appeal to the Court of Appeal, Lords Justice Laws, Rimmer and Sullivan concluded that the proposed badger cull was legal and should go ahead.[30] The Court of Appeal rejected the appeal made by the Badger Trust and upheld the earlier decision by Mr Justice Ouseley, holding that the cull was legal. This result has left Natural England free to go ahead with the badger cull. Outside legal challenges there remains considerable opposition from many pressure groups against the cull. Its implementation is likely to continue to become a focus for protest and disruption. In the final analysis, the question is whether any cull will prove to be cost effective.

Policy-making scientific debate and badger culling

The scientific evidence that a badger cull is likely to be effective in controlling bTB in cattle is much contested. The NFU has lobbied strongly on behalf of its members for a cull, believing that this will result in disease control and protect the economic interests of farmers. There is also support from the British Veterinary Association, and the British Cattle Veterinary Association is in favour of the cull. The former regards any cull as part of a balanced package of measures for dealing with the reservoir of disease in the wildlife. Opposing the cull are the Badger Trust and the Wildlife Trust, the former is active in pursuing legal action against the government. Other organisations focus on the practicality of a cull and a humane method of culling has been discussed by the RSPCA. There are concerns that the shooting of badgers might prove unduly cruel and ineffective. Shooting badgers is likely to be difficult and, to be effective, the actual number of badgers in a specific location needs to be determined so that the necessary threshold of 70 per cent is reached. This is generally regarded to be the percentage required for the cull to be effective. There is scientific evidence that the cull in selected areas will increase the propensity of badgers to migrate to other areas and thus spread disease. Regional and national coordination will be required. There is also the need for regular culls to be undertaken to ensure that a reduction on the badger population is maintained.

The cost of carrying out the cull is estimated to be £562,000 at £1,000 km^2 per year. In addition to the badger cull, there are also a number of policy initiatives included within the TB Eradication Programme such as:

- cattle surveillance and control measures;
- good biosecurity in order to reduce the disease and the transmission between cattle and badges and badgers and cattle;

---

30 *R (on the application of the Badger Trust) v Secretary of State for the Environment* [2012] unreported.

- measures to tackle TB in non-bovine farmed species, such as alpaca and sheep;
- advice and support for farmers, and the development of monitoring and reporting arrangements;
- the development and use of an effective vaccination programme.

Many of the weaknesses highlighted in criticism of the cull have been considered by the government in its consultation documents. Public opinion has also been difficult to harness in favour of the cull and is likely to be influenced by the media and by the activity of pressure groups. Lord Krebs, who advised the original trial, considered that any cull might only result in a reduction of bTB incidence by 12–16 per cent over a nine-year period and is doubtful of the efficiency of the cull. Culls are intended to take place over a six-week period and result in a reduction of the badger population by 70 per cent. Inevitably, the co-operation of the farming community in the cull area is an essential part of the government's strategy. In the final analysis, the combination of stakeholders, the government and the various organisations must co-operate to ensure an effective policy. The legal analysis is also likely to be important in terms of process and consultation. The central issue in any legal challenges will involve the question of effectiveness and cost. The cost of compensation for bTB continues to rise, placing further pressure on developing an effective strategy.

Events in October 2012 have underlined the main challenges in this area of policy making. The Court of Appeal, having rejected the Badger Trust's challenge, provided the legal basis for implementing the badger cull in England. This has proved to be highly problematical. On 17 September 2012, a licence was issued for the cull to take place in the West Gloucester area, one of the two selected sites (the other being West Somerset). Farmers were required to undertake under the terms of the licence the costs of shooting badgers, while the government would take responsibility for licensing and monitoring the cull. The policy also includes biosecurity and monitoring measures. The cost of shooting has proved more complicated, as the original estimate of the number of badgers proved defective. Under the terms of the badger-cull licences, the aim is to achieve eradication of roughly 70 per cent of the badger population, if the cull is to be regarded as effective. Scientific discussion[31] has proved to be contentious amongst the wider scientific community. Professor Ian Boyd, Defra's Chief Scientific Officer, and Nigel Gibbons, the Chief Veterinary Officer, have argued in favour of the badger cull.[32] In mid-October 2012, Sir Patrick Bateson, President of the Zoological Society, together with a number of prominent scientists, wrote to leading newspapers[33] suggesting that the badger cull under current circumstances is likely to be ineffective. A group of 30 senior scientists wrote

---

31 Defra, *Badger Culling Pilots: Independent Expert Panel*, 18 October 2012.
32 'Letters to the editor', *Guardian*, 18 October 2012.
33 'Letters to the editor', *The Times*, 17 October 2012.

to the Sunday papers complaining that there is little scientific support for the cull and arguing that the original trial in 2007 showed the problems of making a badger cull effective.[34] An e-petition undertaken for the HM Government website attracted over 158,000 signatures by 18 October 2012. This triggered a backbench debate scheduled for 25 October 2012, resulting in a debate that approved the motion calling on the government to stop the cull and implement alternatives, such as a vaccination policy for both badgers and cattle. This was approved in the debate.

The Badger Trust also commenced fresh judicial review proceedings on 19 October 2012. Their claim was that there is an unlawful cull based on the failure by the government to conduct a sufficient cost-benefit analysis. The claim also asserted that the approach to the number of badgers to be taken in the cull is irrational. The Badger Trust lost their case and this has left the way clear for a badger cull in England.[35]

In contrast to the position in England, the Welsh Government has undertaken a badger vaccination project within a defined area.[36] This involves vaccinating badgers. The policy includes removing the sources of infection, including badgers, though testing, removing infected animals and increasing surveillance and biosecurity measures. This is the first major badger vaccination policy and the outcome of the policy remains to be evaluated. Implementation began from May 2012 and concluded in November 2012.[37] The second phase has begun and is being undertaken at present.

The EU has also been concerned about the control measures and has suggested improved biosecurity measures and also effective eradication measures.[38] This adds pressure on the UK to ensure the adequacy of testing and control measures. It remains to be seen whether or not the badger cull will be eventually implemented, given the public debate and issues about its effectiveness.[39] In the House of Commons on 23 October 2012, the government announced a postponement of the cull until 2013. There had been problems in starting the cull and the number of badgers found in the cull areas was greater than expected.

---

34   'Letters to the editor', *Observer*, 14 October 2012.
35   'Badger Trust considers further cull legal challenge', *Guardian*, 22 October 2012.
36   House of Commons Library, 'TB vaccination of Badgers SNSC6647', 28 November 2012.
37   Welsh Assembly Government, 'New Bovine TB Eradication proposals announced by Welsh Rural Affairs Minister', 20 September 2010. See *Bovine TB Eradication Programme IAA Badger Vaccination Project, Year 1 Report*, Cardiff: Welsh Government, 2013.
38   See EU Commission, *Final Report of an Audit Carried out in the United Kingdom from 5 to 16 September 2011 in order to evaluate the operation of the bovine tuberculosis eradication programme*, DG(SANCO) 2011-6057, March 2012.
39   House of Commons Library, 'Badger Culling, SNSC – 5873', London: House of Commons Library, 23 October 2012. See also Library Notes SNSC 6447 on TB Vaccination and SNCC 6801 on Bovine TB Statistics.

Sustainable future regulatory strategy

Economics and changing nature of the farming industry

Developing a sustainable regulatory strategy for animal health and welfare must be considered within the economic framework of farming, specifically farm income. However, the statistical data are often difficult to quantify and estimate for future strategic development. Farm incomes are considerably influenced by the volatile movement of sterling relative to the euro and, as Single Farm Payment is calculated in euros, this has a knock-on effect. There is also a knock-on effect of one sector of farming on another. For example, the high grain prices in 2010 and 2011 undoubtedly increased incomes of cereal farmers, whereas the impact of higher grain prices on livestock farming led to a reduction in the incomes of farmers who used grain for feed. Some sectors may experience reduced prices for their products, and dairy farmers have faced reduced incomes.

The past two decades have witnessed the farming industry adapting to many challenges. Disease outbreaks and demands on animal owners to improve animal health and welfare have added to costs. Environmental concerns have also led to improvements in standards and practices amongst farm owners. Higher costs on fuel, feed, fertilizer and electricity have also placed pressure on farming budgets. There has also been a gradual decline in farm holdings and farm numbers. Taken together, such pressures have resulted in the intensification of farming and farming methods. The pressure on production levels and demands for food and biosecurity all indicate that farming practices are likely to follow the industrial model of production. This includes streamlining costs and reducing overheads. The economies of scale allow farmers to increase output and achieve a lower cost for each unit of meat product or milk. The main result is likely to be upward pressure on farm production and this is likely to favour larger farms and consolidation of smaller ones. The impact in certain key sectors, such as milk and pork production, is noted above.

There is considerable support for the development of super farms. There are recent examples from applications in Nocton, Lincolnshire for 8,000 dairy cows and a 25,000 indoor sow units at Foston in Derbyshire. In England, a permit is needed if livestock capacity exceeds certain specified limits.[40]

The development of super farms raises many issues in terms of the governance of animal health and welfare issues. There is opposition to large farms from organisations such as the World Society for the Protection of Animals. The main general concerns are local environmental issues in terms of pollution control, and planning and consumer decisions for local communities are also relevant.

Specific concerns are about the concentration of a large number of animals at one site. Waste and its disposal as well as the impacts of slurry and manure in

---

40 Currently, 750 sows, 200 production pigs over 30kg, 40,000 poultry including pullets, turkeys, ducks and guinea fowl.

terms of odours are issues that will have to be addressed. Related environmental issues in terms of the generation of greenhouse gases (GHGs) (methane, carbon dioxide and nitrous oxide) must be addressed. The decrease in livestock numbers between 1990 and 2007 resulted in some significant GHG reductions, but this may change with the fact that the increase in intensified farming may raise emissions. The operation of intensive farming may provide an opportunity to address the problems of emissions. This may be facilitated by the larger farms if appropriate steps are adopted.

Animal welfare issues arise with indoor housing and this may result in some benefits. The benefits are to provide a single organisation, modern facilities, specialist advice and greater biosecurity that may provide higher standards of animal health and welfare compared with smaller units. There is also a good opportunity to provide cost-sharing arrangements, which would facilitate financial assistance from stakeholders in order to provide high standards. However, there is a question as to whether or not intensified large farms might increase disease risk and thereby threaten food supplies.

Significance of the CAP

There are reforms to the CAP to take effect in 2014.[41] This is an important date because it is when the new entrant Member States will become full members of the CAP. The CAP budget is to be frozen at around £47 billion a year. A new framework is proposed to take account of the 27 Member States.

Future strategy must take account of the close links between pricing, milk production, competition and farming policy. The CAP has an important effect on this sector especially in terms of competition policy. Milk quotas are still in force in the EU and the 2008 CAP Health Check remains in place until April 2015. The dairy sector is vulnerable to trade liberalisation, especially for milk products in terms of cheese and butter. This is also the case for trade liberalisation and competition from Brazil and Argentina which relies on the EU to provide protection against full access from competitors outside the EU. The beef sector has also been vulnerable to the CAP reform from 2003 with the introduction of the Single Farm Payment replacing the previous beef suckler payment regime. The Environment, Food and Rural Affairs Committee report *Proposals for the Dairy Sector and the Future of the Dairy Industry* (July 2011) explains that the changes will have enormous significance for future policy making. There are a number of strands to the new policy. Market management schemes are built into the new proposals, including risk management and a more holistic approach to the food chain and its organisation. Climate change is given importance as is the promotion of ecosystems, as well as education and poverty reduction. The aim is that 25 per cent of the rural development envelope will be devoted to

---

41 See EU Commission, *The Common Agricultural Policy after 2013*, Brussels: EU Commission, 2012.

agri-environmental schemes. Monitoring and compliance will be increased with regular four-yearly reports. Framing future animal health and welfare policy making will need to adapt to changes in the CAP.

Significance of supermarkets

The role of supermarkets is often the determining factor in the economy of farming. Supermarkets are important stakeholders in the rural economy. In April 2008, the Competition Commission concluded its final report and recommendations on the grocery sector. The Coalition Government in its Programme for Government, in May 2010 proposed that an Ombudsman might be introduced in the Office of Fair Trading to advance the Grocery Supply Code of Practice recommended by the Competition Commission report. The Grocery Supply Code of Practice set out a number of elements that apply to corporate groups within the UK retail grocery sector with a turnover in excess of £1 billion per year. Retailers are obliged to sign up to a fair dealing provision that includes a number of agreements. The Competition Commission published a draft Order for consultation in February 2009, further strengthening the Groceries Supply Code of Practice. Since then many retailers rejected the idea of a statutory code. Despite this rejection the Coalition Government has taken forward the idea of an Ombudsman with specific statutory powers.

Lastly, there is the overall question of consumer choice and behaviour. There are severe financial pressures especially in the current economic climate to keep food prices low. This leaves the question of how to pay for high standards of food hygiene and the costs of improved animal health and welfare. Consumers might be willing to pay for high quality standards but their ability to pay may be seriously in doubt. This raises doubts over policy making in this area.

Cost-sharing responsibility and insurance: regulatory lessons

We see in Chapter 6 how cost sharing has developed as a policy driver in the future regulation of animal health and welfare. Value for money is also linked to obtaining good value for the money spent. How the strategy can be judged value for money is more difficult to calibrate in its early 'phased in' period. Efficiency, if measured in terms of short-term economy and effectiveness may be very differently judged if evaluated on longer-term goals. It is also unclear how value for money is going to be always compatible with animal health and welfare. Longer-term capital investments may prove more efficient and effective than a short-term fix. It is impossible to predict the next farming disease crisis. Indeed the current bTB in cattle may be so expensive to eradicate that it would be more effective to import milk and dairy produce on one calculation, but less effective if the need is to preserve a capability for the animal industry as a whole. The better approach would have been to calibrate the cost sharing and responsibility concept in terms of what is sustainable. Sustainability provides an acceptance of the role of the market (a key issue in who pays) but calculates many additional issues, such as green farming that is less harmful to the environment, but also the link between investing in animal welfare as a way of promoting animal health.[42]

The adoption of a really responsive approach to risk regulation is favourably disposed to cost sharing. The cost and responsibility equation allows for shifts in the allocation of different relationships over time. Conditions vary as does the likelihood of disease, and a variety of flexible options are needed. Partnerships may be favoured but at other times co-regulation and the shifts in costs from the public to the private purse need to be adaptive. Incentives as well as penalties are important and, as prevention is better than cure in many instances, knowing what to do and finding out the correct information is vitally important. Vaccination strategies may be the most effective, but the cost and take up variable. There are also many unknown dynamics of regulation that need to be factored into the analysis of how best to regulate. Behavioural changes amongst farmers and the variations in the rates of diseases and their prevalence are also required. Sustainability strategies must be advanced with value for money as a guiding principle, but there is a need to have a fresh start from previous attempts to engage in the regulation of the industry. Transparency is a much needed quality, but correct and independently variable risk assessment is critical to the success of a cost-sharing and responsibility strategy. The future is also one where the EU strategy must be considered in terms of variables in policy making in this area. Public confidence must be set ahead of lobbying groups and vested interests amongst stakeholders.

There is also the insurance principle.[43] There are good reasons to think that insurance offers a number of important advantages to the cost-sharing endeavour – it provides a useful method of contribution, engages with different stakeholders and allows advantageous premiums that encourage good practices over bad ones. It also links together some of the existing cultural norms that affect the industry at present, namely that in all but name the public purse has supported a public insurance in the various compensation schemes for many animal keepers. If the insurance principle is negotiated with the insurance industry through a phased use of public underwriting, the catalyst for change might be introduced consistent with a sustainable farming industry.[44]

It is clear that the use of cost sharing and responsibility offers an important regulatory mechanism in the area of animal health and welfare. This is an important achievement and intended to link costs and responsibility sharing to animal health and welfare. We saw in Chapter 2 how, in the past, animal health and

---

42 *ENDS Report 430*, November 2010, p. 6, and also in evidence to the Environmental Audit Committee.

43 Generally, see England Advisory Group on Responsibility and Cost Sharing, *Responsibility and Cost Sharing for Animal Health and Welfare: Final Report*, London: Defra, December 2010, section 5, p. 63.

44 Ibid., para 5.33, p. 71.

welfare has not been well considered or adequately addressed. The economic dimension has made animal health a high priority but this is generally not as clearly evident when it comes to welfare. The needs of a robust regulatory structure should, however, be placed in the context of how regulation is currently perceived by government and regarded by various stakeholders and commentators.

The primary focus is to ensure that the various stakeholders work more effectively *together* and that there is a clear and transparent understanding of costs and benefits of animal health and welfare. Coordination is therefore essential, as is the co-operation between the competing interest groups and stakeholders. There are opportunities for market competition in respect of the EU legal framework for trade in live animals and animal products, with the aim of establishing a single market in animals and animal products. This is consistent with achieving public health and food safety as part of the rationale to promote animal health. The economic consequences of disease and its control contribute to the need to achieve a harmonised system of animal health measures, disease surveillance, diagnosis and control. Setting targets and monitoring standards are therefore envisaged as essential prerequisites for the successful functioning of the market economy. Without checks and balances, the market economy can be destructive, as recent events in financial services sector have shown. Monitoring and enforcement strategies are also a key part of any regulatory activities. There is a need for Defra as a public body to provide resources, communication and expertise that engages with the private sector. It is fundamental to good regulation that the following issues are settled: setting clear roles and responsibilities; achieving partnership between stakeholders; and ensuring that prevention is integral to the benefits of animal health and welfare, which also includes ensuring effective delivery and enforcement of animal health and welfare standards.

Animal health and welfare sets specific challenges for regulation and policy making. The farming industry comprises large and small operators. There are professional services such as Animal Health (formerly the SVS) and private vets. Already mentioned above is the role of supermarkets, and the range of regulation must take account of their role and the opportunity they may provide to engage with animal health and welfare, while defraying costs from the public to the private sector.[45] There is also a strong culture of subsidy and preferential treatment of agriculture. This has its roots in the Second World War, but this agricultural 'exceptionalism' has been eroded as new policy emphases have taken hold. It is essential that any regulatory preference should engage with the wide range of specialisms that cover the agricultural sector, including areas such as disease control, food quality and environmental matters.

---

45 Gunningham, N., 'Enforcing environmental regulation' (2011) *Journal of Environmental Law* 169.

Conclusion: risk-based regulation

Responsibility and cost sharing provides a basis for sharing the costs of compensating farmers for animals/products that are compulsorily destroyed where there is a notifiable disease outbreak. The main factors that may influence the future disease threat must be considered. Prevention and the necessary surveillance must ensure that the early signs of disease are noted and steps taken to address the problem. This raises issues about who pays, including policy issues related to insurance and the willingness of government to encourage cost sharing. This will also require biosecurity issues to be addressed and responsibility of animal owners encouraged. A pivotal role is to be played by the veterinarian profession, and the recently published report by Philip Lowe is largely supportive of this approach.[46] The sustainability of farmed animals must also be addressed in the context of new challenges in terms of climate change, which is one of the most pressing challenges.[47] This is likely to result in the emergence of new diseases in new locations and new transmission methods. The likely increase in vector borne diseases and parasites will set new challenges in identifying and taking steps to address new diseases. Additionally, climate change must be addressed through measures to reduce agricultural sourced pollution. Developing an appropriate strategy requires a pluralist legal strategy. Legal instruments that combine flexibility and incentives are required, with a mix of adaptation and mitigation. Policy making for the future, specifically reform of the CAP post-2013, needs to address the problem through cross-compliance conditions to farm subsidies and the inclusion of climate change considerations in the development of animal health and welfare strategies. Carbon stores and policy making that sets targets for the agricultural sector are required. Currently, the agricultural sector contributes only 7 per cent to UK GHG emissions (nitrous oxide 54 per cent and methane 38 per cent, whereas CO_2 amounts to only 8 per cent).

The EU role in terms of expansion and harmonisation is in the direction of setting a simplified framework in which there is greater convergence in international standards. CAP reform must also be considered in terms of future policy and strategy. The integration of CAP reform to animal health and welfare strategy is important. A new Basic Payment Scheme will replace the existing Single Payment Scheme. The new scheme will be subject to 'cross compliance' respecting certain common standards including animal health and welfare, and also environmental rules. There will also be specific greening measures.

The future question is how best to adopt suitable regulatory strategies. Clearly, an interdisciplinary strategy is needed from the analysis offered above. As we saw in Chapter 2, different regulatory strategies have been used and analysed in

---

46   Lowe, P., *Unlocking Potential: A report on veterinary expertise in animal production*, London: Defra, 2009.
47   Rodger, C., Franks, J. and Lowe, P., 'Editorial: implementing climate change policy for agriculture – what role for the law?' (2011) *Environmental Law Review* 245.

the past. In the aftermath of the financial crisis[48] in 2008, there is some scepticism about their effectiveness. The UK risk-based regulation[49] accepted in the Hampton Report[50] and used quite widely has become intermeshed with the Coalition Government's policy of reducing regulatory burdens. In that context, risk-based and responsive regulatory strategies have become generally accepted as a means of implementing policy while taking account of excessive costs. Responsive regulation has become an important part of future strategy, but this has also become more flexibly interpreted resulting in a combination of measures and strategies. It is clear that evaluating the most suitable strategy is difficult when attempting to decide on what might work best. There are a number of tentative conclusions. The experience of financial regulation has shown that, while rules and deterrence can change the culture of an organisation, they do not necessarily prove to be most effective. Organisations have a habit of developing a culture of regulatory resistance which can prove to be counter-productive. There is also some evidence that the perception of regulation and its application may prove the most effective. Gunningham observes:

> Risk based regulation has the attraction of enabling regulators to prioritise their regulatory efforts and to maximise cost effectiveness. Nevertheless a number of serious challenges confront the risk based strategy – above and beyond the degree of sophistication of the risk assessment and quality of information on which the assessment and management of risk can be based.[51]

Designing and implementing a future regulatory strategy will require taking account of a diversity of experiences and practices. The analysis offered here is that just as animal health and welfare must embrace the governance of animal diseases, the governance of diseases relates to the suitability of particular contexts. This includes different sectoral needs, variations in regulatory drivers – such

---

48 National Audit Office and Comptroller and Auditor General, *HM Treasury: Maintaining the financial stability of UK banks: update on the support schemes*, HC 676, Session 2010–2011, London: NAO, 2010. National Audit Office and Comptroller and Auditor General, *HM Treasury: Stewardship of the wholly-owned banks: buy back of subordinated debt*, HC 706, Session 2010–2011, London: NAO, 2011.

49 Black, J., 'Tensions in the regulatory state' (2007) *Public Law* 58. McEldowney, J.F., 'Managing financial risk: the precautionary principle and protecting the public interest in the UK' in Labrosse, J.R., Olivares-Caminal, R. and Singh, D. (eds), *Risk and the Banking Crisis*, Cheltenham: Edward Elgar, 2011. McEldowney, J.F., 'Defining the public interest: public law perspectives on regulating the financial crisis' in Labrosse, J.R., Olivares-Caminal, R. and Singh, D. (eds), *Financial Crisis Management and Bank Resolution*, Abingdon: Informa, 2009, pp. 103–132.

50 Hampton, P., *Reducing Administrative Burdens: Effective Inspection and Enforcement Final Report*, London: HM Treasury, 2005.

51 Gunningham, op. cit., n. 44.

as economic, social and welfare considerations including the CAP – and also the significance of climate change to animal health and welfare.[52]

There are also practical realities of attempting to develop best practice in the sector. There is a tension between developing effective regulation while maintaining a legitimacy of purpose. There are high political risks when the next disease outbreak occurs of regulation and/or best practice not being effective and public opinion having to be addressed. There is also the sensitivity of the farming community and the voice of pressure groups. Compromise and flexibility are needed when policy making and future regulatory strategy is considered. The recent badger-cull debate has underlined the challenges of implementing effective policy making in this area amidst public debate and scientific uncertainty.[53]

52 House of Commons Library, 'Agriculture and climate change, SN/SC/3763', London: House of Commons Library, 26 January 2012. See also the climate change page on the Defra website, www.defra.gov.uk/environment/climate (accessed 27 March 2013).
53 See House of Commons Library Standard Note: Badger Culling: Policy to 2008 SN/SC/3751 (15 February 2011).

8 Conclusions

Animal health and welfare for the twenty-first century

Introduction

This study of the governance of disease in farmed livestock coincides with a period of increasing interest in the livestock industry and its importance in the everyday life in Britain. The agri-food sector accounts for 7.1 per cent of the business sector and 14 per cent of national employment. There is growing consumer spending[1] on food, and heightened concerns about raising food prices – a major factor in inflation – are also related to climate change and pressures on the food supply. This has been highlighted by the Government's Chief Scientist's *Global Food and Farming Futures Foresight Projects* that identify UK farming as vulnerable to global markets and economic circumstances.

Outbreaks of animal disease have a number of diverse social, biological, environmental, economic and legal impacts. Increased reliance on livestock especially in the UK comes during a period of heightened threat of exotic disease. Bluetongue and the Schmallengberg virus are examples of diseases, that, although not commonly seen in the UK, illustrate the changing nature of disease threats. In the case of bluetongue in sheep and cattle, during 2007, the government worked closely with the farming community and developed successful control strategies for the disease. Engaging with the key stakeholders at an early stage provided the government with an understanding of how to communicate and best address the disease. Co-operation with the veterinary profession and engagement with stakeholders, including supermarkets and the public, helped to create a strategy that included a vaccination delivery plan for dealing with outbreaks. However, endemic disease remains a more important limitation to production, and there has been relatively little change in understanding or variation in approach.

We suggest that the way in which animal diseases are categorised as endemic or exotic can lead to inconsistency and incoherence in how diseases are managed and how responsibilities are allocated. The classification of disease as eliminated,

---

1 Defra, *Progress towards a Sustainable Future for Livestock farming*, London: Defra, April, 2012. Figures suggest increasing consumer spending on food.

exotic or endemic, especially for economically significant diseases, is complex and more quantitative than qualitative. It also may give rise to legal implications in terms of controls and procedures. A disease may be classified from (at a minimum) epidemiological, political, policy, legal and economic perspectives. Moreover, the classification may be limited in time, location,[2] species, strain, managed versus wild populations, etc. Social scientific (e.g. legal, policy, political and economic) classification may further need to distinguish between reality, an assessment based on sufficient validated evidence, and/or beliefs and expectations (which themselves vary in incidence and prevalence).

Zoonotic diseases are particularly challenging as the disease pathways for the varied pathogens involved are highly complex and hard to contain for policy makers. Contemporary approaches on how each animal disease is considered are often self-reinforcing and historically derived, making changes difficult to implement and manage, and the current situation difficult to escape. This may result in considerable variation in how farmers are held responsible for the overall health and welfare of animals and can have considerable impact on their livelihoods. Prioritisation of livestock diseases requires careful consideration of sometimes competing needs. These include the need to protect public health and the protection and promotion of the welfare of animals as well as the protection of the general interests of the wider economy, environment and society. Diseases that are transmissible between animals and humans, such as salmonella from poultry or *Campylobacter* from pigs, are a serious threat to public health.

Valuable lessons on how to manage outbreaks of disease may come from an understanding of previous outbreaks, and learning from the past should become an important priority for government in ensuring that basic knowledge and information is effectively used. Communication of complex information and uncertainty about risk is challenging but essential to ensure public confidence and government policy. Media attention given to information can prove particularly problematic for government, stakeholders and policy makers. The culling of badgers to reduce bTB in cattle in England may lead to considerable polarisation of public opinion and litigation. Contested scientific data may act against the public's acceptance of expert evidence. In contrast in Wales, it is proposed to vaccinate badgers on a trial basis. The differences in policy making in England and Wales in the example of bTB serves to underline the significance of devolution in the UK. This has the potential of opening up opportunities for policy experiments and policy learning. It may also add to the complexity of the decision-making process, making it more complex. Competing claims made about science underlying policy decision making in different jurisdictions may well serve to question the role of government, and its impartiality and credibility may be lost. A particular challenge to any framework is the heterogeneity between farmers in terms of their experience of a disease and its impact. If a disease is controlled, it is clear that farmers without the disease in their herd have competitive

---

2 Market segment, geographical or political region, epidemiological area, etc.

advantages and those who remove the disease will enjoy economic benefits. Other farmers will also benefit from a reduced risk of moving infection into their herd. Total elimination of disease is not always possible, leaving farmers with the potential risk for the re-introduction of the disease from the meta-herd, i.e. the national herd.

Combining sciences: law, science, policy and economics of animal health and welfare

As outlined in Chapter 2, legislative initiatives to address animal health and welfare issues have progressed significantly from the eighteenth and nineteenth centuries. Legislation provides a rapidly changing framework that must take account of developments in disease control and scientific knowledge. Animal health and welfare have become more intertwined, although this has been a struggle, and the balance between animal health and welfare is often under strain. In fact, the appropriate approach is to ensure that health and welfare issues are integral in policy making as a whole. Economic considerations, as well as philosophical and cultural attitudes are much in evidence. The law is diffuse, complicated and often subject to policy makers' action responding to the spotlight of rival interests – the consumer, the animal keeper, the veterinarian, the supermarket and the government – to name but a few. Gary Francione,[3] a famous American academic, is sceptical about how effective legal welfarism might be when applied to animals, as the human/animal conflict is too readily resolved in favour of human interest.

The legal framework is entirely a compromise filled with contradictions and often defined in practice by economic and political realities. Conor Gearty[4] questions how the obsession about human mastery and individual property rights so entrenched in western society can be overcome for animals to be properly treated. Philosophers have struggled to find an adequate conceptualisation of universal collective values over individual rights. Legal protection has often stopped short of a fully integrated approach between animal health and welfare. Stepping outside the discipline of law and political science, it might be possible to find common cause with a more sociological approach. From this perspective, animal health and welfare is intrinsically bound up by the climate change debate. This provides a useful link from man to nature and from nature to animals. Human rights and environmental protection come together to provide a common platform where unspoilt natural resources are considered in the context of sustainable development and environmental justice. This has a promising ability to link the protection of animal health and welfare even more closely together.

3 Francoine, G., *The Animal Rights Debate: Abolition or Regulation?*, New York, NY: Columbia University Press, 2010.
4 Gearty, C., 'Can animals have "human rights" too?', LSE Working Paper Series, London: London School of Economics, January 2008.

Sceptics may find this too optimistic and prefer to consider the governance of animal health and welfare as the main focus of their concerns outside the parameters of philosophical and sociological analysis.

Scientific research informs this study but the science is framed in terms of the economic, political and legal implications of policies and regulation. The collaborative nature of the research and its interdisciplinary nature provides a challenging environment for the development of a shared methodology and approach.

An important aspect of the approach taken in the book is to consider as a case study how researchers drawn from different specialist disciplines in the social sciences as well as from the biological sciences should engage. The work has helped to identify the challenges facing interdisciplinary research and how such research is best undertaken. There are also benefits in framing research questions in a more comprehensive way when considered from an interdisciplinary perspective, allowing a more comprehensive approach than would otherwise be the case. Different disciplines have their own subject loyalties that find expression in the way their findings are approached. Providing coherent engagement between different specialisms requires identification of key issues, discussion of collaborative efforts and recording of findings in a way that is transferable between disciplines. Effective collaboration is essential at a time when policy makers are engaged in an extensive consideration of how best to regulate animal health and welfare.

The biggest benefit of the interdisciplinary approach is that the problems that can be considered are not constrained by disciplinary boundaries. Indeed, different disciplines must first argue and agree what the problems actually are, and it is this process that results in a broader understanding of the issue. It is far more likely that the problem is framed in a way that it addresses the real world if there have been many disciplines involved in the discussion. The resulting understanding of the problem will develop questions that no single discipline can answer on its own. This is not a moot point, because answering a well-framed question is far more likely to be a real-world solution. The alternative is that each discipline develops its own version of the problem, and questions it can answer, the solution to which is a set of further discipline-nested problems and questions.

In a broad sense, the contributions in the book fit the socio-legal framework that is characterised as the law in context approach. Instead of exclusively studying law and legal rules, materials and writing as an autonomous system, the law in context approach examines the way law and lawyers work in specific social, economic or scientific contexts. Developing research that seeks to understand animal health and welfare from the perspective of all the disciplines provides an opportunity to integrate socio-political, economic, scientific and legal thinking. This encourages co-operation but also *highlights* the strengths and weaknesses of any collaboration and of making policy. The study also provides a model of how to interpret complex, integrated research outcomes and how to evaluate what has been achieved as well as raising future possibilities.

How do science, law and policy interrelate? The book has offered a case study of animal health and welfare which covers government policy, the role of regulation and the science base for the eradication of various animal diseases. Within the policy and legislative constraints, the role of farmers, veterinarians and ministers as well as civil servants has been examined. A study of the governance of animal disease, how diseases are currently managed and how management has arisen – including action taken by the individual farmer and how the government intervenes through regulatory legislation – are essential for understanding the integration of science in policy and strategy making, which involves coordination of the assessment of success and failure of disease outcomes and the idea of disease elimination being seen as a public good.[5] The methodology used in the book addresses the broader analytically and more policy focused approach favoured by social scientists and will help scientists to recognise how they must engage with the policy implications of their findings. As Philip Lowe and others have noted, in general there is a need to 'recalibrate' the instruments that have emerged as part of the European agri-environmental policy.[6] By adopting broad perspectives that collaborate across disciplines, a common methodology is considered. The various scientific strategies for the control of infectious diseases are studied. The study of the governance of animal disease shows how diseases are currently managed and how management has arisen, including action taken by the individual farmer and how the government may intervene through regulatory legislation. This requires coordination of success and failure and the idea of disease elimination results in a public good.[7] These issues have been considered in the findings of the research.

In the context of animal disease, one of our central contentions may be summarised as follows: that livestock pathogens can be analysed in both their socioeconomic and epidemiological environment. Given that both natural and social processes are at work and interact with each other, we constructed a classification of cattle diseases combining political and epidemiological dimensions.[8] This can be considered as a dynamic system and could serve as part of a policy toolkit contributing to the development of decision making, facilitating interventions that are proportionate and governance that is appropriate to each pathogen. Such a methodology offers a theoretical and empirical application of the interdisciplinary approach, yielding results that could not be obtained by a discipline working on its own.

5   See the Farm Animal Welfare Council website, www.fawc.org.uk. Brambell, F.W.R., *Report of the Technical Committee to Enquire into the Welfare of Animals kept under Intensive Livestock Husbandry Systems*, December 1965, London: HMSO, 1965.
6   Rodger, C., Franks, J. and Lowe, P., 'Editorial: implementing climate change policy for agriculture – what role for the law?' (2011) *Environmental Law Review* 245.
7   See n. 5.
8   See Carslake, D., Grant, W., Green, L.E., Cave, J., Greaves, J., Keeling, M., McEldowney, J., Weldgebriel, J.H. and Medley, G.F., 'Endemic cattle diseases: comparative epidemiology and governance' (2011) 366 (1573) *Philosophical Transactions of the Royal Society B* 1933–1942.

Understanding and assessing the risk management of animal health and welfare

The epidemiology of endemic disease is determined by biological, social and economically motivated processes that operate at different levels. This has a number of aspects. The risk of infection is determined by the prevalence of infection in the herds or premises to which the animal belongs throughout its life. In an individual herd, the pattern of infection is determined by contamination of the herd premises and transfer of infection between farms especially through animal movements. This has consequences within the meta-herd. It is clear that some diseases such as BVD must move between herds to persist since their biological characteristics mean that they will naturally fade out in all but the larger herds. There are other diseases that can persist in the smallest of herds and are transported from herd to herd through movements of infected animals.

Many influences on control of diseases currently operate at the herd level by the individual farmers. Information about disease flows in networks through the influences of veterinary advice, other farmers and the government. Individual farmers make choices that are determined by the technical ability to diagnose, treat and vaccinate, often combined with perceived potential commercial and welfare consequences of the disease. There are many ways in which individual farmers may lead to changes at the meta-herd level, including vaccination, that may have beneficial implications. It is also possible that there may be detrimental effects such as selling infected animals to other herds or materially affecting their productivity.

It is clear that farmers without the disease in their herd have competitive advantages over other farmers. Removing disease will also result in economic benefit but will also benefit other farmers from a reduced risk of moving infection in their own herd. This may lead to a free-rider effect, namely that some farmers by doing nothing receive benefits from the actions of others without bearing the costs of controls.

Disease threats are always present, and it is unrealistic not to realise this. Even where farmers eliminate disease from their herd, there will always be the possibility of reintroduction from the meta-herd requiring a concerted effort at prevention and control. Uncertainty in agriculture may lead to inappropriate risk transfer and hedging of risks. The unplanned actions of one farmer may lead to uncertainty and cause farmers to take unnecessary preventative actions. This goes against the efficient allocation of resources and effective use of resources.

Regulating animal health and welfare

In Chapters 6 and 7 we evaluated the role of cost sharing and responsibility sharing as it fits a strategy to develop a regulatory system suited to animal health and welfare issues. It also takes account of the current economic climate. Our conclusions are that good governance regulation based on needs and effectiveness derives from the allocation of responsibilities and costs. This offers economic and legal mechanisms to encourage dialogue between stakeholders linked to animal health and welfare strategies, with the potential for private and public sectors to co-operate in a sustainable approach to regulating risk. As we explained, our research considers the principles of more effective regulation including taking decisions closely related to fact finding; transparency and fairness; minimisation of costs and market distortions; and proportionality in decision making.[9] Cost sharing is a form of co-regulation consistent with the strategy of moving costs from the public onto the private sector. This will help sustain the shift from Defra's long experience as broadly a 'publicly' supported insurance provider for animal health and welfare to one that is firmly formulated with stakeholders, including the private and public sectors working together. This will also assist the operation of informal working groups, strategy groups and individual consultation arrangements, as mutual and beneficial interests may combine. There is considerable merit in Julia Black's suggestion that regulators need to observe, adapt and engage in self-critical learning that engages with the regulatory problem and changing social and political environment.[10]

The setting up of the AHWB is likely to allow Defra to combine its role as a government department developing and implementing policy with its role as a broker between business and government. This is likely to require considerable robustness in the way the AHWB performs its role, in relation to responsibility, powers and duties. The model of containing a regulatory structure within Defra also marks a shift in the regulatory State. Shifting regulatory responsibilities within the relevant government department is likely to create a different regulatory culture than an external, independent and statutory-based formulation of regulation which has been the custom of the regulatory structures in the UK, post-privatisation in the 1980s.[11] This form of regulation is intended to be collaborative, engage with stakeholders and provide an interconnection between government, private and public sectors as well as the market. Instead of seeing regulation as a delegated form of government activity, the aim is to encourage contracts and market-led solutions that avoid red tape and unnecessary regulation as part of the complex interrelationship between stakeholders. All this is highly ambitious and it remains to be seen whether or not it will be effective. A key issue will be the question of accountability and whether or not there is sufficient transparency and oversight.

It is clear that animal health and welfare has, in the past, not been well considered or adequately addressed. Cost and responsibility sharing offers a co-regulation strategy that connects private and public sectors. Lessons from the PFI and

---

9 Defra Consultation Paper (2007). The Consultation Paper is part of a strategy set out by Defra in *The Animal Health and Welfare Strategy for Great Britain*, London: Defra, 2004.

10 See Julia Black, 'Paradoxes and failures: "new governance" techniques and the financial crisis' (2012) 75(6) *Modern Law Review* 1037–1063, p. 1062

11 See Oliver, D., Prosser, T. and Rawlings, R. (eds), *The Regulatory State*, Oxford: Oxford University Press, 2010.

existing forms of co-regulation must be taken into account. Sharing costs also means shifting levels of responsibility including information competences, objectives and responses. More examination is required of how this form of co-regulation will meet animal health and welfare demands. The regulatory style and design of the various regulatory instruments to be established by the AHWB must be mapped out in full. This should take account of the general historical context of the role of the state in the regulation of business and society. Addressing the history of past attempts to regulate animal health and welfare is the primary challenge facing the new body. This includes adopting the most appropriate regulatory strategy to take account of risk-based regulation and the precautionary principle discussed in Chapter 7. It is important to understand how future policy strategy might be best shaped by acceding to a hybrid approach to regulation drawing on different types of regulation. Finding the best mix of regulation will ensure that the need for flexibility is met. Really responsive regulation provides a sufficiently adaptable and nuanced approach within a framework that is both flexible and sufficiently robust to address the needs of enforcement and compliance. Placing emphasis on enforcement and compliance gives really responsive regulation the appropriate framework for evaluation, in order to take forward and improve animal health and welfare strategies.[12] In addition to the regulatory arrangements, there is a need to ensure that regulating animal health and welfare embraces risk assessment and various levels of safety linked to the precautionary principle. This includes policy making that engages with both experts and public opinion, decision making at national and European levels, stakeholder participation and the inclusion of economic and legal regulatory instruments. These are high ideals, given the current state of public finances and doubts about the viability of the eurozone economies. This may cast general doubts over the ambition of the decision making at the European level. Cost-sharing principles must be analysed and assessed in the context of ownership of policy making.

In Chapter 5 we considered steps necessary to address the main animal diseases, including bluetongue, FMD, bTB and BVD. There are also issues arising out of the eradication of BSE in cattle. Exotic and endemic diseases; disease prevention, preparedness and control; animal health and welfare and policy delivery were examined. Biosecurity and compliance as well as the implementation of risk assessment strategies were also addressed. The increasing need for certification and control of exports and import border controls were also considered. Sharing information and data is also increasingly important, as is co-operation within the EU. Surveillance and monitoring are also important as is disease control. There are wider EU and international regulatory requirements that need to be addressed, and setting a balance on proportionate responses must

12   Ibid.

be achieved. The recent experience of the farm assurance schemes is illustrative of the problems of implementation strategy and the challenges of introducing new economic instruments in farming.

Policy making and future strategy: animal health and welfare

Policy makers must address animal health and welfare issues from the perspective of the limited resources available between both public and private sectors for the prevention, eradication and management of diseases. The process of prioritisation must take account of the varied impacts of disease on animal health and welfare, as well as the broader environment and human health. Establishing the rationale about aims and objectives is important, not least because of the different levels of government that are relevant. The main focus of the book is on animal health and welfare in England, although throughout the book, there are relevant references to Wales, Scotland and Northern Ireland. It is clear that animal diseases do not recognise geographical or constitutional boundaries, and the creation of Devolved Administrations outside England requires close collaboration at both policy making and implementation levels. Northern Ireland's land border with the Irish Republic makes the development of policy within Northern Ireland particularly challenging. The challenge will be to operate at all levels of government with sufficient effectiveness to ensure that best practice is agreed and implemented throughout the UK and also the EU. What should be the principal characteristics of a governance framework that is able to cope both with existing disease challenges and with new ones as they emerge? Clearly, it must be sufficiently flexible to respond to unanticipated challenges, but flexibility depends on other conditions. It must be evidence based, although this is not always straightforward when there is contestation about the evidence, as the case of bTB shows. It must be well resourced, not just in terms of finance, but also the availability of veterinary and other relevant expertise. Flexibility needs to be reflected in resourcing to avoid conflicts between strategic objectives; for example, the re-emergence of brucellosis would require prompt action and, without the availability of additional resources to deal with such a challenge, resources would need to be taken from other activities. Both the basic resource requirements and such flexibility are a challenge in a period of fiscal consolidation. Any strategy needs to involve the Devolved Administrations and also take account of EU regulations and policy, as well as any international trade implications. Above all, the governance framework must be responsive, not just in terms of listening to the views of various stakeholders, but also engaging effectively with them, not just to devise solutions, but to secure their involvement in implementation, as happened in the case of bluetongue. This can help to overcome some of the resource challenges. A successful framework needs to avoid a 'top down' approach, but also to avoid paralysis in decision making which is a particular risk in endemic diseases such as bTB. There is no simple formula that can meet all these requirements, but there has been a willingness to move beyond existing ways of thinking and established approaches.

It is clear from the study that the lack of a fully integrated approach that uses natural, economic and social scientific evidence can have detrimental effects on effective policy making. Setting policy priorities requires both epidemiological and political dimensions to be addressed, and recognises that diseases are not independent. Control interventions for one disease will have impacts on others. For example, the BSE crisis that led to a ban on meat exports to the EU and beyond removed many of the incentives that farmers had to control diseases such as infectious bovine rhinotraceheitis. Conversely, where policies exist that enhance control of many diseases simultaneously, they should be prioritised where there are multiple benefits.

The vulnerability of farmed animals to disease has potential impact on the economics of farm production. This may disrupt markets and threaten trade. It may also affect tourism, for example when there are exclusion zones. Lastly, there are important questions raised about protecting international trade during a notifiable disease outbreak. The operation of EU controls on the export of live animals and animal products may have a severe effect on public confidence and trust on UK products, as well as economic consequences.

The EU *Animal Health Strategy 2007–2013* takes forward the principle that prevention is better than cure, and includes prevention and control mechanisms. Disease prevention includes surveillance, control at source and biosecurity. Traceability of cattle movements as well as import and trade controls are important. There are also import and trade controls that may ensure prevention through detection.

The use of vaccination may provide solutions such as a vaccine for bTB, but research in this area has not to date resulted in an effective vaccine. In Wales, there are hopes that a vaccine for badgers might prove effective. But there is also the problem of catching the badgers to inject them, which is difficult and expensive. There are also important lessons in terms of husbandry and production systems. The breeding of resistant livestock or the effective use of genetically modified and cloned animals may also assist in future control measures, but carry their own set of problems. This may provide solutions for the future, dependent on scientific development.

The way forward is to ensure that policy makers have all the information needed to take decisions and make effective policy. They must avoid relying all small subsets of specialists and a limited range of stakeholders' interests. Decision making must be transparent and the range of stakeholders' interests must be fully addressed. But equally there is a risk of policy paralysis if one tries to square all stakeholders. This involves careful communication and the ability to view the problem from an interdisciplinary perspective. The language of communications must seek to clarify and explain, rather than to confuse and adopt technical language that only serves to reinforce specialist knowledge.

Policy makers must also be aware of human behaviour and how strategies to improve health and welfare are best addressed. Some stakeholders may be

unwilling to take action to reduce risk and may prefer to pass all the responsibilities onto farmers who are unable to reduce the risk because of costs or
lack of access to specialist information. There is plenty of information available,
not least online: applying it to the specific farm in a cost-effective way may
be the real challenge. Responsibilities also devolve to regulators and the
government to ensure that there is adequate engagement with stakeholders.
Bluetongue shows how one might go beyond that. Co-operation is needed and
flexibility required to cope with the fast changing nature of animal health and
welfare in periods of economic uncertainty. The role of the media is likely to
be critical in the communication of policy, and the value of well-targeted information to the public should not be underestimated. Negative influences need
to be addressed in improving standards and the media and public opinion can be
important here. For example, the demise of the battery hen came about largely
because of media pressure, and concerns about the rise of *E. coli* 0157 led to
better food hygiene.

It is important to emphasise that when developing new strategies and
policies, they require much more clarity and transparency in order to raise public
confidence and also, at the same time, provide useful lessons that can transfer
across disciplinary boundaries. The twenty-first century with globalised
markets, fragile public finances and vulnerable agriculture creates uncertainty
emphasised by climate change and increase in prevalence in animal diseases.
This must be recognised by policy makers. Successful long-term disease control
to improve livestock production, health and welfare must operate at the meta-
herd level, with co-operative concerted action from all farmers who exchange
livestock.

Lastly, there are significant research implications for policy makers that
emerge from the study. The status of diseases, i.e. their categorisation, should
be challenged and the allocation of resources to specific diseases should take
into account the true impacts of the diseases. The potential for policy to influence
the disease including market developments and farmer behaviour should be
included in all decisions. It is clear that efforts to control endemic disease will
be sub-optimal if left primarily to the decision of the individual farmer. Policy
makers must provide the necessary arrangements to create co-operation and
concerted action when required. The focus on the individual farmer should
include relevant rules for the adoption of precautionary and control measures that
discourage behaviour which spreads disease.

Supermarkets, by ensuring high-quality food and own-brand marketing,
have the potential to set controls on the quality of food products through the
sourcing of products from quality assured farms. There are a number of factors at
work. Livestock buyers must made aware of disease risk and infections from
herds. Better disclosure of information is needed on sellers of animals, including
a more objective assignment of risk. Policy making needs to address the needs of
different stakeholders, including balancing the role of supermarkets. Monitoring
information and disease control need to be undertaken on a systematic and
comprehensive basis.

Conclusions

RELU support for this study has facilitated consideration of the impact of biological, economic and political processes and legal arrangements on the efforts of producers and government to control animal disease or mitigate its consequences. Persistent or endemic diseases of livestock are numerous and common, and set many challenges for policy makers and regulators. It must be accepted that disease in farmed livestock is a constant whatever measures, laws or regulatory practices are adopted. Variables such as policy making, the resources available and the strategies adopted may help mitigate the consequences of disease, but not always wholly eradicate it. Animal welfare is an important means to achieve improvements in animal health, and good practice may help to reduce disease occurrence and produce economic benefits through more productive herds. The research undertaken for the study indicates that there are often unrealistically high expectations amongst stakeholders. Equally important is not to underestimate the risks of regulatory failure. Regulators need to be able to recognise and identify any unintended consequences, side-effects or counterproductive consequences of the regulatory system they employ. This requires transparency and open debate undertaken in the political culture of contemporary society. There are lessons for politicians in recognising the limitations of any performance evaluation or regulatory regime.

Animal disease has been considered in this book from a number of perspectives, but essentially from the implicit presumption that it is, like human disease, a suffering that should be avoided where possible. An alternative approach would have been to consider the value or worth of animals and what is lost by disease. However, we believe that any approach would reveal the same central message: that animal disease and its control involve a complex interaction between biological and human spheres, of which economics, politics and law are key. To argue from an extreme, it is theoretically possible to eliminate most obligate pathogens with current scientific understanding and technology – what is missing is the necessary political will and legal framework. Endemic diseases, especially those that persist biologically and against which interventions could be implemented, persist only because the economic, legal and political frameworks allow them to. These human activities respond to animal disease, sometimes resulting in elimination of infection, so the 'successful' endemic disease is one that (subconsciously) creates its own environment in all spheres. If the ultimate aim is to remove animal disease,[13] then a system needs to be created that is able to appropriately manipulate the biological, political, economic, legal and social factors. However, control of endemic animal disease typically suffers from two

---

13   There are biological arguments (the 'hygiene hypothesis') that would argue that infection has beneficial effects, and an economic perspective would argue that this should only be an aim if the benefits outweigh the costs. Consequently, the desired outcomes of an idealised animal disease control system are not simply defined.

opposing problems. First, it does not have the political profile to attract research and surveillance funding to demonstrate the burden of disease, and its economic impact. Second, this lack of data and knowledge prevent its political profile being increased.

The setting up of the AHWB[14] for England offers an important opportunity to set the terms of the relationship between public and private sectors in the financing of the surveillance, detection and prevention of animal diseases. Coordination of various policies and strategies is essential if regulation is to be effective. Increasing the scope and variety of regulation on the keeper of animals and the various stakeholders must be accompanied by an extensive toolkit of regulatory ideas and devices. Regulating animal health and welfare through the AHWB brings the potential of a new approach to governance. This will enable stakeholders and the public to be engaged in an important collaboration at a period when science is doubted, government and politicians are not trusted, and various regulators under the light touch regimes of the past have been thought inadequate.[15] The AHWB also needs to apply a systematic framework for risk and cost sharing. Stakeholders must be engaged in the development of this framework and the legitimacy of the AHWB is required to ensure public support and confidence.

Placing the best scientific advice available at the heart of animal health and welfare is fundamental to the success of any new regulatory system. This entails prioritising scientific methodology and ensuring transparency so that accountability mechanisms are in place. Cross-disciplinary and collaborative studies are essential. This creates the most appropriate relationships within a regulatory system, and supports professional judgment and responsibility. At the apex of any new regulatory body for animal health and welfare are the political, economic and societal issues that make up decision making.[16] At the outset, public accountability requires that sound science is openly discussed and available; that political choices are fully explained and justified; and that when choices are wrongly taken there is an appropriate feedback to ensure that better decision making takes place in the future. This is essential in the context of addressing the various challenges – social, economic and political – set out in the book, as well as meeting all the expectations that come from engaging with stakeholders and scientific evaluation.

Lastly, looking to the future, animal health and welfare considerations must fit within the mix of agri-environmental concerns.[17] Market instruments are unable

---

14 Defra, *Consultation on a New Independent Body for Animal Health*, London: Defra, 2009, p. 15.

15 Lodge, M., 'Accountability and transparency in regulation: critiques, doctrines and instruments' in Jordana, J. and Levi-Faur, D. (eds), *Politics of Regulation: Institutions and Regulatory Reforms for the Age of Governance*, Cheltenham: Edward Elgar, 2004, pp. 124–144.

16 Hampton, P., *Reducing Administrative Burdens: Effective Inspection and Enforcement Final Report*, London: HM Treasury, 2005. Macrory, R., *Regulatory Justice: Making Sanctions Effective: Final Report*, London: Cabinet Office, November 2006.

17 Burrell, A., '"Good agricultural practices" in the agri-food supply chain' (2011) *Environmental Law Review* 251.

to develop the scale and specificity required. The fragility of the agricultural market in the UK and the vulnerability of different sectors to external market competition from outside the EU give rise to a number of serious challenges. There is an important educational function of shaping farmers' views and approaches to disease and its eradication. In the current context of higher food prices, there is also a pressing need to mitigate climate change and develop legal controls on land use that are sustainable. The CAP post-2013 may offer the potential to make the link between cross-subsidies for agriculture based on serious compliance to ensure green credentials that support regulatory change. Integrating animal health and welfare priorities into this complex problem[18] of climate change is likely to be one of the greatest challenges of the twenty-first century. Finding the correct context in which to make agricultural issues central to climate change mitigation must confront the costs of animal foodstuffs and the general uncertainties that are intrinsic to climate change. Agricultural practice is one of the most important means for delivering sustainable animal health and welfare, and must engage with regulatory law and practice based on sound science. The visual and aesthetic landscape of the country is shaped by agriculture, can support biodiversity and enhances the lives of many citizens.

18 Cardwell, M., 'European Union agricultural policy and practice: the new challenge of climate change' (2011) *Environmental Law Review* 271.

Bibliography

Aldred, J., 'Ethics and climate change cost–benefit analysis: stern and after' (2009) 14(4) *New Political Economy* 469–488.

Anderson, I., *Foot and Mouth Disease 2001: Lessons to be Learned Inquiry Report*, London: The Stationery Office, July 2002.

Anderson, I., *Foot and Mouth Disease 2007: A Review and Lessons Learned*, London: The Stationery Office, March 2008.

Appleby, M.C., 'Tower of Babel: variation in ethical approaches, concepts of welfare and attitudes to genetic manipulation' (1999) 8 *Animal Welfare* 381.

Appleby, M.C., *What Should We Do About Animal Welfare*, Oxford: Blackwell Science, 1999.

Ayres, I. and Braithwaite, J., *Responsive Regulation: Transcending the Deregulation Debate*, Oxford: Oxford University Press, 1992.

Baekbo, P., Kristensen, C.S. and Larsen, L.E., 'Porcine circovirus diseases: a review of PMWS' (2012) 59 *Transboundary and Emerging Diseases* 1865–1682.

Baldwin, R., 'Is better regulation smarter regulation?' (2005) *Public Law* 485–511.

Baldwin, R. (ed.), *Law and Uncertainty: Risks and Legal Processes*, London: Kluwer Law International, 1997.

Baldwin, R. and Black, J., 'Really responsive regulation' (2008) 71 *Modern Law Review* 59–64.

Baldwin, R. and Cave, M., *Understanding Regulation*, Oxford: Oxford University Press, 1999.

Barnes, R., *Property Rights and Natural Resources*, Oxford: Hart Publishing, 2007.

Barrett, S., 'Global disease eradication' (2003) 1(2–3) *Journal of the European Economic Association* 591–600.

Barrett, S., *Why Cooperate? The Incentive to Supply Global Public Goods*, Oxford: Oxford University Press, 2007.

Beck, U., *Risk Society: Towards a New Modernity*, London: Sage, 1992.

Beckerman, W., 'Sustainable development: is it a useful concept?' (1994) 3(3) *Environmental Values* 191–209.

Beecher-Monas, E., *Evaluating Scientific Evidence*, New York, NY: Cambridge University Press, 2007.

Begon, M., Harper, J.L. and Townsend, C.R., *Ecology. Individuals, Populations and Communities*, 3rd edn, Oxford: Blackwell, 1996.

Bennett, R., 'The "direct costs" of livestock disease: the development of a system of models for the analysis of 30 endemic livestock diseases in Great Britain' (2003) 54(1) *Journal of Agricultural Economics* 55–71.

Bennett, R.M. and Cooke, R.J., 'Costs to farmers of a TB breakdown' (2006) 158 *Veterinary Record* 429–432.

Bennett, R.M. and Ijpelaar, J., 'Updated estimates of the costs associated with 34 endemic livestock diseases in Great Britain' (2005) 56 *Journal of Agricultural Economics* 135–144.

Bentham, J., *An Introduction to the Principles of Morals and Legislation*, London, c. 1789.

Bickerstaff, K. and Simmons, P., 'The right tool for the job? Modelling, spatial relationships and styles of scientific practice in the UK foot and mouth crisis' (2004) 22 *Environment and Planning (D)* 393–412.

Bishop, P., 'Badgers and bovine tuberculosis: the relationship between law, policy and science' (2012) 24(1) *Journal of Environmental Law* 145–154.

Black, J., 'Paradoxes and failures: "new governance" techniques and the financial crisis' (2012) 75(6) *Modern Law Review* 1037–1063.

Black, J., 'The emergence of risk based regulation and the new public risk management in the UK' (2005) *Public Law* 512–549.

Bracken, J.I. and Oughton, E.A., '"What do you mean?" The importance of language in interdisciplinary research' (2006) 31(3) *Transactions of the Institute of British Geographers* 371–382.

Brambell, F.W.R., *Report of the Technical Committee to Enquire into the Welfare of Animals kept under Intensive Livestock Husbandry Systems*, December 1965, London: HMSO, 1965.

Broom, D.M., 'Indicators of poor welfare' (1986) 142 *British Veterinary Journal* 524–526.

Brooman, S. and Legge, D., *Law Relating to Animals*, London: Cavendish Publishing, 1997.

Brownlie, J., Clarke, M.C., Howard, C.J. and Pocock, D.H., 'Pathogenesis and epidemiology of bovine virus infection of cattle' (1987) 18 *Annales de recherches vétérinaires* 157–166.

Bryson, B. (ed.), *Seeing Further: The Story of Science and the Royal Society*, London: The Royal Society, 2010.

Burnett, J., *Plenty and Want: A Social History of Food in England from 1815 to the Present Day*, 2nd edn, London: Routledge, 1989.

Burns, Lord (Chair), *Report of the Committee of Inquiry into Hunting with Dogs in England and Wales*, Cm 4763, London: The Stationery Office, 2000.

Burrell, A., '"Good agricultural practices" in the agri-food supply chain' (2011) 13(4) *Environmental Law Review* 251–270.

Camm, T. and Bowles, D., 'Animal welfare and the Treaty of Rome – a legal analysis of the protocol on animal welfare and standards in the European Union' (2000) 12 *Journal of Environmental Law* 197–202.

Cardwell, M., 'European Union agricultural policy and practice: the new challenge of Climate Change' (2011) 13(4) *Environmental Law Review* 271–295.

Carslake, D., Grant, W., Green, L.E., Cave, J., Greaves, J., Keeling, M., McEldowney, J., Weldgebriel, J.H. and Medley, G.F., 'Endemic cattle diseases: comparative epidemiology and governance' (2011) 366(1573) *Philosophical Transactions of the Royal Society B* 1933–1942.

Carson, R., *Silent Spring*, New York, NY: Fawcett Crest, 1962.

Carter, G.R. and Wise, D.J., *Essentials of Veterinary Bacteriology and Mycology*, 6th edn, Chichester: John Wiley & Sons, 1993.

Case, P., 'Police warn badger cull could spark clashes', *Farmers Weekly*, 24 November 2011.

Clapp, B.W., *An Environmental History of Britain*, London and New York, NY: Longman, 1994.

Clark, S.R.L., *The Moral Status of Animals*, Oxford: Clarendon Press, 1977.

Cohen, R., *Global Diasporas*, London: University College Press, 1999.

Collins, H., Evans, R. and Gorman, M., 'Trading zones and interactional expertise' (2007) 38(4) *Studies in History and Philosophy of Science Part A* 657–666.

Dawkins, M.S., *Animal Suffering. The Science of Animal Welfare*, London: Chapman & Hall, 1980.

Department for Environment, Food and Rural Affairs, *Bovine TB Eradication Programme for England*, London: Defra, July 2011.

Department for Environment, Food and Rural Affairs, *UK Bluetongue Control Strategy*, PB13752, London: Defra, 1 December 2008.

Department of Trade and Industry, *Building Businesses Not Barriers*, Cmnd 9794, London: HMSO, 1986.

Department of Trade and Industry, *Lifting the Burden*, Cmnd 9571, White Paper, London: HMSO, 1985.

Denhardt, R.B. and Denhardt, J.V., 'The new public management: serving rather than steering' (2000) 60(6) *Public Administration Review* 549–559.

Diamond, J., *Collapse: How Societies Choose to Fail or Succeed*, New York, NY: Viking Penguin, 2005.

Doremus, H. and Tarlock, D., 'Science, judgment and controversy in natural resource regulation' (2005) 26 *Public Land and Resources Law Review* 1–37.

Drewry, G., 'The new public management' in Oliver, D. and Jowell, J. (eds), *The Changing Constitution*, 4th edn, Oxford: Oxford University Press, 2001, pp. 168–189.

Dunnet, G., *Badgers and Bovine Tuberculosis*, London: HMSO, 1986.

Eastwood, D., 'Amplifying the province of the legislature: the flow of information and the english state in the early nineteenth century' (1989) 62 *Historical Journal* 275–294.

Ellis-Iversen, J. and Hoegeveen, H., 'Barriers and motivators for zoonotic control on cattle farms', Society for Veterinary Epidemiology and Preventative Medicine, London, 1–3 April 2009, pp. 177–187.

Emmerson, C., Johnson, P. and Miller, H. (eds), *The IFS Green Budget: February 2012*, London: Institute for Fiscal Studies and Oxford: Oxford Economics, 2012.

England Advisory Group on Responsibility and Cost Sharing, *Responsibility and Cost Sharing for Animal Health and Welfare: Final Report*, London: Defra, December 2010.

Enticott, G., 'The ecological paradox: social and natural consequences of the geographies of animal health promotion' (2008) 33(4) *Transactions of the Institute of British Geographers* 433–446.

Enticott, G., Donaldson, A., Lowe, P., Power, M., Proctor, A. and Wilkinson, K., 'The changing role of veterinary expertise in the food chain' (2011) 366(1573) *Philosophical Transactions of the Royal Society B* 1955–1965.

EU Commission, *A New Animal Health Strategy for the European Union (2007–2013) where 'Prevention is better than cure'* (COM 539 (2007) final).

EU Commission, Communication on the European Union Strategy for the Protection and Welfare of Animals 2012–2015 (COM (2012) 6 final).

Evans, E.P., *The Criminal Prosecution and Capital Punishment of Animals*, London: Heinemann, 1906.

Everson, M. and Vos, E. (eds), *Uncertain Risks Regulated*, Abingdon: Routledge-Cavendish, 2009.

Fish, R., Austin, Z., Christley, R., Haygarth, P.M., Heathwaite, L.A., Latham, S., Medd, W., Mort, M., Oliver, D.M., Pickup, R., Wastling, J.M. and Wynne, B., 'Uncertainties in the governance of animal disease: an interdisciplinary framework for analysis' (2011) 366 (1573) *Philosophical Transactions of the Royal Society B* 2023–2034.

Fisher, E., 'Drowning in numbers: standard setting in risk regulation and the pursuit of accountable public administration' (2000) 20 *Oxford Journal of Legal Studies* 109–130.

Fisher, E., *Risk: Regulation and Administrative Constitutionalism*, Oxford: Hart Publishing, 2009.

Francione, G.L., *Animals, Property and the Law*, Philadelphia, PA: Temple University, 1995.

Fraser, D., 'Science, values and animal welfare: exploring the inextricable connection' (1995) 4(2) *Animal Welfare* 13–117.

Frey, R.G., *Interests and Rights*, Oxford: Oxford University Press, 1980.

Froderman, R., 'Introduction' in Froderman, R., Klein, J.T. and Mitcham, C. (eds), *The Oxford Handbook of Interdisciplinarity*, Oxford: Oxford University Press, xxix–xxxix.

Gardner, H., *The Mind's New Science*, New York, NY: Basic Books, 1985.

Garner, R., *Animals, Politics and Morality*, Manchester: Manchester University Press, 1993.

Garner, R., *Political Animals, Animal Protection in Britain and the United States*, Basingstoke: Macmillan, 1998.

Gearty, C., 'Can animals have "human rights" too?', LSE Working Paper Series, London: London School of Economics, January 2008.

Gearty. C., 'Do human rights help or hinder environmental protection?' (2010) *Journal of Human Rights and the Environment* 7–22.

Giddens, A., *Modernity and Self-Identity: Self and Society in the Late Modern Age*, London: Polity Press, 1990.

Giddens, A., *The Third Way*, Cambridge: Polity Press, 1998.

Gilbert, M., Mitchell, A., Bourn, D., Mawdsley, J., Clifton-Hadley, R. and Wint, W., 'Cattle movements and bovine tuberculosis in Great Britain' (2005) 435 *Nature* 491–496.

Gompertz, L., *Moral Inquiries on Situation of Man and of Brutes*, London, 1824.

Gore, A., *An Inconvenient Truth*, Emmaus, PA: Rodale Press, 2006.

Gouldon, A. and Murphy, J., *Regulatory Realities. The Implementation and Impact of Industrial Environmental Regulation*, London: Earthscan Publications Ltd, 1998.

Grant, W., 'Intractable policy failure: the case of bovine TB and badgers' (2009) 11(4) *British Journal of Politics & International Relations* 557–573.

Grant, W., *Pressure Groups and British Politics*, Basingstoke: Palgrave Macmillan, 2000.

Greaves J. and Grant, W., 'Crossing the interdisciplinary divide political science and biological science' (2010) 58(2) *Political Studies* 320–339.

Green, L.E. and Medley, G.F., 'Mathematical modelling of the foot and mouth disease outbreak of 2001: strengths and weaknesses' (2002) 73(3) *Research in Veterinary Science* 201–205.

Green, L.E., Kaler, J., Wassink, G.J., King, E.M. and Grogono Thomas, R., 'Impact of rapid treatment of sheep lame with footrot on welfare and economics and farmer attitudes to lameness in sheep' (2012) 21 (supplement 1) *Animal Welfare* 67–72.

Greenstein, R.J., 'Is Crohn's disease caused by a mycobacterium? Comparisons with leprosy, tuberculosis and Johne's disease' (2003) 3(8) *The Lancet Infectious Diseases* 507–514.

Gunn, G.F., Stott, A.W. and Humphry, R.W., 'Modelling and costing BVD outbreaks in beef herds' (2004) 167 *The Veterinary Journal* 143–149.

Gunn, G.J., Hefferman, C., Hall, M., McLeod, A. and Hovi, M., 'Measuring and comparing constraints to improved biosecurity amongst United Kingdom farmers, veterinarians and the auxillary industries' (2008) 84(3–4) *Preventative Veterinary Medicine* 310–323.

Gunn, G.J., Saatkamp, H.W., Humphry, R.W. and Stott, A.W., 'Assessing economic and social pressure for the control of bovine viral diarrhoea virus' (2005) 72 *Preventive Veterinary Medicine* 149–162.

Gunningham, N., 'Enforcing environmental regulation' (2011) 23(2) *Journal of Environmental Law* 169–201.

Gunningham, N., 'Regulating biotechnology: lessons from environmental policy' in Somsen, H. (ed.), *The Regulatory Challenge of Biotechnology*, Cheltenham: Edward Elgar, 2007.

Gunningham, N.A. and Grabosky, P., *Smart Regulation: Designing Environmental Policy*, Oxford: Oxford University Press, 1998.

Haack S., *Defending Science*, Amherst, NY: Prometheus Books, 2007.

Haack, S., *Defending Science within Reason: Between Scientism and Cynicism*, Amherst NY: Prometheus Books, 2008.

Haack, S., *Evidence and Inquiry: Towards Reconstruction of Epistemology*, Oxford: Blackwell, 1993.

Hampton, P., *Reducing Administrative Burdens: Effective Inspection and Enforcement Final Report*, London: HM Treasury, 2005.

Hardin, G., 'The tragedy of the commons' (1968) 162 *Science* 1243.

Harremoës, P. *et al.* (eds), *The Precautionary Principle in the 20th Century: Late Lessons from Early Warnings*, London: Earthscan, 2001.

Harris, G., *Seeking Sustainability in an Age of Complexity*, Cambridge: Cambridge University Press, 2007.

Harvey, D., 'RELU special issue: editorial reflections' (2009) 27(2) *Journal of Agricultural Economics* 329–336.

Haskell *et al.*, *Research Project: Animal Welfare and Climate Change: Impacts, Adaptations and Risks* (AW0513), Scottish Agricultural College, 2011.

Heffernan, C., Nielsen, L., Thomson, K. and Gunn, G., 'An exploration of the drivers to bio-security collective action among a sample of UK cattle and sheep farmers' (2008) 87(3–4) *Preventive Veterinary Medicine* 358–372.

Hennessy, D., 'Coordinating to eradicate animal disease and the role of insurance markets', Working Paper 07-WP 45, Iowa State University, Iowa, 2007.

Hindmoor, A., 'Explaining networks through mechanisms: vaccination, priming and the 2001 foot and mouth crisis' (2009) 57 *Political Studies* 75–94.

Home Office, *Code of Practice for the Housing and Care of Animals used in Scientific Procedures*, HC 107, London: HMSO, 1989.

Home Office, *The Ethical Review Process*, London: HMSO, 1998.

Horan, R.D., 'Economics and ecology of managing emerging infectious animal diseases' (2007) 89(5) *American Journal of Agricultural Economics* 1232–1238.

House of Commons Agriculture Committee, *Animal Welfare in Poultry, Pig and Veal Calf Production*, HC 406, London: HMSO, 1981.

House of Commons Agriculture Committee, *Badgers and Bovine Tuberculosis*, HC 233, London: The Stationery Office, 1999.

House of Commons Agriculture Committee, *Badgers and Bovine Tuberculosis*, HC 92, London: The Stationery Office, 2001.

House of Commons Agriculture Committee, *The UK Pig Industry*, HC 87, London: HMSO, 1999.

House of Commons Agriculture Committee, *The UK Poultry Industry*, HC 67, London: HMSO, 1994.

House of Commons Environment, Food and Rural Affairs Committee, *Badgers and cattle TB: the final report of the Independent Scientific Group on Cattle TB*, Fourth Report of Session 2007–08, HC 130-1, London: The Stationery Office, 2008.

House of Commons Library, *The Food Standards Bill: Bill 117 of 1998–99*, Research Paper 99/65, 18 June 1999.

House of Commons Library, 'Agriculture and climate change, SN/SC/3763', London: House of Commons Library, 26 January 2012.

House of Commons Science and Technology Committee, *The Government's review of the principles applying to the treatment of independent scientific advice provided to government*, Third Report of Session 2009–10, HC 158-I, London: The Stationery Office.

Hughes, O., *Public Management and Administration*, 2nd edn, Harlow: Longman Pearson, 1998.

Independent Scientific Group on Cattle TB, *Bovine TB: The Scientific Evidence*, Final Report of the Independent Scientific Group on Cattle TB, Defra: London, June 2007.

Jordan, L., *The Eradication of Bovine Tuberculosis*, London: HMSO, 1933.

Josling, T., Roberts, D. and Orden, D., *Food Regulation and Trade*, Washington, DC: Institute for International Economics, 2004.

Julia Black, "Paradoxes and failures: "new governance" techniques and the financial crisis" (2012) 75(6) *Modern Law Review* 1037–1063.

King, Sir D., *Tuberculosis in Cattle and Badgers: A Report by the Chief Scientific Adviser*, London: London, 2007.

Krebs, J. and the Independent Scientific Review Group, *Bovine Tuberculosis in Cattle and Badgers: Report by the Independent Scientific Review Group*, London: Ministry of Agriculture Fisheries and Food, 1997.

Kuchler, F. and Hamm, S., 'Animal disease incidence and indemnity eradication programs' (2000) 22 *Agricultural Economics* 299–308.

Lawrence, J., *On the Rights of Beasts in A Philosophical Treatise on Horses and on the Moral Duties of Man towards the Brute Creation*, London, 1796.

Lawton, J.H., 'Ecology, politics and policy' (2007) 44(3) *Journal of Applied Ecology* 465–474.

Legwood, G. (ed.), *Veterinary Ethics: An Introduction*, London: Continuum, 2000.

Lindberg, A., Brownlie, J., Gunn, G.J., Houe, H., Moenning, V., Saatkamp, H.W., Sandvik, T. and Valle, P.S., 'The control of bovine viral diarrhoea virus in Europe: today and in the future' (2006) 25(3) *Rev. sci. tech. Off. Int. Epiz.* 961–979.

Linzey, A., *Why Animal Suffering Matters*, Oxford: Oxford University Press, 2009.

Lodge, M., 'Accountability and transparency in regulation: critiques, doctrines and instruments' in Jordana, J. and Levi-Faur, D. (eds), *Politics of Regulation: Institutions and Regulatory Reforms for the Age of Governance*, Cheltenham: Edward Elgar, 2004.

Lowe, P. and Goyder, J. (eds), *Environmental Groups in Politics*, London: Allen & Unwin, 1983.

Lowe, P. and Phillipson, J., 'Reflexive interdisciplinary research: the making of a research programme on the rural economy and land use' (2006) 57(2) *Journal of Agricultural Economics* 165–184.

Lowe, P. and Ward, N., 'New Labour, new rural vision? Labour's rural white paper' (2002) 72(3) *Political Quarterly* 386–390.

Lowe, P., Phillipson, J. and Lee, R.P., 'Socio-technical innovation for sustainable food chains: roles for social science' (2008) 19 *Trends in Food Science and Technology* 226–233.

Lowe, P., Whitman, G. and Phillipson, J., 'Ecology and the social sciences' (2009) 46 (2) *Journal of Applied Ecology* 297–305.

Lyall, C., Bruce, A., Tait, J. and Meagher, L., *Interdisciplinary Research Journeys*, London: Bloomsbury Academic, 2010.

Macdonald, D.W., Riordan, P. and Matthews, F., 'Biological hurdles to the control of TB in cattle: a test of two hypotheses concerning wildlife to explain the failure of control' (2006) 131 *Biological Conservation* 268–286.

Macleod, M. *et al.*, *Review and Update of UK Marginal Abatement Cost Curves for Agriculture: Final report*, Prepared for the Committee on Climate Change, 2010.

MacNeil, M., Sargent, N. and Swan, N. (eds), *Law, Regulation and Governance*, Oxford: Oxford University Press, 2003.

Macrory, R., *Regulatory Justice: Making Sanctions Effective: Final Report*, London: Cabinet Office, November 2006.

Macrory, R., *Regulatory Justice: Sanctioning in a Post-Hampton World: Consultation Document*, London: Cabinet Office, May 2006.

Malthus, T.R., *Principles of Population*, London, 1798.

Marsden, T., Lee, R., Flynn, A. and Thankappan, S. *The New Regulation and Governance of Food*, Abingdon: Routledge, 2010.

Marzano, M., Carss, D.N. and Bell, S., 'Working to make interdisciplinarity work: investing in communication and interpersonal relationships' (2006) 57(2) *Journal of Agricultural Economics* 185–197.

May, P.J., 'Regulatory regimes and accountability' (2007) *Regulation and Governance* 8–26.

McEldowney, J.F., 'Defining the public interest: public law perspectives on regulating the financial crisis' in Labrosse, J.R., Olivares-Caminal, R. and Singh, D. (eds), *Financial Crisis Management and Bank Resolution*, Abingdon: Informa, 2009, pp. 103–132.

McEldowney, J.F., 'Managing financial risk: the precautionary principle and protecting the public interest in the UK' in Labrosse, J.R., Olivares-Caminal, R. and Singh, D. (eds), *Risk and the Banking Crisis*, Cheltenham: Edward Elgar, 2011.

McEldowney, J.F. and McEldowney S., *Environment and the Law*, Harlow: Longman, 1996.

McEldowney, J.F. and McEldowney, S., *Environmental Law*, Harlow: Longman Pearson, 2010.

McEldowney, J.F. and McEldowney, S., *Environmental Law and Regulation*, London: Blackstone and Oxford: Oxford University Press, 2001.

McNeill, D., 'On interdisciplinary research: with particular reference to the field of environment and development' (1999) 53(4) *Higher Education Quarterly* 312–332.

Ministry of Agriculture, Fisheries and Food, *Animal Health: A Centenary 1865–1965*, London: HMSO, 1965.

Ministry of Agriculture, Fisheries and Food, *Animal Health, The Report of the Chief Veterinary Officer*, London: The Stationery Office, annual publication.

Ministry of Agriculture, Fisheries and Food, *Guidance on the Welfare of Animals (Transport) Order 1997*, London: The Stationery Office, 1998.

Moran, M., *The British Regulatory State: High Modernism and Hyper-innovation*, Oxford: Oxford University Press, 2004.

Morgan, B. and Yeung, K., *An Introduction to Law and Regulation*, Cambridge: Cambridge University Press, 2007.

Moses, J. and Knutsen, T., *Ways of Knowing: Competing Methodologies in Social and Political Research*, Basingstoke: Palgrave Macmillan, 2007.

Mungall, C. and McLaren, D. (eds), *Planet Under Stress*, Oxford: Oxford University Press, 1990.

National Archives, MAF 287/101, 'Animal health division working party to consider nationalised veterinary service', London.

National Audit Office and Comptroller and Auditor General, *Department for Business, Innovation and Skills: Delivering Regulatory Reform*, HC 758, Session 2010–2011, 17 February 2011, London: NAO, 2011, pp. 4–5.

National Audit Office and Comptroller and Auditor General, *Department for Environment, Food and Rural Affairs: Managing front line delivery costs*, HC 1279, Session 2010–2012, 22 July 2011.

Nicholson, E.B., *The Rights of An Animal. A New Essay in Ethics*, London: C. Kegan Paul and Co., 1879.

Nielsen, V.L., 'Are regulators responsive?' (2006) 28(3) *Law and Policy* 395–416.

Ogus, A., *Regulation, Legal Form and Economic Theory*, Oxford: Clarendon Press, 1993.

Oliver, D. and Drewry, G., *Public Service Reforms*, Oxford: Oxford University Press, 1996, pp. 1–15.

Oliver, D., Prosser, T. and Rawlings, R. (eds), *The Regulatory State*, Oxford: Oxford University Press, 2010.

Olson, M., *The Logic of Collective Action*, Cambridge, MA: Harvard University Press, 1965.

Orwin, C.S. and Whetham, E. H., *History of British Agriculture 1846–1914*, 2nd edn, Harlow: Longmans, 1971.

Ostrom, E., *Governing the Commons: The Evolution of Institutions for Collective Action*, Cambridge: Cambridge University Press, 1990.

Packer, R., *The Politics of BSE*, Basingstoke: Palgrave Macmillan, 2006.

Parker, C., *The Open Corporation: Effective Self-Regulation and Democracy*, Cambridge: Cambridge University Press, 2002.

Pattison, I., *The British Veterinary Profession 1791–1948*, London: JM Dent, 1993.

Philipson, T., 'The welfare loss of disease and the theory of taxation' (1995) 14 *Journal of Health Economics* 387–395.

Phillips, L., Bridgeman, J. and Ferguson-Smith, M., *The BSE Inquiry: The Report*, London: The Stationery Office, 2000.

Phillipson, J. and Lowe, P., 'Towards sustainable food chains: harnessing the social and natural sciences' (2009) 19 *Trends in Food Science and Technology* 224–225.

Phillipson, J., Lowe, P. and Bullock, M., 'Navigating the social sciences: interdisciplinarity and ecology' (2009) 46 *Journal of Applied Ecology* 261–264.

Plumb, H., *The Plumb Line: a Journey through Agriculture and Politics*, London: Greycoat Press, 2001, p. 64.

Pogge, T., *World Poverty and Human Rights: Cosmopolitan Responsibilities and Reforms*, Cambridge: Polity Press and Malden: Blackwell, 2002.

Rachels, J., *Created from Animals*, Oxford: Oxford University Press, 1990.

Radford, M., *Animal Welfare Law in Britain*, Oxford: Oxford University Press, 2001.

Regan, T., *The Case for Animal Rights*, London: Routledge, 1983.

Reyher, K.K, Haine, D., Dohoo, I.R. and Revie C.W., 'Examining the effect of intramammary infections with minor mastitis pathogens on the acquisition of new intramammary infections with major mastitis pathogens – a systematic review and meta-analysis' (2012) 95(11) *Journal of Dairy Science* 6483–6502.

Richardson, B.J. and Wood, S., *Environmental Law for Sustainability*, Oxford: Hart Publishing, 2006.

Rodger, C., Franks, J. and Lowe, P., 'Editorial: implementing climate change policy for agriculture – what role for the law?' (2011) 20 *Environmental Law Review* 245.

Rootes, C., 'Nature protection organisations in England' in Markham, W.T. and van Koppen, C.S.A. (eds), *Protecting Nature: Networks and Organizations in Europe and the United States*, Cheltenham: Edward Elgar, 2007.

Royal Society for the Prevention of Cruelty to Animals, *Annual Review*, Horsham: RSPCA, annual publication.

Royal Society for the Prevention of Cruelty to Animals, *Farm Animal Welfare*, Horsham: RSPCA, 1995.

Salt, H., *Animals' Rights Considered in Relation to Social Progress*, 1892; reissued London: Centaur Press, 1980.

Sandoe, P. and Simonsenm, H.B., 'Assessing animal welfare: where does science end and philosophy begin?' (1992) 1 *Animal Welfare* 257–267.

Santarosa *et al.*, 'Optimal risk management versus willingness to pay for BVDV control options' (2005) 72 *Preventive Veterinary Medicine* 183–187.

Schön, D.A. and Rhein, M., *Frame Reflection: Toward the Resolution of Intractable Policy Controversies*, New York, NY: Basic Books, 1994.

Scott, C., 'Accountability in the regulatory state' (2000) 27(1) *Journal of Law and Society* 38–60.

Scott, C., 'Regulation in the age of governance: the rise of the post-regulatory state' in Jordana, J. and Levi-Faur, D. (eds), *The Politics of Regulation*, Cheltenham and New York, NY: Edward Elgar, 2004.

Seals, M., *Animal Health and Welfare Board for England Presentation*, January 2012, www.defra.gov.uk/ahwbe.

Sen, A., *The Idea of Justice*, London: Penguin, 2009.

Spencer, A., 'One body of evidence, three different policies: bovine tuberculosis policy in Britain' (2011) 31(2) *Politics* 91–99.

State Veterinary Service, *National Scrapie Plan for Great Britain: Scheme Brochure*, London: Defra, 2006.

Steele, J., *Risks and Legal Theory*, Oxford: Hart Publishing, 2004.

Stern, N., *The Economics of Climate Change*, London: HM Treasury, 2006.

Stiglitz, J., *Globalisation and Its Discontents*, New York, NY: W.W. Norton and London: Allen Lane, 2004.

Stiglitiz, J., *The Price of Inequality*, London: Allen Lane, 2012.

Stocks, C., 'Too risky: Hilary Benn decides against a badger cull', *Farmers Weekly*, 11 July 2008.

Stott, A.W., Jones, G.M., Humphry, R.W. and Gunn, G.J., 'Financial incentive to control paratuberculosis (Johne's disease) on dairy farms in the United Kingdom' (2005) 156 *Veterinary Record* 825–831.

Stott, R., *Darwin's Ghosts*, London: Bloomsbury, 2012.

Sumner, D.A., Bervejillo, J.E. and Jarvis, L.S., 'Public policy, invasive species and animal disease management' (2005) 8(1) *International Food and Agribusiness Management Review* 78–97.

Sunstein, C., *Risk and Reason*, Cambridge: Cambridge University Press, 2002.

Szmaragd, C., Wilson, A., Carpenter, S., Mertens, P.P.C., Mellor, P.S. *et al.*, 'Mortality and case fatality during the recurrence of BTV-8 in northern Europe in 2007' (2007) 161 *Veterinary Record* 571–572.

Taig, T., *The Development and Use of Scientific Advice in Defra*, London: TTAC Limited, 2004.

Tester, K., *Animals and Society. The Humanity of Animal Rights*, London: Routledge, 1991.

Thaler, R.H. and Sunstein, C.R., *Nudge: Improving Decisions About Health, Welfare and Happiness*, New Haven, CT: Yale University Press, 2008.

Todd, P., 'The protection of Animals Acts 1911–1964' in Blackman, D.E., Humphreys, P.N. and Todd, P. (eds), *Animal Welfare and the Law*, Cambridge: Cambridge University Press, 1989 pp. 13–36.

Turvey, C.G., 'Conceptual issues in livestock insurance', Working Paper No. WP-0503-005, Food Policy Research Institute, Rutgers University, 2003.

Vernon, M.C. and Keeling, M.J., 'Representing the UK's cattle herd as static and dynamic networks' (2009) 276 *Proceedings of the Royal Society B* 469–476.

Vogel, D., *National Styles of Regulation*, Ithaca, NY: Cornell University Press, 1986.

Vogler, J., *The Global Commons: A Regime Analysis*, Chichester: Wiley, 1995.

Warleigh-Lack, A. and Cini, M., 'Interdisciplinarity and the study of politics' (2009) 8(1) *European Political Science* 4–15.

Welsh Assembly, *Final Report of the Rural Development Sub-Committee Inquiry into Bovine Tuberculosis*, Cardiff: Welsh Assembly, 2008.

Westacott, E., *A Century of Vivisection and Anti-Vivisection*, Rochford: CW Daniel Ltd., 1949.

Whatmore, S., 'Generating materials' in Pryke, M., Rose, G. and Whatmore, S. (eds), *Using Social Theory: Thinking Through Research*, London: Sage, 2003, pp. 89–104.

Whatmore, S., Ward, N. and Lane, S.N., 'Environmental knowledge controversies: competency groups as an experimental methodology', paper presented at the British Association for the Advancement of Science, University of Newcastle, meeting panel, 'Working together Across Disciplines: challenges for the natural and social sciences', York 2007.

White G., *The Natural History of Selborne*, Mabey, R. (ed.), London: Penguin Books, 1977 (first published 1788–1789).

Williamson, K., Lowe P. and Donaldson, A., 'Beyond policy networks: policy framing and the politics of expertise in the 2001 foot and mouth disease crisis' (2010) 88(2) *Public Administration* 331–345, 343.

Williamson, T., *The Transformation of Rural England: Farming and the Landscape 1700–1870*, Exeter: University of Exeter Press, 2003.

Wilkinson, K., 'Evidence based policy and the politics of expertise: a case study of bovine tuberculosis', Centre for Rural Economy Discussion Paper Series No. 12, April 2007, Centre for Rural Economy, Newcastle.

Winichokoff, D., Jasanoff, S., Busch, L., Grove-White, R. and Wynne, B., 'Adjudicating the GM food wars: science, risk and democracy in world trade law' (2005) 20 *Yale Journal of International Law* 81–123.

Woodbine, K.A. *et al.*, 'Seroprevalence and epidemiological characteristics of *Mycobacterium avium* subsp. *paratuberculosis* on 114 cattle farms in south west England' (2009) 89 *Preventive Veterinary Medicine* 102–109.

Woods, A., *A Manufactured Plague: The History of Foot and Mouth Disease in Britain*, London: Earthscan, 2004.

Woods, A., '"Partnership" in action: contagious abortion and the governance of livestock disease in Britain, 1885–1921' (2009) 47(2) *Minerva* 195–216.

Zuckerman, Lord, *Badgers, Cattle and Tuberculosis*, London: HMSO, 1980.

Index

Note: the reference 6n21 refers to note 21 on page 6.